History of the Town of Uttoxeter

Francis Redfern

HISTORY
OF
UTTOXETER.

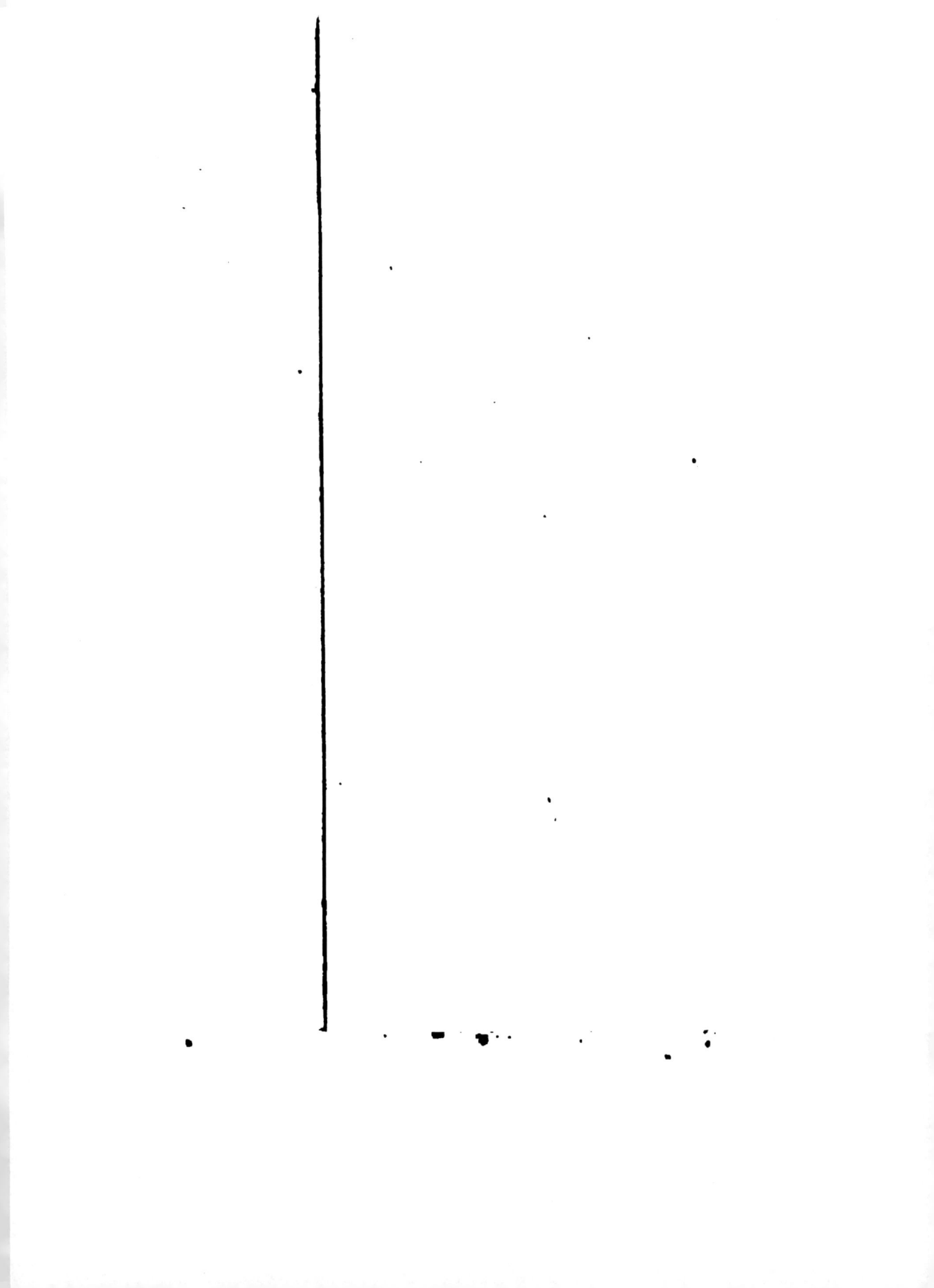

THE TOWN OF UTTOXETER

DESCRIBED, A.D. 1658.

HISTORY

OF THE

TOWN OF UTTOXETER;

WITH

NOTICES

OF

PLACES IN ITS NEIGHBOURHOOD.

BY

FRANCIS REDFERN.

LONDON: J. RUSSELL SMITH, 36, SOHO SQUARE;

UTTOXETER: PUBLISHED BY THE AUTHOR;

DERBY: L. JEWITT, " TELEGRAPH" OFFICE, WARDWICK.

1865.

TO THE

RIGHT HONOURABLE THE

EARL OF SHREWSBURY AND TALBOT,

My Lord,

In dedicating this work to your Lordship, I cannot but express the deep sense I feel of the kind manner in which you have permitted me to issue it under the sanction of your name. The circumstance of your Lordship being one of the lords of the manor: with the way in which this town and neighbourhood expressed their sympathy with your Lordship during the arduous trial for the just recovery of the Shrewsbury Peerage, and the Alton estates ; and the almost unexampled enthusiasm which the town of Uttoxeter displayed on your Lordship's taking possession of your princely inheritance, in the vicinity of Uttoxeter, all so demonstrative of the esteem in which your lordship is held by all classes, were some of the inducements (with the additional one, that one of your Lordship's ancestors Walter Chetwynd, Esq., of Ingestre, did good service towards a history of this county) which led me to ask your lordships kind patronage to this my book ; and I sincerely trust it will prove, as I have striven it should, that that kind condescension which you have shown has not been bestowed unworthily.

I have the honour to be, with deep respect,

Your Lordship's

Most obedient and faithful servant,

FRANCIS REDFERN.

PREFACE.

THE HISTORY OF UTTOXETER, now for the first time submitted to the public, owes its existence to the visit paid to the town a few years ago by that distinguished author, Nathaniel Hawthorn, who, out of admiration for the genius of Dr. Samuel Johnson, came into Staffordshire to visit the places at Lichfield rendered memorable by circumstances in the Doctor's life, and to see the spot—interesting above all others in connection with his name—which he consecrated by his penance and tears at Uttoxeter. In this latter object he was unsuccessful, for no one was able to point out the spot. It had not been described in books, and he returned, lamenting that the place had not been permanently marked by a fitting memorial, The visit to Uttoxeter of so remarkable a person, from a distance of three thousand miles, for such a purpose, and the appearance shortly afterwards of an article from his talented pen, created an anxiety in the town to recover a knowledge of so deeply interesting a site. The de-

sired information was not, however, elicited, although
the matter became a subject of discussion in the
press.   I consider myself fortunate, through my own
enquiries, in being enabled to put the identity of the
place of the Doctor's penance beyond question.   The
discovery interested me, and I was led by curiosity,
from gathering up some of the traditions of the
town, to a more serious enquiry into its pre-historic
annals and authentic history.   I had not, at first, even
the most remote conception of writing a history, nor
am I aware of any stimulus that I received, further
than the discovery about Dr. Johnson.   My research-
es, in the course of time, brought me a considerable quantity of material, when, as I found no history
of the town existed, I bethought me I might attempt
to write one.   Thus the present history of Uttoxeter
has merged into shape.

Of the importance of a history of a market-town
so ancient as Uttoxeter there cannot be any doubt.
Mr. Ward, the laborious author of the " History of
Stoke-upon-Trent," has said, " Every commercial district, large parish, borough, or rural circle, should
have its particular history ;" and a writer in the
" Manchester Examiner," February 18th, 1862, in
noticing the " Annals of Kendal," evinces his own
love of local lore—a love somehow embedded in human nature generally—by these encouraging obser-

vations—" There is scarcely a village or market-
town throughout Great Britain that would be void of
interesting material for historical record, if earnest
enquiry were made by some local student."

The execution of the work is a subject of which
the public must be the judge—it must speak for itself. But I may venture to say that I have not
spared any pains to make it complete and interesting,
and I hope that I have succeeded in this in a manner not only to ensure it a welcome in the neighbourhood, but to give it a generally favourable reception. To the critic, I beg to observe that it is not
the production of a person either devoted to a literary
calling, or living in worldly ease. Being employed
as I am, at a mechanical trade, I have been able to
devote but very little time to its compilation except
at nights, after the suspension of labour. In award-
ing to it, therefore, praise or blame, I would beg that
the circumstances under which the History has been
produced may be considered. Only for these circumstances I would not so far have referred to myself; but these rendered it necessary, and I must
plead them as an apology for doing so.

In the prospectus which I issued, I promised an
appendix to the present volume, and its non-appear-
ance will require a word of explanation. After, as
I thought, I had finished the work, the " Survey of

Uttoxeter," in MS., by Peter Lightfoot, physician, fell into my hands, and knowing very well what the labour of re-writing the book would be, I resolved to add what interesting matter it contained in an appendix. I, however, afterwards, changed my determination; and in writing the History over again, so as to include in it what was valuable in the "Survey," I have been enabled, likewise, to improve it in many other respects. I have, already, some reason to believe that the work will not be uninteresting and useless, and this is some satisfaction, if there is no other, for the toil it has involved.

The notices of the places in the neighbourhood are brief, but as a whole I think they will be found more complete in the mention of what is curious, and more generally interesting, than any other similar notices that have yet appeared.

The old plan of Uttoxeter, taken by Dr. Peter Lightfoot, in 1658, of which a fac-simile is given, will be found very interesting; and the number of engravings will greatly enhance the attraction of the book. The old Grammar School of Alleyne I have not had engraved, although it was promised; for as it was not the original school-house, but a very plain and more modern brick building, it did not possess sufficient interest for an illustration. To compensate for this, I have, however, substitued several other subjects of antiquity of real interest.

My thanks are due to Messrs. Blair, Jervis, and Gould, for so kindly allowing me the use of their copy of Lightfoot's " Survey of Uttoxeter," made in 1658, and for permission to copy the plan attached to it. I have also to acknowledge the kindness of the Rev. Henry Martin, burser of Trinity College, Cambridge, in furnishing me with copies of the manuscript notes of Sir Simon Degge to his own copy of Dr. Plot's " Staffordshire," preserved in Trinity College Library : and they are also due to W. T. Lightfoot, Esq., of Sandhurst, Kent, for some interesting particulars relating to the family of the Rev. Thomas Lightfoot, vicar of Uttoxeter, and to his descendants.

CONTENTS.

CHAPTER I.

Introductory Remarks—Natural Scenery—Interesting Geological Notice—Etymology of Uttoxeter.

CHAPTER II.

The Celtic, Romano-British, and Anglo-Saxon peric ' .

CHAPTER III.

Doomsday Survey of Uttoxeter—Its Feudal Tenure, &c.

CHAPTER IV.

Uttoxeter during the Civil War, and Rebellion—Dr. Samuel Johnson's Penance—Peace of 1802—Royal Visits—Birth of W. J. Fox, Esq.—Peace Rejoicings.

CHAPTER V.

Lord Shrewsbury's Peerage—Trial for Alton Estates—Festivities at Uttoxeter on Lord Shrewsbury taking possession of Alton Towers.

CHAPTER VI.

History of Uttoxeter Church—Early period of a Church in Uttoxeter—Instance of Martyrdom in Uttoxeter, &c.—Altar-tombs—Church Inscriptions—Cemetery.

CHAPTER VII.

History of Dissent in Uttoxeter—Quakers—Catholics—Independents—Wesleyan Methodists—Primitives—Plymouth Brethern.

CHAPTER VIII.

Distingnished Persons :—Thomas Alleyn—Dr. Lightfoot—Sir Symon Degge—Lord Gardner—Mary Howitt—Samuel Bentley—Captain Astle—Edward Rudyard, &c.

CHAPTER IX.

Extent of Uttoxeter—Its quaint appearance—Noted Buildings
of Antiquity—Court Leet—Fires which have happened—
Population since 1662—Persons noted for their longevity.

CHAPTER X.

Ancient Families :—The Mynors—The Degges—Floyers—Normans—The Lightfoot Family—The Milwards.

CHAPTER XI.

Ancient Customs—Sacred Wells—Omens and Superstitions—
Sports and Pastimes—Civil Usages.

CHAPTER XII.

Antiquity of Uttoxeter Markets—Curious particulars of butter
pots—Trial about tolls, &c.—Manufactures and trade—
Printers and Books—Tradesmen's tokens.

CHAPTER XIII.

Libraries—Mechanics' Institute—Town Hall.

CHAPTER XIV.

Public Schools—Alleyne's Grammar School—Alleyne's will,
&c.—National School—New Day School.

CHAPTER XV.

Uttoxeter Charities.

CHAPTER XVI.

NOTICES OF PLACES IN THE NEIGHBOURHOOD OF
UTTOXETER.

Loxley—Stramshall—Leigh—Feelde—Chartley Castle—Abbotts
Bromley— Blythfield — Woodford — Woodlands — March-
ington—Houndhill—Draycott—Newborough—Handbury
— Faulde — Tutbury — Sudbury — Doveridge — West
Broughton — Marston — Somersall — Eaton — Norbury —
Alton—Tean—Croxden—Checkley—Toot Hill and Beam-
hurst—Rocester—Denston—Crakemarsh—Blount's Hall
Kingston—Needwood Forest.

LIST OF ILLUSTRATIONS.

(The whole of the Illustrations are by Mr. Llewellynn Jewitt, F.S.A.)

PLAN OF UTTOXETER, FROM " LIGHTFOOT'S SURVEY."

LORD GARDNER'S HOUSE.

BIRTH-PLACE OF MARY HOWITT.

SAMUEL BENTLEY'S HOUSE.

UTTOXETER CHURCH.

UTTOXETER OLD CHURCH, NOW TAKEN DOWN.

ALTAR TOMBS, UTTOXETER CHURCH.

REMAINS FOUND AT SUDBURY.

PORTRAIT OF THOMAS ALLEN.

NORMAN PITCHER, WITH ARMS OF FERRARS.

SEAL OF ROBERT DE FERRARS.

ANCIENT BUTTER-POTS.

TRADERS' TOKEN, WILLIAM CARTWRIGHT.

———————, ROBERT GILBERT.

——— ———, JOHN HALSEY.

———————, WILLIAM LATHROP.

——— ———, JEFFREY POWER.

———————, WILLIAM WAKELIN.

THE WHITE BEAR INN.

DR. JOHNSON AND CAPTAIN ASTLE.

AUTOGRAPH OF SAMUEL BENTLEY.

CELTIC CINERARY URN, TOOT HILL.

ROMAN URN, TOOT HILL.

——— VESSEL, HIGH WOOD.

CHECKLEY, " DANISH MONUMENTS."

CHECKLEY FONT.

KINGSTON OLD CHURCH.

ROCESTER, INCISED SLAB.

ROCESTER " FRAME YARD."

———, SPEAR HEAD.

TORQUE, FROM NEEDWOOD FOREST.

TISSINGTON—THE " HALL WELL."

TISSINGTON—THE " TOWN WELL."

ANCIENT HUNTING HORN.

HISTORY OF UTTOXETER.

The past and present here unite,
Beneath time's flowing tide,
Like foot-prints hidden by a brook,
But seen on either side.

Definition of Local History—General characteristics of Uttoxeter—
The etymology of its name—Scenery and Geology of its neighbourhood.

LOCAL HISTORY in its most restricted sense is a
description of any single town or village, and it forms
a portion of the topographical history of a county or
kingdom. The subjects upon which it treats are
often strangely diversified. Old customs and popular
superstitions have to be described, side by side with
graver matters of antiquity and family history. It
does not offer a theatre ample or stirring enough for
the general historian, who aims at piling up goodly
tomes on national history, and its themes may be
deemed too insignificant for the exercise of his genius;
but it has, nevertheless, features of very great interest, and not unfrequently they are of a kind to at-
tract general notice. Matters which come within its
scope are often of great importance to the general
historian, and possess interest for the most erudite

B

scholars and persons devoted life-long to the most
useful studies.   One of its greatest charms, however,
lies in the simple fact that it *is* Local History—the
history of a locality with which one is intimately acquainted, and with which our sympathies are closely
connected.   The mental pleasures to be realised by a
knowledge of what has transpired in any locality
where Providence has placed us, are very great, and
most persons feel a laudable and just pride, in being
familiar with such events as have occurred in their
neighbourhood, or of having the means for the acquisition of such knowledge within their reach, and
they guard their memory of them with the care they
would bestow on a rare treasure.   Wherever the
birthplace of a person happens to be—whether a
town or village shrines that sacred spot we in England call our home—where we have passed our earliest and happiest days, and where our forefathers
have for generations slept,—a description, or a history of the spot touches those chords of the heart
and affections which ever thrill at the mention of
what is most precious and dear to us—

> My earliest Home ! how fondly swells my heart
> As at thy lowly door I enter.—*S. T. Hall.*

Such thoughts as these naturally arise, while at-
tempting, for the first time, to collect together the
materials, and to prepare the history and description
of so interesting a town as Uttoxeter—a town which
has borne the quaintest of aspects by which it will be
known so long as "Woodleighton" and "My Own
Story" exist—a town of great antiquity, and famous

for its former position in the honor of Tutbury; for its markets; for the trying part it took during the civil wars; and for the number of distinguished persons to whom it has given birth. All these, with many other circumstances connected with its history give an air of importance to Uttoxeter, and invest it with a two-fold interest to those living in its neighbourhood, or who are associated with it by birth or even by less powerful ties of attachment.

> Uttoxeter, sweet are thy views!
>   Each scene of my fond boyish days,
> Past pleasure in fancy renews,
>   While gratitude sings in thy praise;
> Here plenty with copious horn,
>   Dispenses her bounties around,
> And rosy thy sons like the morn,
>   In health and in spirits abound.
>
> Thy buildings, what though they are plain
>   And boast no magnificent dome,
> Enough for the wise may contain,—
>   Enjoying true plenty at home;
> How happy thy poor who enjoy
>   Possessions o'er want to prevail,
> Whose hills daily bread can supply,
>   And sweet milky tribute the vale.—*S. Bentley.*

Uttoxeter is situated on the eastern borders of Staffordshire (derived, according to Sir Symon Degge's notes to Plott, from *Stadeford*, the strand shore or bank of a ford) in Totmanslow south, and in the ecclesiastical jurisdiction of the See of Lichfield. It is distant fifteen miles from the county town, and about one hundred and forty from London. The parish consists of Crakemarsh, Creighton, Stramshall, the Woodlands, and the liberty of Loxley, and con-

tains about 10,000 acres of land; 2,460 of which are
in the township of Uttoxeter; 1,735 in Loxley; 1,066
in Crakemarsh; 1,274 in Stramshall, and 2,419 in
the Woodlands.

Uttoxeter has an elevated position, to which is due
its famed salubrity. The market place lies in a central part of the town, and the main streets have a
direct communication with it. These are, High
Street having a northern direction, from which, at
Uttoxeter Heath, are branch roads to Ashbourne and
the Potteries; Carter Street and Balance Street towards the west, for Stafford and Abbots Bromley;
the Doveridge road on the east for Derby and Burton; and Schoolhouse Lane or Bridge Street, (in which
is situated the passenger station of the North Staffordshire line of railway,) on the south, leading to
Marchington and other villages. The Stone-way is
reached by Smithy Lane out of High Street, and
Tinker's or Susan's Lane out of Carter Street. There
are two lanes taking a southward direction from
Balance Street, which, although formerly but little
frequented, have latterly become busy thoroughfares
for traffic from the railway luggage station. These
are called Pinfold Lane and Spicer's, Spiceall, or
Petticoat Lane. The passenger station at Uttoxeter
on the Churnet Valley line of railway is at Bull's
Bank on the Doveridge road.

The derivation of the name, Uttoxeter, has never
been satisfactorily ascertained, and has formed a perplexing question to the etymologist. Indeed, but few
persons have attempted it, but have contented them-

selves with simply acknowledging the difficulty with which it is surrounded. The *Wotocheshede* of Doomsday book has been supposed to be derived from *Wudu* (wood) and *Seade* (shade)[1] but then this has been asserted not to have been the name of Uttoxeter as spelt by the Saxons. There are few, perhaps not any, towns whose name has been spelt in such a variety of ways, and this of itself is sufficient to make its solution perplexing to most people. It is written Uttoxeshather, Utcester, Uttokcester, and Ulcester, besides its common form of Uttoxeter; and in converse it is pronounced as Utceter, Uxeter, and Utcheter as well as popularly, Uttoxeter. Assuming the name in Doomsday book to be incorrect,—and it is well known that great difficulties occur in correctly appropriating the names of places as they are written in that invaluable document—it is so from one of two causes, either that the Norman scribes wilfully perverted the spelling of places through their antipathy to the Saxons, or did so through their ignorance of the langauage from which, chiefly, the names of places had been derived. There would, therefore, appear to be no alternative but to accept the name as given by Leland, Camden, and Hollinshead, and which Camden states is its Saxon name; this is, Uttok–cester. The termination is of course from the Latin castrum, a camp, and the prefix has been stated to be derived from the Saxon *mattock*, a term significant of any place having been disforested or cleared of trees by

_____

[1] Ward's History of Stoke-upon-Trent.

the mattock, or some similar implement of husbandry. As, however, places where such operations
by such implements have been effected, are, literally,
both on the Continent and in England, called
field[1] or *felled place*, that opinion will not be received. The Saxon word *stocca*, meaning the trunk
or stem of a tree, appears much more likely to be its
origin. If so, Uttoxeter may signify a town built of
wood or on stocks, or surrounded by a stockade,
where the Romans previously had a camp. The
prefix has also been supposed to mean an *out-take*
from the forest of Needwood; but this can scarcely
be on the opinion that the site of Uttoxeter was a
British settlement, and afterwards a Roman station
before the Saxon occupation of it, for the Saxons
would not have given it a name to imply an out-take
from a wood unless it had been made by themselves.
Neither, for the same reason, can it signify an out-take
from a chase for which the word forest was anciently
used. It is more agreeable to suppose that the expression means that the town was taken out of a
camp, or that it is expressive of a camp from which
the Romans have departed.[2] Another view, however, remains to be taken of the prefix, which is
afforded in another name by which Uttoxeter is designated. That name is Tocester,[3] about the meaning of which there can be no dispute, the *To* evidently
being a variation of Toot or Teut, and implying the

[1] Paedutes in Hogg's Instructor.
[2] Verstigan's Restitution of Decayed Intelligence.
[3] Grand Gazeteer.

Tootcester, or castra situated near the altar dedicated to Teut. I am inclined to believe that this is the meaning intended to be conveyed in the *Woto* in Doomsday book. The castra of the Romans is also to be seen in the *cheshede* in the same ancient survey, for wherever the Roman Stativæ [1] were and were so called, the word *sede* was understood, which meant the same thing as camp.

The neighbourhood of Uttoxeter is exceedingly pleasant, its scenery being greatly diversified and filled with sylvan beauty. Its immediate vicinity is remarkable for the number of old lanes, as well as footpaths along the fields, so primitive and rural in their character, and so tempting for a quiet stroll at almost any season and in almost any state of feeling. The High Wood, a little distance to the south of the town, (so called because of its elevation, and from its having formed part of Needwood Forest,) affords some really fine prospects of the surrounding country. From hence, Needwood Forest, extending along undulating cliffs sweeping down to the south, lifts itself into view, although its grandeur becomes more evident as it is approached, particularly in the Woodlands, at the new church, where the scene is one of the richest magnificence. It is, however, to the north from the High Wood that the view is the most extensive and varied. Uttoxeter presents itself on an eminence rising out of a vast basin, the church spire shooting high above all other surrounding buildings.

[1] Shaw's History of Staffordshire.

More to the north the prospect takes in the Moor-
lands of Staffordshire, with the continuous range of
the hills of Wever, whose huge proportions

> Swell from each broken scene below.—*Vales of Wever*.

to about 1,500[1] feet above the sea.   Although these
hills have such an imposing look from a distance,
they lose much of their appearance of magnitude when
the spectator sees them in . closer proximity above
Wootton ; so true it is—

> That distance lends enchantment to the view.

This disadvantage is easily accounted for; an elevated
tract has to be gone over before their vicinity is
reached.   Besides these there are many other inviting
patches in the landscape.   Doveridge has a delightful
appearance on the right.   The spire of the village
church is beheld—

> Peering through tufted trees.—*Vales of Wever*.

and the declevity from the seat of Lord Waterpark
has a highly pleasing effect from the woody surface
which so tastefully adorns it.   Eaton Banks, a little
more distant, deserve so poetic a name, for the scenery
from the High Wood would be imperfect, and the
neighbourhood devoid of one of its greatest charms,
without the imposing woods by which they are
crowned—

> Painting with verdure all the scene.—*Vales of Wever*.

Eaton Woods were threatened with complete anni-
hilation in 1797, subsequent to the death of their
owner; the axe had made considerable havoc, but ere

---

[1] Pitt's Agriculture of Staffordshire.

it was too late the exterminating summons was arrested, and the portion now existing preserved for the admiration of all lovers of the picturesque. Thomas Gisborne, in his "Vales of Wever," and Francis N. C. Mundy, in his "Needwood Forest," have emulated each other in lamenting the fall of the woods, which had begun, and in perpetuating their friendship with their deceased proprietor, Godfrey Clarke, Esq., in the following lines in their poems :—

Ah! Eaton! soon thy woodlands gay
Shall live alone in Mundy's lay,
On Fancy's page immortal bloom,
And spurn the sawpit's yawning tomb.
Oftimes the Bard, where Needwood low'rs,
Sigh'd as he view'd your conscious bowers,
Ponder'd o'er Clarke's untimely bier,
And Friendship dropped a tuneful tear.
Hence, Eaton, when thy woods dethron'd
Stoop from the heights they long have crown'd,
Dryads and Fauns, a sylvan train,
At eve shall mourn thy parting reign,
In pale procession climb the steep,
And o'er thy withering hours weep;
Then shall the blue-ey'd nymphs of Dove
Glance at thy naked realms above,
Lean on their silver oars, and hear
The dulcet dirge with feeling ear.—*Vales of Wever.*

Yes, Eaton banks, in vain I strive
To hide the griefs your oaks revive :
Bow thy tall branches, grateful wood !
Afford me blossom, leaf, and bud.
He, for whose memory these I blend,
Thy late lost master, was my friend.
Fall, gentle dews! fresh zephyrs, breathe !
Spread, cooling shades! preserve my wreath !
Alas, it withers ere its time !—
So faded he in manly prime :
But Virtue, scorning Friendship's aid,
Rears its own palms which never fade.—*Needwood Forest.*

From the High Wood the valley of the Dove is exposed to view for some miles, and the river is seen winding its way southward, through luxuriant fields, and by many a pleasant spot on its banks. Owing to the opening of this valley to Ashbourne, Brassington moors and remoter portions of the mountainous tract of north Derbyshire can also be dimly observed in the blue mists of the horizon.

There are many charming woody declivities lying about Loxley, but they must be visited to be appreciated. They may be most favourably viewed on the way to Bramshall and on reaching the ridge on the west side of that village.

Perhaps the most interesting features belonging to the valley of the Dove by Uttoxeter are its vast extent and its fertility. Here it expands into many thousand acres of the most productive meadow and grazing land. Leland testified that " there be wonderful pastures by the Dove." This characteristic of the valley has also given existence to various popular sayings, one of which is that " if a stick be laid down there over-night in spring it will not be found for grass the next morning," and in being taken as the standard by which to judge of other land in the kingdom, it has been said, " it is nearly as good as Dove land." It has been further asserted, and probably without any exaggeration, that before the land in the country was cultivated, there was no fat meat in it but what came from the Dove. The wonderful qualities of the land so eulogised are owing to the floods of the river—"the British Nile"—which are sometimes sudden and of considerable extent, nearly inundating the whole valley, and carrying off sheep and sometimes cattle before any danger is suspected. A single night, by the melting of snow on the hills, or by a heavy fall of rain, which soon swells both the rivers Churnet and the Dove as well as the Tean brook, which unite their separate volumes before reaching Uttoxeter, readily serves to cause these unexpected floods which produce the fertility which has given such fame to the land at Uttoxeter and along the valley for many miles. Hence the saying—" In April, Dove's flood is worth a king's good."[1]

> Down yon mid dale the British Nile,
> Fair Dove, comes winding many a mile,
> And from her copious urn distils
> The fatness of a thousand hills.—*Needwood Forest.*

The geology of the neighbourhood of Uttoxeter, an account of which it may be thought ought to have preceded the description of its scenery, may not afford any very striking points of interest except to those engaged in a patient study of the science. Uttoxeter is built upon what is geologically termed the *drift* formation, which belongs to the upper tertiary epoch and immediately beneath the materials of the alluvium. The whole of this kingdom, as well as Europe, except the highest parts, have been submerged beneath the sea, and the drift is taken as evidence of a strong current from north to south. It consists of boulders and clay, large blocks of rock,

[1] See Plotts', Shaw's. and Nightingale's Histories of Staffordshire, and Leigh's History of Lancashire, Cheshire, and Derbyshire.

and accumulations of gravel. The larger materials are considered to have been conveyed from their native position in the north in vast masses of ice, which on dissolving have deposited their stony freight at great distances south of where they are naturally found. The gravel contains small boulders, supposed to have been deposited towards the close of the subsidence of the watery element. Uttoxeter itself stands upon a bed of gravel, which appears to terminate at the lower edge of the town, on the south. The hills immediately at each side of the town are of clay and marl. The High Wood running along the south of Uttoxeter consists of clay with large boulders, and in some places, gravel and sand, and others marl. Amongst the boulders are large quantities of slightly abraided pieces of limestone, and on the top of the High Wood may be found portions many pounds weight. In going along the road from the High Fields, these may be observed lying out on the road sides, and can scarcely have been conveyed there by any natural laws than those which accompanied the drift period. At Oldfield, where excavations for a new residence have recently been made, pieces of rounded rock, half a hundred weight or more in size, have been dug up. The gravel and boulders afford specimens of most kind of rocks, and from amongst them I have picked up several limestone specimens containing encrinites and bivalves. I have also seen several broken pieces of fossil bone of considerable thickness from the gravel or drift at Uttoxeter, and their vicinity has been marked by appearances, intermingling with the debris, very much resembling pieces of oxidized copper, bluish in colour, as if they had originally been small and thin copper coins. A very deep drain, perhaps ten or twelve feet deep, was being made in Carter Street last summer, in the previously undisturbed strata, when several fragments of bone of great thickness were met with, as well as the other appearances described. These would appear to be the result of the carbonization of animal substances, similar to those recently discovered by Mr. E. Brown, at Burton-on-Trent, an account of which was read at a recent meeting of the "Midland Scientific Association," at Derby.[1] In Marchington Woodlands the tertiary system has afforded a remarkable fossil of the proboscidian tribe, found beneath a bed of marl twenty-one feet in thickness, which, from its dark boggy appearance, must have originally been the bed of an ancient lake. The fossil was found by the late Mr. Hall, while sinking a well, but he was prevented from making further search for water by coming upon this dark inky-looking sediment. The whole skeleton of the fossil animal was supposed to have been there embedded, but no part of it was got away with the exception of what was supposed to be the horn of an elk, and it was wrenched off by the aid of a horse and chain. The size of the so-called horn is four feet six inches long, but it has been longer. It is about twelve or fourteen inches in circumferance, and its concentric formation, weight, and slight cur-

[1] Printed in the "Reliquary" Quarterly Journal, vol. 2, p. 206.

vature only indicate it to be an appendage of some other gigantic creature—perhaps of the mastodon. When found it was stated to have been richly gilded, an appearance produced by the presence of pyrites or sulphuret of iron. With an account of an interesting discovery shortly to be noticed, I sent a description of the so-called horn to the late Mr. T. Bateman, who was of opinion that it was a tusk of one of the extinct mastodons or of the Asiatic elephant, and if so was of greater antiquity than the remains usually found in bogs or near water courses. The beautiful metallic appearance he also regarded as singular, as it is more generally to be found upon fossils of the eocene, the lower tertiary, and oolite days. The tusk is preserved by the son of Mr. Hall.

The valley of the Dove consists of the alluvium or post tertiary accumulations in which horns, said invariably to be those of the extinct elk, but which are antlers of the deer, are frequently met with. They have been found at Eaton, and twelve feet in the earth at Rocester. One of the most interesting discoveries yet made in this superficial deposit by the Dove, and not recorded before, took place a few years since at the Eyes, near Sudbury, in a cutting then in process of making. Along with the antlers of a deer were two trunks of bog-oak—each twenty feet long— and a human skull. The skull is that of a female. This discovery gives rise to several interesting speculations, and had the late learned Mr. Bateman been spared, it probably would have formed the subject ot a paper in the "Reliquary," in continuation of a

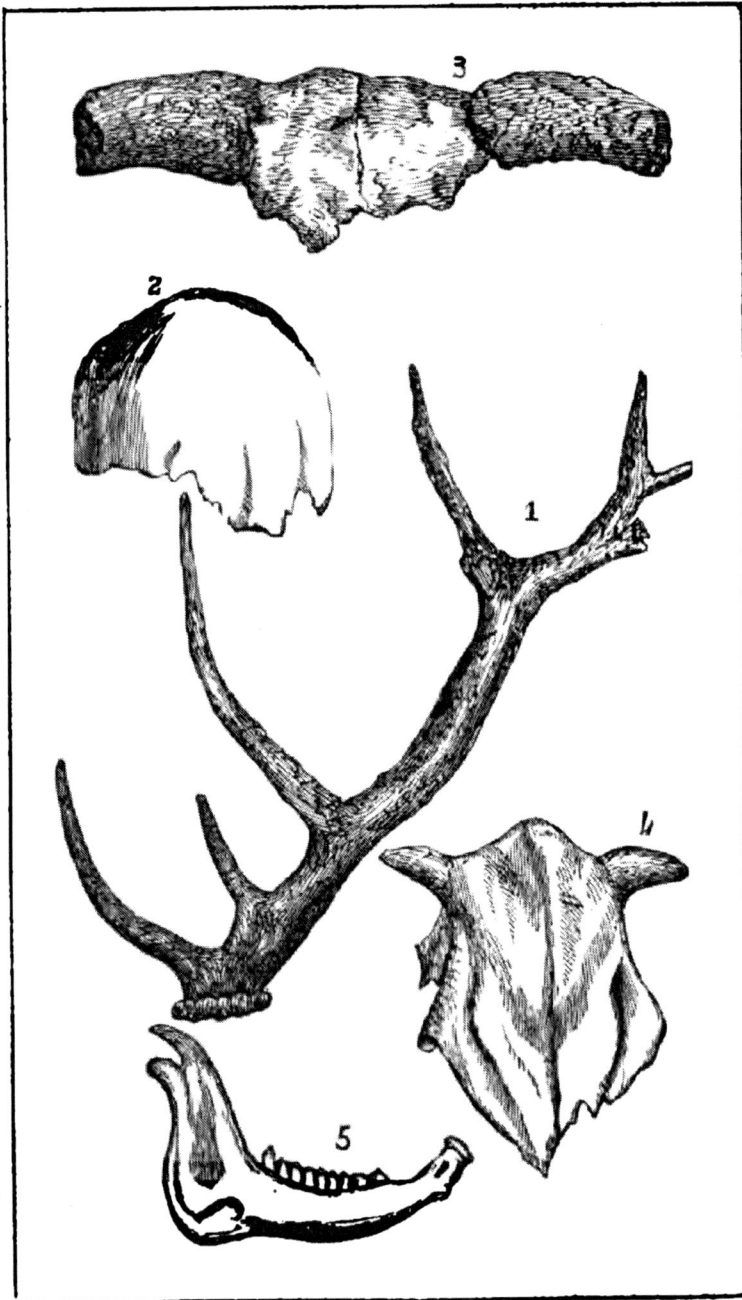

REMAINS FOUND AT SUDBURY.

previous interesting and valuable one by him on the
" Extinct Animals of Derbyshire in their relation to
Man," which appeared in that valuable antiquarian
miscellany. Whether the person, of whom the skull
is a portion of the remains, became accidentally entombed in a bog, or was the victim of the Scandinavian
punishment of being buried alive in a bog, (to which
females were subjected) it would be difficult to decide.
It may be said, however, that the discovery does not
clash with, but adds confirmation to, the accounts of
the late appearance of man upon the present scene,
and associates him with this island, and this neighbourhood in particular, at a very remote period. The
skull and antlers are preserved amongst other curio-
sities at Sudbury Hall, the seat of Lord Vernon.

Mineral springs are indicative of particular strata,
and of these there are several within a few miles of
Uttoxeter. Penny-croft well, close to Uttoxeter on
the north, and Moat spring near Buttermilk hill, are
both sulphurious. A spring at Messrs. Copes, at
Pinfold lane, is chalybeate, or contains iron. Near
Draycott mill is a saline spring—the salt pit of the
nuns at Hanbury. One purely vitriolic exists on
Needwood Forest, near Hanbury, and alluminous
waters are found at Draycott.

THE CELTIC, ROMANO-BRITISH, AND ANGLO-SAXON PERIODS.

And this, then, is the place where Romans trod,
Where the stern soldier revell'd in his camp,
Where naked Briton's fixed their wild abode,
And lawless Saxons paced with warlike tramp.
John Bolton Rogerson.

IT has been common for topographical writers to suspect that Uttoxeter was a British settlement before the Roman occupation of this island. None, however, have yet attempted to furnish any information or reason in support of such a suspicion. Of course there is no historical evidence to be had, but at the same time there are various interesting circumstances which may be advanced, which strongly favour it. The tribe dwelling in this territory, according to Ptolemy, were the Cornavii, a term meaning "holy district or country of the priesthood," and strikingly indicative of the general prevalence of Druidical practices for which the then abounding woods and forests, in which they took place, were so favourable. The Cangi, or Woodlanders, who were herdsmen of this tribe, inhabited Cannock Chase which is affirmed to have joined Needwood forest, and to have reached even the banks of the Dove. [1] So that it may reasonably be supposed that for the advantage of the flocks and herds of the extensive pasturage by the Dove, they might select so tempting a spot as Uttoxeter as the site of their residence in such huts as they erected.

However, there is decisive evidence both of the existence of the ancient Britons in the neighbourhood of Uttoxeter, and also of the observance of Druidical rites. These facts not only strengthen the likelihood of Uttoxeter having been a settlement of this ancient people, but are a matter of considerable importance, and invest the place with such an interest as the more imposing Celtic remains in the Peak of Derbyshire, and the relics of a similar nature in other parts, possess. Toot Hill, on Uttoxeter High Wood, has associations of a similar interesting character, although it has only, till now, been mentioned as a Roman tumulus.

The name of Toot Hill implies that it was dedicated to the Celtic deity, Teutates, as an altar. The name of this heathenish god is derived from Du Tath or Deus Taautus. Tot, Toot, or Teut, is an Ætheopic word, signifying dog-star, and it is supposed that the Toth of Egypt, deified in the dog-star, was transferred to the Phœnecians who derived their astronomical knowledge from Egypt. The Phœnecians carried on commercial transactions with this island,

---

[1] Whittaker's History of Manchester.

C

particularly in tin, and it has been observed that the superstitious worship of this deity was left by them amongst the barbarous islanders. At the same time the Druidic rites of the Celts have been accounted for as having been preserved amongst them from their common origin in the east. It has also even been surmised that some Egyptians had become established amongst them as among other rude nations, and had thus given a peculiar Egyptian character to the Druidic rites of this distant island. Stukely, in his "Stonehenge Described," conceives that the Druids came here from the east in the time of Abraham.[1] The chronological accounts fix the arrival of the Celts in Britain about one thousand six hundred years before the Christian era, and their migration over the Bosphorous and spread over the western parts of the old world upwards of two thousand years before Christ, or about the time when Abraham is supposed to have lived. The same heathenish deity was worshipped by the Greeks under the name of Hermes, and by the Romans as Mercury.

Each of the fabulous gods had offices assigned to him peculiar to himself. Teutates, amongst the Britons, was regarded as the god of messengers and travellers. The tumuli which were dedicated to him, as Toot Hill was on Uttoxeter High Wood, stood on elevated and precipitous places. The reason of this was, as Cæsar relates, that travellers might have guidance and protection along the roads and track-

[1] Stonehenge Described by Dr. Stukely.

ways, and become prosperous in their commercial enterprises.

On Toot Hill, as on all such eminences in the kingdom, the sacred or Beltane fires were kindled and flamed thrice a year at the great festivities of the Druids, in honour of Baal or the sun. One of a prodigious character was lit on May eve on these hills, and produced a remarkable light over the whole country. Fires were again made on Midsummer-eve, and on the eve of the first of November. The last was accompanied with sacrifices and festivities. On this day the people of the country out of a religious sentiment inculcated by the Druids, completeley extinguished their fires to rekindle them the same eve, for the ensuing year, by a portion of the consecrated fire from the sacred altars. This was a duty which the head of every family was rigidly obliged to observe, and it was expected that by such observance good luck and prosperity would attend them till the return of the eve of the first of November. For the privilege of obtaining the use of this holy fire they had, however, to pay an annual due to the Druids, [1] which if they ommitted to discharge by the last day of October ensuing, they had no prospect than to live the winter through without fire. No neighbour was permitted to give them any, or allow them the use of theirs—if they did, it was at the risk of excommunication, a fate, as managed by this religious priesthood, worse than death.

---

[1] A small coin said to be worth about threepence.

At the sacred fires on the first of November it was customary for some person of distinction to take in his hands the entrails of the animal sacrificed, and walking barefoot over the coals thrice, carry them to the Druid, who waited at the alter dressed in a whole skin. If he passed through the ordeal unhurt it was considered a favourable omen, and he was applauded; if otherwise, it was received as an augury of calamity to the whole community. The midsummer fire and sacrifices were for the purpose of obtaining a blessing on the fruits of the earth now becoming ready for gathering, as were those on the first of May that they might grow prosperously. Those of the last of October were a thank-offering for finishing the harvest.[1]

From Hollingbury being situated close to Toot Hill, it is not improbable that it took its name from another hill or altar dedicated to Belanus or Baal. This is the name under which the Celts worshipped the sun, and the worship of Teutates was generally united with it. In another part of the county there is a hill called Hilbury Hill contiguous to a Toot Hill. Indeed, in the survey of Uttoxeter, taken about 1658, by Peter Lightfoot, physician, it is in one place called Hill or Hollingbury indifferently. There are several mentions, moreover, of a Hollin Hall in descriptions of land on the High Wood as in the following instances:—"One tenement and barn and one close adjoining to the High Wood against Hollin Hall," and, "One tenement and two closes adjoining

---

[1] Toland's History of the Druids.—Hones Every Day Book.

to the High Wood and the lane over against Hollin Hall." These references, without the slightest doubt, are to Hollingbury, and confirm the supposition that there was an altar there to Baal as well as one to Teut.

In the name of Ashcroft,[1] a close near the High Fields in a direct line with the High Wood, is also indicated another place of Druid worship. The ash was a tree sacred to the Druids. In the most ancient of languages the word ash signifies fire, and the remnants of fires are to this day called ashes, and therefore the places, where these fires, made chiefly of ash were kept, and have ash in the prefix of their name, as in Ashkelons, and Ashfield, they may properly be concluded to be sites where these ancient rites were observed. There is also a meadow, near Uttoxeter, which anciently bore the name Beale[2] or Bean meadow, but now only the latter, which suggests the still greater prevalence in the neighbourhood of Uttoxeter, of the worship of Baal.

The doctrines of the Druids, out of which arose their rites just described, although the account may appear somewhat too favourable, have been remarked upon[3] as more refined and rational in their nature than those of most other religious bodies. They taught the immortality of the soul and a future state of rewards and punishment. Their morality was at

---

[1] So called in Lightfoot's survey.
[2] The Survey of Peter Lightfoot, physician, of Uttoxeter.
[3] Ireland illustrated.

once mild and strict, and their denunciation of the
sins they specified was unremitting; but their opinions
of the Deity were vague and erroneous. They had
an imperfect perception of one pervading essence
which revelation teaches Christians to worship under
the name of God, but they worshipped the sun as a
personification of his power, and used fire as an em-
blem of his nature in their worship; besides, they did
not regard the Divinity as a being of such stainless
purity as we reverence; still, this species of Baal
worship—which originated in the East, where
God himself, according to scripture, (Hosea, c. ii. v.
16) was at one period worshipped under the name of
Baal—was infinitely superior in simple and lofty
truth to that of the Greeks and Romans. In course
of time it became corrupted by teaching a plurality
of Gods. In many parts of the united kingdom, vestiges of the rites of the Druids may still be traced.

Having described some of the Druidical customs
with which Toot Hill has been associated—on which
indeed they have taken place—it only remains to be
described as a place of sepulture. Various modes
of burial, very different to those in use at present,
have been practiced in times past. Sometimes the
sepulchres assumed the character of vast barrows, as
the Pyramids of Egypt; as the grave of Semiramis;
upon which, as amongst the Etruscans, art and
wealth were lavished without any restriction. The
tumuli, or loose tombs, meaning graves, which exist
as artificial hills, are numerous in this kingdom,
many of which have been raised at the expense of

much labour and time. They are chiefly of Celtic formation, but they have often been taken advantage of by the Romans and Anglo Saxons for places of sepulture.[1] Toot Hill, as its name and associations show, is a Celtic grave-hill, and its form is of the most ancient type, being a long tumulus—and in age is perhaps coeval with the Pyramids themselves. Having obtained permission to open it in May 1860, I secured the aid of a man for a considerable part of one day, starting very early in the morning on the ninth of that month to the interesting research. I found myself, from early usage, a tolerable adept both with the pick and spade. On the second day I employed two men to assist me, and we spent about three parts of it in digging into the mound. On the first occasion I opened it in two places in the centre, and also in two at the east end. At the base of the tumulus in all those openings I came across a bed of charcoal. I also discovered a fragment of coarse pottery, at a depth of two feet, in one of the openings at the east end.[2]

In the subsequent attempt I resolved upon cutting a trench nearly through the tumulus, beginning at its east end; and also to open it in the centre. Here, about nine or ten feet below the surface, the layer of charcoal, of which I have before spoken, again

[1] Ten Years' Diggings in Celtic and Saxon Grave-hills, by T. Bateman.

[2] The fragment of pottery here alluded to is undoubtedly Roman, and has formed a part of a vessel of the form shown on the accom-

presented itself, unaccompanied, however, by any remains.   In commencing the long trench at the eastern
extremity of the hill, and about four yards from its
edge, a stone about six or eight pounds in weight was
found lying at the south side of a small heap of
human remains burnt to ashes, and from an appearance around them, it is not unlikely they had been
deposited in a cloth or skin.   They were about four
feet deep.   Exactly beneath these ashes, about four
feet more, on the ground of the tumulus, I picked up
pieces of calcined bone, charcoal, and some portions
of one of the most primitive specimens of Celtic pottery.   The pieces were quite soft; indeed they had
become of a piece with the clayey bottom of the
hill. [1]   Here were some pieces of raddle and yellow
ochre, and a few flakes of flint.

panying engraving.   It is of the ordinary form, and is interesting as
showing that on this hill interments at various periods have been
made. —L. Jewitt.

(1) The fragments appear to have formed a cinerary urn of the usual
type, as found in the Derbyshire and Staffordshire barrows.   I have

The soil on the top of Toot Hill presents strong evidence of the Beltane fires having been lit upon it. For an inch or two in depth the soil is burnt to redness all over its surface.

The extent of Toot Hill at the base is about seventy feet long and sixty-eight wide, and its height from seven to nine feet or more. The place overlooks the valley of the Dove, and was formerly in the depth of the Uttoxeter ward of the forest of Needwood. A number of trees are growing upon it, and around it are the remains of a holly fence.

Brends, the name formerly of land in the moor of Uttoxeter, may indicate the heathenish rite of interment by cremation.

Besides this, there are many other tumuli in the neighbourhood, and several have been destroyed. There appears to be one close to the Moorhouse, with

carefully examined the few pieces which have been preserved, and have shown in the accompanying engraving the form of the vessel and the style of ornamentation as closely as may be. The ornaments have been indented as usual, in the pottery of this period, with twisted thongs.—*L. Jewitt.*

some massive timber growing upon it. One at Morton was destroyed in 1860; it was of the long description, and no relics were found in it, except a few pieces of bone and a fragment of corroded iron. There has been one at Stramshall, which was destroyed when the new church was built. There is a slight elevation in a field at Lee Hill, Doveridge, which has the reputation of being one, and in the course of the cultivation of the field where it is situated, it has been ploughed over. It is called a Fairy Ring, a name quite singular in its application to a mound of earth. The name of Scownslow Green indicates that there has been a barrow there, and so does Callow Hill. A barrow still exists at Lowfields with trees growing upon it. It is called "Robin Hood's butts," and the place from whence he is said to have shot his arrows from the trusty bow, is placed at the White Gate on the Stubwood. This low is but slightly elevated above the surrounding surface. Fragments of swords are said to have been turned up near it, in the course of draining operations which have been carried on. There is a tradition current among the peasantry, that a battle was at one time fought at Low Fields, and the appearance of the low would lead one to the belief that it is a Saxon barrow, and may form part of a cemetery of that period.

THE ROMANO-BRITISH PERIOD.

So far back as the time of Erdeswick Uttoxeter has been deemed a Roman station, for in giving the distances of Roman stations from Mere, he mentions it as being fifteen miles plain west from Uttoxeter. At one time the learned Camden laboured to fix the Etocetum of Antoninus at Uttoxeter, which has since been proved to be at Wall, where numerous Roman antiquities have been discovered. That the Romans should have had a station at Uttoxeter is not surprising, since they had forty-six military stations and twenty-eight cities of consequence betwixt Perth and Inverness, and London, with a military force of 20,000 foot and 1700 horse for the defence of the colony.[1] Indeed it was the practice with them to have such kind of places along their roads and through the wooded parts of the kingdom for security against surprise from the Britons, as well as to insure proper pasturage, fodder, and water for all kinds of cattle passing and repassing from place to place.[2] The opinion that Uttoxeter was a Roman station is also favoured by the fact that it is situated close to the old Rykeneld street, or old British way, and also known as the *Via Devana*, or road to Ches-

[1] Scotland in the middle ages.
[2] Vegetius.

ter.   In 1789 an attempt was made to trace the course
of this way from Leicester to Chesterton.   It was found
through Needwood forest and followed to within a
mile south of Uttoxeter, but all trace of it was lost
until reaching Checkley and Tean, although it has
generally been supposed to have passed on the west
side of Uttoxeter at about the distance of a mile.[1]

I conceive, however, that by the aid of Lightfoot's
survey of Uttoxeter, I am enabled to show that the
old British and Roman way proceeded close on the
east side of Uttoxeter and not on the west side as previously supposed, and also to point out some remaining portions of it.   I was struck by the occurrence
in the old MSS. of the words Portway or Salter's
Lane, and I felt sure that if I could find out the land
in connection with which they are mentioned, I
should not be far from making out something of the
way itself, although no lane about Uttoxeter is, at
this time, known by such a name.   After spending a
considerable time in trying to find out what was
meant by land or fields in " The Botham field," and
in " The Bromshulf field," I was led to conclude
from the names of distinct fields, though much
altered in their spelling and pronunciation in the
course of two hundred years, that the land at the
west side of Uttoxeter up to Bramshall went under
the designation of Bromshulf field, and that at the
north-east side under the denomination of Botham

(1) See Shaw's Staffordshire ; Uttoxeter Parish Magazine, 1861 ; and
County Histories.

field. As, therefore, certain fields in the Botham field are said in the survey to shoot or abut on, or adjoin the Portway or Salter's lane, particularly the Mastalls near the Flatts and Penny-croft-well (close to a field or two now called the Bottoms), and the Tarhole, the name at that remote period of a small piece of land near where the lower mill was situated (the one where the fulling mill had been, and a little above where the old mill house now is) over Tean brook, the locality of the Portway, when in existence, became no longer doubtful. Adopting the opinion that Moisty-lane at the east side of the High Wood is a part of the Rykeneld Street (though the roads on the High Wood were greatly altered when the enclosures of the moor took place), it must have passed by the east side of Woodville and Uttoxeter, quite touching the latter place at Bull's Bank, and have gone along the bridle way betwixt the residence of Mrs. Jerningham and the Roe Buck, across the fields now called the Bottoms, and so have joined Slade Lane in its course towards Stoke and Chester. Supposing this account is correct, then the old way had a straight direction by Uttoxeter, for the bridle way at Bull's Bank is direct for the road above Woodville, and less than half a mile from it. However, the old Rykeneld street had an existence near the Flatts, and probably in a part of Slade Lane, for the same way is called in other parts both Portway and Salters Lane. This view receives additional confirmation from the fact that portions of the Rykneld, which traversed Derbyshire, are called *Bathom* Gate, and

Darley *Slade*, which have taken their names from the same circumstances as the "Bothams" and "Slade Lane" at Uttoxeter. It is supposed to have taken the name of Salters Way through' having probably been the packway for salt out of Cheshire. Port is no less significant of its having been a portion of the same ancient way. The word is Teutonic, signifying *chief* or *principal*, and prefixed to *way* as under consideration, indicated it to be what it really was, the principal way through the kingdom to Ireland.

Another road of remarkable firmness has gone across three fields called "The Bottoms," and so on to Crakemarsh, as if for Rocester. In the *Big Leasowes* which is separated from the Bottoms by Tean Brook, there is a remarkable site, of more than an acre, of *banks*, moat-like places, and uneven surfaces; and in the same field, where a gravel pit has recently been commenced for private purposes, at about five feet in depth wood and "curious bricks" have been found. The bricks (which have not been preserved) are described to have been "hard as flint." These remains may possibly be those of a Roman villa, and are worthy of extended investigation.

It has just been seen why the Romans selected in various places, posts; for those very reasons the site of Uttoxeter might have been fixed upon for the same purpose. At this point the Rykeneld would emerge from a wooded territory, inhabited by the British tribe who were the last to be conquered, whilst the pasturage by the Dove would supply them with forage to an extent, and in a way, few other places could.

It is to be regretted that the name of Uttoxeter is almost the only evidence (but that is indubitable) of its having been occupied by the Romans. It is, however, supplemented by circumstances already related, and by others to follow. In many places where there have been Roman stations, antiquities, including pottery and coins have been found to confirm reasonable conjecture. In this case but little in the way of antiquities can be mentioned to show that the Romans occupied a station at Uttoxeter, and but one relic of the Roman period besides the piece of pottery from Toot Hill, can be spoken of as having been found in the neighbourhood. Before describing it, however, an old well, which has had a Roman origin ascribed to it, may be mentioned. It was discovered in 1856, by the workmen of Mr. Evans, builder, in the course of getting out foundations for additional back premises at the house of Mr. Britton, which stands between the corner of Carter street and the Old Talbot, in the Market Place. As I did not see the well I transcribe a paragraph respecting it which appeared at the time.[1] "As a party of workmen were engaged a few days since in digging the foundations for a new house in connection with the shop and premises occupied by Mr. Britton, hosier, Market Place, Uttoxeter, which are undergoing extensive alterations, they discovered a short distance underground, a curious old stone well, arched over and about ten yards deep. The stones, of which it is

[1] In the Derbyshire Advertiser.

built throughout, are worn away by the trickling of
the water, and it is of very ancient if not as supposed
of Roman origin; but the Goths and Vandals of the
place filled it up with soil so that the efforts of the
curious to examine this ancient remain will be for
ever precluded."

To this account of the ancient well may be added
a description of remains, discovered a year or two
since, which may perhaps with equal certainty be ascribed to the Romans.   When Mr. Pedley, in Carter
street, was having a *sough* made under his house
floor, three or four separate pavements of boulders,
pebbles, and stones, one beneath the other for four
feet deep, were disturbed.   A number of drain tiles
of the Roman form, with four oblong sides, and the
usual holes down them, were met with.   The work
people thought the discovery very curious and un-
common at the time, but took no further notice of it,
and it was only by accident that I lately became
acquainted with the particulars.   It is not unlikely
that the same remains are continued underneath the
yard at the back of the house.

The relic referred to is a Roman vessel which was
brought to light in 1788, during the enclosure of the
High Wood.   The land there was being cultivated
for the first time, and the vessel was dug up by a
labouring man, and a drawing and description of it
from Mr. Samuel Bentley appeared in the *Gentleman's Magazine.*   As this gentleman had the article
in his possession, it may be presumed that his account
will be the most accurate.   He stated that all the

bottom of the vessel, of which the drawing was an exact copy, was corroded away by time, and as the

Romans had several (?) stations in this neighbourhood, he supposed it to have been a vessel in use amongst them, and consequently to have been of very remote antiquity. He was the more confirmed in his supposition as it bore a very close resemblance to a Roman vessel described in Montfaucon's Antiquities, on plate twenty-four, No. 9. According to the account there given of such vessels, he supposed it to have been used for bringing wine to the table, or else that it had been appropriated to sacrifices. The measure over the top was three inches and-a-half from the lip to the handle, and the handle five inches to the top of the bended part. The metal appeared to have been covered, both inside and out, with a hard and smooth enamel where it was not corroded and chipped, and to have been of a grey colour. The handle had been richly gilt, and the labourer who found it was exceedingly elated, expecting that the whole had been of that precious metal, and was very

D

much surprised when it proved to be only brass.
The vessel, it is further said, was a good deal ham-
mered and scraped to see what the metal was, but
what finally became of it does not appear, unless it
was sent to Mr. Green's museum at Lichfield.   This
Mr. Bentley intended to do, but had some hesitation
on account of the senseless scraping and hammering
it had received.   .

It has not been recorded whether any Roman coins
have been found nearer to Uttoxeter than Newborough, Hanbury, and Rocester.

THE ANGLO-SAXON PERIOD.

During the Anglo-Saxon period, Uttoxeter was included in the kingdom of Mercia, from Myricnarac,[1]
signifying in the Anglo-Saxon language, woodland
kingdom, and therein agreeing with Coritani, the
latinized name of the old British inhabitants, meaning woodland men or foresters.   Uttoxeter having
been a Roman station, was probably occupied by the
Saxons at an early period of their acquaintance with
this island.   Before the villages came into existence,
most of which have had a Saxon origin, the stations

[1] Macpherson's Annals of Commerce.

of the Romans, although partially demolished by the Picts, were invariably first seized upon by the Saxons for dwelling-places. This fact accounts for their hybrid character causing no little perplexity in the derivation (especially when coming through Norman writers) of the word Uttoxeter, and of many other Saxonized Roman places.

There are no remains of Saxon architecture in existence at Uttoxeter, nor any object which can be regarded as a production of their skill in art. If there were any remains in the old church, they have been swept away. Yet there are several interesting circumstances which clearly identify our Saxon ancestors with Uttoxeter. Accounts are preserved, with pictorial representations, of the amusements of the Saxon people, amongst which was that of seeing bears exhibited. A scene of this description, as having taken place in an Anglo-Saxon amphitheatre, is to be found amongst the Harleian manuscripts in the British Museum. The word Bear-Hill, applied to the open space at the east end of Uttoxeter Market-place, and which it had two hundred years back,[1] implies that this pastime was common in Uttoxeter amongst the Saxons, and that either the bears were kept at Bear-Hill, or that the sports with them took place there, or both. As the Saxon people of the town would not be likely to import these creatures for the purpose, it may be presumed they obtained them from Needwood Forest, where, as well as in

[1] Lightfoot's Survey of Uttoxeter, 1668.

other English forests, they existed in common with
the wild boar and wolf.[1]   As a proof of the wolf in-
habiting Needwood Forest in Saxon times, Wolf-
hurst, the name of an enclosed piece of land near
Uttoxeter, may be cited.   The word is Saxon: *Wolf*
being the Saxon name of the animal itself, and *hurst*
that of wood or forest.

Uttoxeter is also associated with Saxon times by a
curious monosylabic compound, thought to be the
nick-name of the place, and applied to a spot at the
east end of Silver Street.   The word is *Hole-in-the-
wall*, in which the Alwynehall may possibly be traced,
implying that one Alwyne, a Saxon thane, had his
residence there.   This little circumstance is of interest, pointing out as it probably may the locality
where one of the Saxon nobility lived, who might
possibly have been one of the influential functionaries
of the day.   It may be useful to add, that the thanes
were of several orders, although it would be useless
to inquire of what degree the Alwyne was who may
be supposed to have lived at the Hole-in-the-wall.
The king's thanes or attendants were of the first
order ; then the thanes of the aldermen and earls,
who were of the highest degree of the Saxon nobility,
and next the inferior thanes who were of the landed
gentry.   Thanes were amongst the members of the
Saxon Whitenagemot, or Parliament, or meeting of
wise men.   One of the qualifications of a Saxon
thane, was a certain amount of landed property, five

(1) See " Reliquary " for 1860-1861.

hides of land being required to qualify one of the highest order. One of the laws of Æthelstan declares, that if a ceorl, or commoner, shall have attained five hides of land in full property, with a church, a kitchen, a bell house, a burgate seat and a station in the king's hall, he shall henceforward be a thane by right. Perhaps the Alwyne at the Hole-in-the-wall was the thane of an Earl—possibly of Earl Algar.

We are further reminded of the Saxon character of the town by the principal entrance to the churchyard being called the "Light Gate." This word is corrupted from *Lice*,[1] the Saxon word for carcass or dead body, and Lich Gate was therefore the name given to the south entrance to the churchyard at Uttoxeter by the Saxons. *Lich* watching, or sitting with the dead, still observed in some places, was originated by the Saxons, but the practice does not appear to be continued at Uttoxeter.

Besides these traces of the Saxons in the town, there are many places in the neighbourhood which bear appellations originating with that people. Of these the following are examples, but some of them have a meaning which is not very evident. *Mansholme*, meaning a place surrounded by water; it is also applied to rising ground or a hill. Sweth*holme*, means the same. *Eaton*, water town; *Winfield*, to win peace; *Hockley*, the termination meaning pasture, and the prefix probably intimating that sports took place there, or from *hoc*, dirt, signifying a dirty field;

[1] So Bede says of Lichfield, from *Lice*, a dead body.

Ryecroft, a slip of ground near a house; Limecrofts, the same; *Shaw*, a wood; *Burndhurst*, which takes its name from a river and wood; *Field*, a feld place, the name of a village; Crakemarsh, a low place, or land overflown by a river or pool, or ditch; Ruffcliff, the side or pitch of a hill, a cragged mountain. *Slade* Lane, a long flat piece or slip of land. The prefixes and terminals to these and many other words, as well as many whole words, testify how generally the Saxons had become settled about Uttoxeter.

THE FEUDAL TENURE OF UTTOXETER.

Hitherto we have scanned the pre-historic period relating to Uttoxeter, and it has proved itself not altogether barren of many matters of interest, both local and general. We are now arrived at that period when local history receives the aid of authentic records, namely, when the survey of the kingdom was taken, by appointment of William the Conqueror, and contained in the Domesday-book, which was finished about 1086. The accounts of places are in a contracted form in the mixed latin of the time. Written out in full and plain English, the portion relating to Uttoxeter is as follows :—" Wotocheshede belongs to the king. It formerly belonged to Earl Algar. It has half a hyde of land. The arable land is ten carucates, with two in demesne and one servant, twenty-four villans, eleven bordars with eleven carucates. There are also sixteen acres of meadow land and a wood two miles long and broad.

It was worth seven pounds in the time of Edward the Confessor; it is now worth eight pounds."

A *hide* of land was one hundred and twenty acres. The arable land designated *carucates*, was plough-land, a *caruca* being as much as was tilled in a year. The villans, who took their name as a class from *villa*, a country farm, were employed in tillage, and are supposed to have been formed by the coalision of the conquered Britons, called Thralls, and of the free Saxon Ceorls.[1] The bordars, or boors, were inferior to the villans, and held small quantities of land on the borders of manors on a base and uncertain tenure.

It is singular that the name of Earl Algar is found in the survey, as he died seven years before the conquest, and was succeeded by his sons Edwin and Morcar, Earls of Mercia and Northumberland, who took up arms on behalf of their countrymen in 1071. Edwin, who would become the owner of Uttoxeter, on the death of his father, was betrayed to the Normans, and his estates were confiscated by the king.[2] This was a fate to which many Saxon noblemen had to submit, whether favourable or otherwise to the accession of William the Conqueror. The king, however, did not long retain Uttoxeter, but along with seven lordships in Staffordshire, and numerous others in Derbyshire, Warwickshire, Nottinghamshire, and Leicestershire, gave it to Henry de Ferrars, Ferers, Ferriers, or Ferrariis, son of Walkeline de Ferrariis, a baron of great wealth and power in Normandy, who

(1) Harland's History of Mamcester (Manchester), 1860.

(2) Henry's History of England, and Ward's History of Stoke-upon-Trent.

accompanied the king.[1] The name of Ferrars was taken from his employment, that of shoeing horses, —not that he was himself a farrier, but was appointed to direct and superintend that business in the nature of *præfectus faborum.* So when, at the time of the Crusades, it became the custom for families to take coat armour hereditarily, a charge of six horse shoes sable, on a field argent, was assumed by this great house.[2]

---

[1] Erdeswick's Staffordshire.

[2] Whether De Ferrars did hold the office of chief of the farriers, and whether or not in virtue of that office he assumed the badge of the horse shoe—or whether it was assumed as a "canting" badge (*armes parlantes* becoming pretty general as early as the reign of Henry II.) from its name, *fer de cheval* for Ferrars, as is generally believed— certain it is that the horse shoe was borne by the family of Ferrars in a variety of ways, and that it is identified with them throughout the period in which they held lands in this county. Mr. Planché, Rouge Croix Pursuivant of Arms, has laboured hard to prove that the Ferrars are not originally entitled to the distinction of the horse shoe, and that it was only borne by them after an alliance with the Marshalls, Earls of Pembroke, but I have no doubt in my own mind that he is wrong in the conclusion he has arrived at. Three, or six, horse shoes are described as the arms of Ferrars—called, of course, by the early heralds, "ferres de cheval"—thus the play on the word "ferres" for "Ferrars" is easily seen. Another bearing of the Ferrars is "Vaire, or and Gules," and I conceive that here (although such a supposition has never heretofore been started by any writer)—is another instance of the "canting," or playful bearings. Vaire being spelt and pronouced "VERRE" is so close an approximation to "Ferrars" as to warrant one in supposing that to that circumstance it owes its adoption as an heraldic bearing of that once powerful family. Again—on a Norman pitcher, recently discovered by me near Duffield, are, besides five horse shoes, two BUCKLES, which were probably also adopted as a badge from the resemblance of the name "fer-mailles" or "Fermaux" to "Ferrars."

It perhaps might be pushing the idea too far to suppose that the

Henry de Ferrars was held in great esteem for his political knowledge, abilities and integrity. The bestowal of these extensive possessions upon him by the king was for the eminent services he had rendered to this monarch. In the settlement of these lands in the honor of Tutbury (by which is meant an estate consisting of several lordships—as the lordship of Uttoxeter—manors and knight's fees), upon this nobleman, the king reserved to himself, or the crown, certain privileges and payments. He, nevertheless, on certain conditions, allowed portions of the same lands to be again given to others for their services, as will be subsequently perceived. Henry de Ferrars was one of the commissioners appointed to take the general survey of the kingdom. He died in the in-

pitcher just described proves that the proper heraldic bearing of the Earls of Ferrars and Derby was 5 horse shoes instead of 3 or 6—but I think there is reason to suppose this to be the case. In the first place, 5 is equally as legitimate and usual a number as 6, and is one which fits the shape of the shield quite as well. It is evident from the disposition of the horse shoes on this jug, that the potter had some special end in view in placing 5 around it,—for he has put 4 of an uniform size, and then to complete the requisite number has had to crowd in a small one by the buckles. The pitcher here described was found in the remains of a Norman pottery, on lands formerly belonging to the Ferrars, and not far from their chief residence, Duffield castle. It has been carefully engraved and described in the " Reliquary," Vol. III., page 216; which engravings, exhibiting both sides of the vessel, I have pleasure in here introducing.

It has generally been believed that the Normans were the first to introduce the practice of shoeing horses into England—but this has long been disproved—and I have myself found iron horse shoes with undoubted Roman remains. That the Normans attached great importance to the art of farriery there can be no doubt, for besides the grants to the Ferrars it is recorded that the Conqueror gave to Simon St. Liz the town of Northampton to provide shoes for his

NORMAN PITCHER, BEARING THE BADGE OF THE FAMILY OF FERRARS.

terval of the years 1080 and 1089. He had by his wife, Bertha, three sons, Eugenulph, William, and Robert. The two former died during the lifetime of their father, so, that he was succeeded by Robert in the possession of Uttoxeter.

To Robert de Ferrars, who was a nobleman of enlightened views, Uttoxeter was indebted, in common with other immediate parts of the Honor of Tutbury, for some of its earliest advantages, arising from improvements in agriculture and trade. With a view to the cultivation of some newly enclosed parts of

horses—that Gamelhere held land in Cukney, Nottinghamshire, for the service of shoeing the king's palfrey upon four feet, with the king's nails, or shoeing materials, as oft as he should be at his manor of Mansfield, and if he put in all the nails the king should give him a palfrey of four marks, or he was to have the king's palfrey giving him 5 marks, as he was also to do if he lamed the horse, pricked him, or shod him straight—that Henry de Avering held the manor of Morton (Essex) by the sergentry of finding a man with a horse value ten shillings, and 4 horse shoes, one sack of barley, and one iron buckle, as often as the king should go with his army into Wales, at his own expense, for forty days.

The horse shoe was painted on the wooden foot quintain and it occurs heraldically on the seal of Walter Marshall, Earl of Pembroke, 1246, in the arms the Company of Farriers, and those of the families of Borlace, Cripps or Crispe, Ferrars, Randall, and Sheyswell, or Shoeswell, &c., &c. It also forms the arms of the town of Oakham, in Rutlandshire—and here again its connection with the Ferrars is remarkable, for the manor, with its regal hall, was held by them, and they had the priviledge, which is still retained as a right although compounded for by money, of claiming from every peer of parliament the first time he passes through the town, a horse shoe to be nailed on to the Castle Gate, and if he refuse, the bailiff of the manor has the power to arrest him and take one by force from his horses foot. In the fine old hall at Oakham, a number of these horse shoes, many of them with the names of the peer from whom claimed are preserved.— *L. Jewitt.*

Needwood forest, and the consumption of their produce, he enlarged Uttoxeter and Tutbury, and built
Newborough.[1] Uttoxeter, according to the Harleian MSS. had 127 burgages, Tutbury 182, and
Newborough 101, the occupiers of which got their
living by some handicraft or trade of merchandise.
At Uttoxeter, iron was manufactured, whilst bleaching was pursued at Newborough, and wool-combing at
Tutbury.   Thus Earl Robert intended the agricultural and trading populations of the district to be
mutually advantageous to each other; the former to
supply the latter with necessary food, while they in
return were to supply the former with the requisite
articles of clothing and implements of husbandry.
Uttoxeter also gained other benefits under this wise
and beneficent Earl; he made it a free borough, by
which is to be understood that the inhabitants were
exempt from servile offices to the lords of the
honour.   He also granted unto them other privileges
which they had not before enjoyed.   They were made
free of all tolls, tonnage, package, poundage, and
other exactions within their possessions.[2]   Liberty

(1) About twenty years ago, an old saw-pit was discovered in Uttoxeter
Market Place, which may reasonably be supposed to have been made
when Uttoxeter was enlarged.   The wall separating the house of Mr.
Norris from the Old Talbot Inn (two of the oldest houses in the
town), was giving way, owing to the decay of the oak sleepers, and to
remedy the matter, it was found necessary to dig ten feet deep for a
foundation for a new wall.   At this depth, the saw-pit, containing
sawdust and curious oak wedges, quite black by the action of the iron
in the earth, was met with, and a similiar discovery was made afterwards, underneath the same premises, when sinking a well.

(2) Harleian MSS.

was given them to cut wood within the Uttoxeter Ward of the forest for fuel, buildings, and fences; known as fire-boot, house-boot and hay-boot, as also to depasture horses and cattle in the forest, and to turn swine therein to consume the acorns, for which a sum of money was paid, called pannage.[1] In the survey of Uttoxeter by Lighfoot, some portion of land on Balance Hill is called swine-pits, either from the woods having at some period extended as far, and in which swine were turned, or from swine having been collected there out of the forest, or fed there with acorns collected for them. The Domesday Survey contains some curious items respecting the feeding of swine in this way, which show their value, and how greatly they were depended upon as a source of profit and food. The return for Middlesex was 16,535 hogs; for Hertfordshire 30,535, and for Essex 95,991. But more curious is it, that a nobleman by his will left 2000 swine to two daughters; another nobleman directs 100 swine and a hide of land to his relations, and 200 swine to two priests, in equal proportions for the good of his soul; whilst another disposes of land to a church, on condition that 200 swine were fed for the use of his wife.

Robert de Ferrars also granted to the monks of Tutbury priory right to make a trench in the moor of Uttoxeter to preserve their fields, and gave them the branches of the willows and osiers which hung over

[1] Sir Oswald Mosley's History of Tutbury.

the water for improvement of their wet lands, which were often injured by floods.

It does not appear who was the wife of this Earl, but beyond the great improvements he made in the Honor of Tutbury, in which Uttoxeter so largely participated, it is mentioned of him that in the reign of king Stephen, he accompanied William Peverel, Earl of Nottingham, and other noblemen who undertook to repel the invasion of David, king of Scotland; and in consequence of the personal valour he then displayed, king Stephen created him an Earl. He died the year after this memorable event, in 1139.

He was succeeded by his son Robert, who in his fathers life-time styled himself "Robertus junior, "comes de Nottinghame." He succeeded his father as Earl of Ferrars, and is said to have been the first who assumed the title of Earl of Derby, being created to that dignity by king Stephen in 1141. But it is also said that it was the *first* Robert who was thus distinguished by Stephen for his conduct at the battle of the standard. This second Robert died in 1184, in the thirtieth of Henry II. He was succeeded by his son William, Earl of Ferrars and Derby, who married Margaret Peveril, and through her inherited estates, to one of which "Higham Ferrars" he added his name. He is said to have died at the seige of Acre in 1190. His son the second William, married a daughter of Hugh Kevillioc, Earl of Chester, and died in 1247. He was created Earl of Derby by king John in the first year of his reign. He was succeeded by his son, the third William, who married Sibilla, daughter of William Marshall, Earl of Pembroke, who in his turn was succeeded by his son Robert, the last Earl, whose course of infidelity to his sovereign, and reckless and open rebellion, ended in his attainder, and the confiscation of his lands, which in 1266 were given by Henry III. to the Earl of Lancaster.

King John was greatly indebted to the second Earl William, for his faithful attachment, and by a special charter created him Earl of Derby. On this occasion the king himself girded him with a sword, and not only had he in the same charter a grant of every third penny in all pleas before the sheriff of the county of Derby, but in the same year and afterwards the honor of Tutbury was extended by the addition of other manors and grants of land. When the Pope had deposed king John, this earl proved his fidelity to him by becoming surety for his fulfilment of those conditions to which the king was obliged to submit. As an additional return for the royal favours he had received, he accompanied the king to Poictou, and both aided him and his successor Henry III. against the rebellious barons, betwixt whom, some years afterwards, from the estimation in which he was held as a peacemaker and lover of justice, he was chosen arbitrator in their quarrels. He died in the year 1247.

His successor, William de Ferrars, Earl of Derby, did homage for Chartley, and it was during his life that some of the wild cattle of Needwood [1] Forest

---

[1] The name of Needwood appears to be a corruption of Neat's wood, or the wood of cattle.

E

were driven into the the park at Chartley, where
their kind have remained more than 600 years. He
was well acquainted with the laws of his country, and,
like his father, possessed those qualities which com-
mended him to the esteem of all who had the privilege
of his friendship. It was this earl (who died from
the effects of an accident in 1254, and was buried in
Merevale Abbey), who granted the following charter
to the burgesses of Uttoxeter, which is dated August
15th, 1252.[1]

"To all men that shall see or hear this present
deed, William de Ferrars, Earl of Derby, sendeth
greeting in the Lord: Know ye, that we have granted
and by this present deed confirmed for us and our
heirs, to all our burgesses of Uttoxeshather, that
they hold from henceforth freely their burgage and
burgages, with the appurtenances in the same town
of Uttoxeshather, as some of them have formerly
been assessed, and others hereafter shall happen
to be, with free ingress and egress, to be held of
us and our heirs to them and their heirs or assigns
and their heirs for ever, as freely and as decently they
shall and may hold the same as free burgesses, with
all liberties, free common, and easements to a free
borough belonging, yielding to us yearly and to our
heirs for every burgage separately twelvepence sterling at two terms of the year, viz.:—one-half at the
Annunciation of our Lady, and the other half at the
feast of St. Michael, for all secular service, custom,

---

[1] Uttoxeter Chronology in MSS.

and exactions to us and our heirs belonging. We
have granted also to the said burgesses and to their
heirs as above said, that they may take within themselves upon their burgages aforesaid chapman and other
free men whom they will, enfeoffing them or granting them other easements within the said borough
without injury to the same, and without hinderance
of us and our heirs, saving our service in all. And
further we will, that none carry on any trading
within the said free common or liberty without
reasonable and accustomed toll. We have granted also
to the said burgesses and their heirs as aforesaid, and
to all being within their commonality, that they shall
be within all our own lands and liberties free from
toll wheresoever they shall pass for ever, saving other
men's charters and liberties made and used before
this deed. All these things aforesaid we have granted within the said commonality of the aforesaid
burgesses for ever, saving to us and our heirs a
reasonable toll of all our said burgesses and their
heirs or assigns, and of all within their commonality
being, when as our lord the king that for the time
shall be shall tax all his boroughs throughout England so as the said tax be gathered by the hands of
two burgesses to the use of us and our heirs, and also
saving to us and our heirs the ovens and market with
their profits, and the site of the borough and market,
and of the court-leet also from them, with pannage and
all other liberties without our said borough, but so as
the said burgesses and all within their commonality
being, have common and herbage within the ward of

Uttoxeshather, where the men of the said town have
been wont formerly to outcommon without our hin-
drance, so as it may be lawful for us and our heirs
to make our profit of all other lands and tenements,
meadows, pastures, woods, marshes, moors, and in
all other places within the aforesaid town and ward,
without contradiction of the said burgesses or their
heirs.   And if it happen that any·burgage belonging
to us or our heirs, by any means or by fire shall be in
lack of occupation or service by the space of one year,
then for want of a tenant the whole commonality
of the burgesses of the said town's street after the
year shall take the said burgage into their hands, and
make the best profit thereof, and answer to us and
our heirs for the farm and service thereof, without
any claim of him or his, who first held the said burgage: wherefore we will and grant for us and our
heirs, that all things aforesaid be observed and kept
to the said burgesses and their heirs for ever.   In
witness whereof this my present writing with the
strength of my seal for me and my heirs I have for-
tified.   These being witnesses: Hugh de Meynell,
Robert de Essebourn, Robert de Punchardun, Richard
de Mortimer, Jeffrey de Caudrey, Robert de Merinton, Thomas (then rector of the church of Uttoxeter),
Robert de Stretton, clerk, Jordan de Grindon,
John de Twyford, clerk, and William de Rolleston.
Dated at Uttoxeter on the day the Assumption of
the Virgin Mary, in the year of the reign of king
Henry, son of king John, the six-and-thirtieth."[1]

[1] Mosley's History of Tutbury.

The last Earl of Derby to whom Uttoxeter belonged was Robert de Ferrers, son of the latter William. The loss of his father whilst he was under age was a great misfortune to him. He grew up without the influence of paternal authority. He was naturally of a perverse mind, and a knowledge of his extensive possessions was not likely to be the most favourable to its subjection. On attaining the age of twenty-one years, he openly rebelled against the king, his extensive estates furnishing him with a considerable number of followers; and in consequence of the depredations he committed, a large army was sent against him under the king's eldest son Edward, who demolished Tutbury castle, laid waste the country round with fire and sword, and involved the peaceful occupiers of the district in great suffering and loss. Uttoxeter being one of the most considerable places within a few miles of the castle, the possesors of its burgages influential, free from all servile offices, but bound to serve the superior lords of the honor in time of war, most likely felt the infliction of the chastisement upon the earl in a severe degree. Still the loss he thus sustained and the misery he entailed upon the guiltless occupiers of the land, had little effect upon him; he continued his rebellion until at length, for his misdemeanors and crimes, the king resolved to punish him. Seeing his doom, he flung himself upon the mercy of his sovereign, who generously pardoned him. He was bound by the most solemn stipulations to rebel no more, but in their very face he was again found in arms against the king. His tenure of power, however, was short. His forces were routed by Almaine, the king's eldest son; he himself was captured and cast into prison, in London, and his lands, by two grants dated June and August, 1266, were given to Edmund, Earl of Lancaster, son of Henry III.

It would be out of place to follow this earl through his useless litigations for the recovery of his confiscated estates after his imprisonment of three years; but it must be observed that soon after he became of age, and previous to the year 1262, he gave to John Tunley one hundred and twenty acres of land upon the Brends in the ward of Uttoxeter, with timber growing thereon, to be held of him and his heirs, unless they should be religious men or Jews, freely, with house boot and hay-boot throughout the ward of Uttoxeter, and rights of common in the forest of Needwood. He also gave liberty the same year, by his letters patent, dated at Yoxall, to Sir Walter Raleigh and his heirs residing at Uttoxeter, to hunt and course the fox and hare within the precints of his forest of Needwood, with eight braches (a particular sort of hound, perhaps the beagle) and four greyhounds.

The accompanying engraving, carefully drawn from the seal in the Duchy court of Lancaster, represents the seal of this last, and truly unfortunate Earl of Derby, of the noble family of Ferrars. The obverse represents the Earl in full armour, clothed in a suit of chain mail, with hauberk closed, and sword drawn. He bears a heater shaped shield emblazoned with

SEAL OF ROBERT DE FERRARS.

his arms, vaire *Or* and *Gules*, and the trappings of his horse are charged with the same bearing. The figure is surrounded with the legend ROB̄S FIL' ET HERES DN̄I WILL'I DE FERRAR' QV̄DA COMITIS DERBEYE. The reverse bears a heater shaped shield of the then arms of Ferrars, vaire *Or* and *Gules*, hanging upon a tree, the foliage surrounding the shield being truly elegant and highly characteristic of the early English period. Around the seal is the legend SIGILLVM ROBERTI DE FERRARIIS COMITIS DERBEYE. The seal, which is here engraved of its full size, is one of the most beautiful and perfect of its period.

Uttoxeter must now be considered as having become transferred to Edmund, Earl of Lancaster, who was a branch of royalty. This Earl claimed various privileges for Uttoxeter (and the same to Tutbury), which were, view of frank-pledge, infangthef, the right of erecting a gibbet and of receiving waives; also a free warren, a market once in seven days, on Wednesday in each week, and an annual fair on the eve and nativity of the blessed Virgin, all of which liberties, rights, privileges, and customs had been held by Robert de Ferrars, the last Earl of Derby.

The events of the life of Edmund, Earl of Lancaster, may be comprised in a very brief summary. In his youth he was invested with the fictitious title, by the pope, of king of Sicily, probably with the idea of deriving a large revenue from this country. Subsequently he was created Earl of Chester, and at the death of Simon de Montfort, at the battle of Evesham, that nobleman's lands, with the honor of Leicester, were granted to him. He accompanied his brother, Edward I., to the Holy Land, but returned in safety. In the twenty-fourth year of this king, he was sent, with the Earl of Lincoln, with twenty-six bannerets to Gascoigne; they set down near Bordeaux, but seeing no likelihood of its surrender, they marched, after some skirmishes, from thence to Bayonne, where they were honourably received. Having, however, many soldiers with them whom they could not keep together, owing to the exhaustion of their treasures, he grew much troubled in mind, and thereby falling sick, he died at the feast of Pentecost, in the year 1296. He commanded that his body should not be buried till his debts were paid; after which, truce being made, his body was carried to England and buried in Westminster Abbey. A monument was erected to his memory, of which there are plates in Gough's Sepulchural monuments of Great Britain.[1] This earl was twice married; by his second wife, Blanche, he had three sons—Thomas, Henry, and John, and one daughter.

Henry, second Earl of Lancaster, the most powerful and wealthy subject in Europe, did much to improve the country surrounding the castle, which he found still suffering from the injuries sustained during the rebellion of the first earl, and he also repaired and beautified the castle at Tutbury. In the second year of Edward II., he had confirmed to him by royal

[1] Shaw's History of Staffordshire.

grant the weekly market on Wednesday, and the fair at Uttoxeter. In the tenth year of Edward II., he was in the Scottish wars, and was commanded to raise two thousand foot, well armed, out of his own lands and fees, and to bring them to Newcastle to the king within one month of the feast of the nativity of St. John the Baptist. He retained Sir Hugh Meynell to serve him in peace and war.[1] He lived in a state of great splendour, and well would it have been for him if his views had been confined to the improvement of his estates and the sumptuousness of his hospitalities. He became general of a confederate army against Edward II.; various recriminations, and some not the most honourable, were inflicted upon him; ultimately he was taken prisoner, and after having been condemned by a counsel of the king's officers, and not by a body of noblemen, he was beheaded at Pontefract in March, 1320, amid great indignities, and in the sequel *canonized*.[2]

Uttoxeter now became a demesne of the crown, although but for a short time, for after having been consigned, with the rest of the estates of the late earl, to the custody of Roger Beler, who was attached to the king's person, the period approached for those extensive possessions to revert to the brother of Thomas Earl of Lancaster. King Edward became the royal captive of Henry, Earl of Lancaster, but afterwards falling into less humane hands, he was barbarously

[1] Shaw's History of Staffordshire.
[2] Dunstanborough Castle, amongst Plates from J. M. W. Turner, R.A.

put to death. The claim of Henry de Lancaster to the estates of his brother, was admitted by prince Edward, who assumed the administration of the state. It was also again recognised in the first year of Edward III., and an act of parliament was passed for revising the attainder of Thomas, Earl of Lancaster, upon the ground that he had not been tried by his peers according to law and Magna Charta. In the same year, 1327, an inquisition was taken of the lands the late earl left at his death, and Uttoxeter is particularly mentioned in connection with those in Staffordshire.

The principal residence of Henry, Earl of Lancaster, was at Leicester. Very few transactions of his life are upon record connected with the honor of Tutbury. He died in 1345, leaving by his wife Maud, Henry who was created Earl of Derby, and subsequently Duke of Lancaster, who was the first English subject, except those of royal descent, who was invested with the ducal title since the conquest. A considerable part of his life was passed abroad in the service of his country, in which he proved himself one of the greatest warriors of his age. He had, however, in his father's lifetime so distinguished himself as to be made captain general of the king's army in Scotland.[1] His chivalrous exploits formed a theme of exultation to every Englishman, and produced a paralysing dread in the hearts of his opponents. His life was terminated by the plague, at Leicester, on the 24th of

[1] Shaw's History of Staffordshire.

March, 1361. This nobleman left two daughters, Maud and Blanche, co-heiresses of his extensive possessions. Those which formed the earldoms of Derby and Lancaster fell to the share of Blanche. Uttoxeter was included in this division, it being in the honor of Tutbury. This lady became the wife of the famous John of Gaunt, who inaugurated an era of almost fabulous splendour at his castle at Tutbury, which he had restored to its former strength and beauty, after it had lain in ruins and neglect since the death of Thomas, Earl of Lancaster. The whole of the honor felt the benefit of the change; husbandry and trade received an impetus, and the deadly nightmare of depression for forty years, produced by circumstances already described, and the absence of the princely earls from their turreted home for that period, at once fled. At this time, namely, in 1370, Uttoxeter had 140 burgages which made a rental of £7, 2s. There were also two forges and a plot of land rented at 2s. 6d. a year. The rent of assize of free tenancy, with one bow and one sparrow hawk, were valued at £15, 8s. 11d. A meadow, called Wolricheshey, was let at 6s. 8d. The rent of assize of free tenants amounted annually to £24, 6s. 8d. The free fishery in the Dove, with another fishery in the Pool of Uttoxhather, was estimated at £1, 5s. a year. There was a payment of 12s. by ancient custom at the two great courts; and at the feast of St. Martin, another payment of 5s. as a poll-tax of young men. Twenty-one acres of land and one rood of meadow were valued at £1, 4s. annual rent. The pleas and per-

quisites of the court produced £1, and a watermill
there was rented at £5, 6s. 8d.   The sum total being
£61, 5s. 5d.   At this time Needwood forest was
divided into five wards, of which Uttoxeter had one.
In the Uttoxeter ward the sale of lime-tree bark was
valued at 6s. 8d. a year ; the pannage of hogs at
6s. 8d., and the perquisites of the wood-mote at 5s.
There was in this ward a hay, called the moor of
Uttoxeter, which was worth in herbage and acorns
£2 a year, and the amount of the ward was £3,
18s. 4d.

After the death of his first wife, John of Gaunt,
who had become Duke of Lancaster and Earl of Richmond, married Constance, Queen of Castile, and after
the demise of this lady, Catherine Swinford became
his third wife.   John of Gaunt died on the third of
February, 1399.   By his Duchess Maud, he had one
son, Henry, who was created Duke of Hereford.   But
instead of being peacefully permitted to succeed his
father in the Lancastrian estates, King Richard III.,
who had already followed him with persecution into
banishment, seized upon the goods of John of Gaunt,
and issued orders for the rents and revenues of his
possessions to be received for himself.   The nation,
however, was greatly incensed with the king's be-
haviour towards the duke of Hereford, and as he
passed through the city of London, on horseback, on
leaving the kingdom, he was followed by forty
thousand persons, who bewailed his fate and their
own in the most moving manner.   The duke's attorney insisted upon the right of the claim, which

Richard would on no account listen to. The imbecility and incapacity of the king (whom recent historians have attempted to rescue from a good deal of reproach), together with his repeated instances of oppression and tyranny, at length completely alienated the affections of his people, and by almost universal consent he was judged no longer worthy to manage the affairs of the realm. By the advice of parliament he resigned the throne, and the Duke of Lancaster, son of John of Gaunt, was chosen king in his stead, by the name of Henry IV. Consequently, Uttoxeter was now connected with the crown by right.

Still, "uneasy is the head that wears a crown." Henry IV. had several disaffected subjects in different parts of the kingdom. His policy, however, in attaching to his interests a large number of his feudal tenants, served him most effectually in suppressing rebellion amongst the noblemen, whose fidelity was thus relied upon in the several offices to which they were appointed. Amongst these were Sir Nicholas Montgomery, of Sudbury (an ancestor of Lord Vernon), who held the office of constable of Tutbury Castle, and warden of the chase of Needwood, with a salary of £20; Sir John Bagot, Knight, who for other services received forty marks from Uttoxeter; together with Sir John Gresley, Baronet, and Sir Avery Lathbury. The most formidable of the king's disloyal subjects, was the Duke Northumberland. Although defeated, he maintained considerable influence in the north of England, from whence he issued a proclamation, a copy of which found its way into Staffordshire, where, with several gentlemen and others the newly elected king was supposed not to be in great favour. Riotous proceedings were commenced against the king's tenants and offices in this county, and they were continued even after the Duke of Northumberland was slain and the rebellion at an end. Two of these gentlemen were Hugh de Erdeswick and Thomas de Swinnerton, who armed a number of men and made a violent attack upon John Blount, steward of the king's manors at Newcastle-under-Lyme. He was son of John Blount, to whom John of Gaunt gave Barton Park upon the outlawry of Bakespur, whose cause the family of Erdeswick, who lived at Sandon, espoused. Hugh de Erdeswick made a second attack with an armed force upon John Blount, at Lichfield, and nearly succeeded in murdering him. In the first attack the Mayor of Newcastle was intimidated from taking proceedings against the parties for fear of losing his life. For a second attack by Erdeswick, a warrant was issued for his apprehension by the chief steward of the Duchy, and he and his attendants were bound to keep the peace. On that very day, however, he and three brothers of the name of Mynors, of an ancient family of that name then at Uttoxeter, armed themselves and attendants with lances, and made attacks on numerous others of the king's tenants and servants with the intention of killing them. Amongst these other victims of their malice were persons at Rollstone, Dunstall, Newcastle, and Marchington, who only saved themselves by a spirited resistance or a lucky escape. At Uttoxeter they broke open the house and destroyed the furniture therein of an old forester, named John Passman, a faithful servant of the Duke of Lancaster. They also threatened the life of the miller at Uttoxeter mill, if he continued longer to work there, and attempted to kill Thomas de Belton, a tenant of the Duchy. These tumultuous proceedings lasted about a year, when they were suppressed by legislative interference.

After the lords of the Honor of Tutbury had been raised to the throne, a great depreciation took place in the value of their lands and possessions. The reason of this was that in consequence of their absence from the castle, there was a less demand for the produce of the neighbourhood. From the survey taken in the reign of Henry V., preserved in the office of the Duchy Court of Lancaster, it appears that Uttoxeter continued in the Honor of Tutbury. The same survey, which is contained in a beautifully engrossed vellum book, called the " Coucher," shows that Uttoxeter had suffered from the same cause. The number of burgage houses at Uttoxeter had decreased from one hundred and forty to one hundred and thirty-eight, and the rents from £7, 2s. 0d. to £6, 17s. 8d. The two forges, which are mentioned in the previous survey, appear to have been abandoned, as no mention is made of them in the " Coucher."

On Edward IV. gaining the ascendency over Henry VI., he granted the Honor of Tutbury, which he dissevered from the rest of the paternal estates, to

F

George, Duke of Clarence, who is chiefly known for
his whimsical choice of being immersed in a butt of
Malvoisie wine.   King Edward, however, annulled
the grant, owing to the Duke joining the Earl of
Warwick in a rebellion against himself, and issued a
warrant in the thirteenth year of his reign to resume
the possession of these estates, which were accordingly
granted in that year to Thomas, Archbishop of Canterbury and other trustees, to hold for the king during
his absence in France.

The chase of Needwood now began to be regarded
as a royal forest, but the keepers of the various wards
rendered themselves exceedingly disagreeable to the
occupiers of the lands on the borders of the chase, by
heavily amercing them, for driving the deer back
within their boundaries, from whence they often
escaped, and did much damage to the crops.   But
when it was shown that the levy of these fines was
unjust, and the keepers thereby lost this means of
enriching themselves, they did not hesitate to commit
unwarrantable havoc with the timber growing within
the forest.   In the reign of Henry VIII., one of
these officers was detected in an offence of this description.   As a consequence of this, further inquiries
were made into the extent of the evil, when it was
discovered that keepers of the various wards had cut
down and sold large quantities of timber, and the
keeper of Uttoxeter ward eight hundred and forty-
one loads in a single year.   In the first year of the
reign of Queen Elizabeth, Uttoxeter ward was disforested and the deer in it destroyed; but at the

same time it contained more and better timber than any other.

The first most extensive dismemberment of the great possessions of the earl of Derby, was made by James I., by making grants of various lordships in Derbyshire. King Charles I., whose scruples were less and necessities greater than those of his predecessor, did not hesitate to make grants of his territories lying in the vicinity of his castle. The manor ·of Uttoxeter and other appendages of the Duchy of Lancaster, were disposed of on May 24th, 1625, to Lord William Craven, Sir George Whitmore, Sir William Whitmore, and Mr. Gibson. These gentlemen immediately caused a survey of the manor of Uttoxeter to be made, and resold it to the inhabitants of the town for £3120, who conveyed to the various occupiers their interest in the same. The timber then growing in Uttoxeter High Wood was about this time sold for the king's use, by Sir to Thomas Degge and Richard Startin, who again Edward Mosley, the attorney-general of the Duchy, sold it in lots to others. Ten years subsequently to this an attempt was made to enclose the High Wood, which had before been known as Uttoxeter Ward, on ·the forest of Needwood. A greater part of the n-habitants of Uttoxeter enjoyed, however, common rights thereon, and therefore strenuously opposed the project. From private documents in the possession of Sir Oswald Mosley, it appears that in consequence of this, Sir Edward Mosley preferred an information in the Duchy court against the principal persons who had made this attempt, stating that as his Majesty was seized of the said common in his demesne as of fee, being parcel of the Duchy of Lancaster, and as the townsmen of Uttoxeter had destroyed all his deer, fowls and wood, &c., and that as the defendants claimed right of common there, although they had no such right, and did stop and interrupt his majesty from replenishing the same with deer and birds of game, and also from improving the same, he prayed to have writs of privy seal directed to the projectors of this attempt to appear in the Duchy Court to answer the premises, and to abide the order of the said court.

Writs were served, in pursuance of this application, upon the parties, and they all, with one exception, answered upon oath that they admitted the king's title to the common, but disclaimed all knowledge as to how the fowls and wood had been destroyed. They also added that the freeholders had usually enjoyed a right of common there, and if his Majesty was desirous of enclosing a part for his own use, they hoped they might be permitted to compound for and purchase the same. When this answer was returned into the Duchy, the chancellor found it to be insufficient, owing to one of the defendants not having agreed to it. An order to this effect was issued, that as all the said defendants excepting one had consented that his Majesty should enlose a part of the common, all the other resident inhabitants should express their consent in writing, to satisfy the court that they were all willing to submit to such an arrangement. A commission was then directed to Sir Edward Mosley, Sir Edward Vernon, Simon Every, Esq., Walter Vernon, Esq., George Parker, and Thomas Ayloffe, Esqs., to take the subscriptions of the freeholders, and to enclose what part should be agreed upon. Sir Edward Mosley, Mr. Every and Mr Ayloffe, who were all in the king's service, then came to Uttoxeter and threatened the inhabitants with inevitable ruin in case they refused to sign. By these means six more of the inhabitants signed, and twenty more gave in their names as consenting parties. When the certificate of the commissioners as to these consents being obtained had been returned into the Duchy court, a second commission came from thence for the enclosing of half of the said common for the king's use. This was immediately carried into effect under the superintendence of Mr. Ayloff, and an injunction was granted to prohibit commoners from exercising their right of common in the other half of it, until the king's further pleasure was known. Thus was Uttoxeter Ward finally dissevered from the remaining part of the forest. The other was divided amongst the freeholders of Uttoxeter in lieu of their right of common. The king's moiety was in March, 1639, granted to Mr. Nevil, one of the officers of the king's bed-chamber. The quantity of land thus apportioned, amounted to 500 acres. Mr. Nevil, for several years, received rent for his portion without interruption ; but a few years before the commencement of the civil wars, a party of soldiers who had been impressed against their will, burnt the rails, destroyed the fences and laid the ground waste; yet for this trespass several of the townspeople were prosecuted in the Star Chamber, and had not the political convulsions which followed put a stop to the proceedings, the greater part of the inhabitants would have been subjected to a continuance of vexatious lawsuits respecting it.[1]

A common or waste on the High Wood, probably distinct from any of the land above mentioned, was estimated at 369a. 2r. 5p.[2] whilst some other portion called the Moor of Uttoxeter, belonged to the Duke of Rutland, and was held by lease by the Rev. Thomas Lightfoot, about the same time.

Part of the common granted, says Mr. Samuel Bentley, in a note to his poems, from the crown to the poor of Uttoxeter, was enclosed by act of parliament in 1788, for the purpose of aiding the poor's rate of the parish, which then pressed heavily upon it. The enclosure was effected under the directions of a body of trustees, by whom the old workhouse was erected, as appears from the following inscription on the large round sandstone (now in my backyard), which was placed in the front wall of the building. " This workhouse was rebuilt by the trustees for enclosing the common within the constablewick of Uttoxeter, 1789. Thomas Garner, builder." This workhouse was taken down and the present one erected about a quarter of a century back. It occu-

(1) Mosley's History of Tutbury.

(2) MSS. Survey of Uttoxeter, by Peter Lightfoot, 1668.

pies about three roods of land, cost £3900, and accommodates about two hundred persons. Before the erection of these workhouses, a number of houses were employed for the purpose at the bottom of Spicer's Street.

UTTOXETER DURING THE CIVIL WAR AND REBELLION.

ALTHOUGH the opening of the civil war of the middle of the seventeenth century served so well the inhabitants of Uttoxeter in saving them from ruinous proceedings in the dreaded Star Chamber, in respect to their common rights, yet it came upon them otherwise with two-fold severity, which continued a number of years. Uttoxeter, being situated betwixt various places which were garrisoned for the king —as Alton Castle, Wootten Lodge, and Tutbury Castle—the inhabitants were not only harrassed by a continual apprehension of a siege, but also suffered excessively by the exactions of the contending parties as temporary success placed either one in the ascendant. The accounts of the constables of Uttoxeter during this stirring time, are still extant, and afford a vivid picture of the amount of oppression the townspeople and those in the neighbourhood were suffering under. Raising large sums of money and furnishing provinder and provisions for Tutbury, Lichfield, Alton, Wootton Lodge and Stafford, but chiefly for Tutbury, was a daily occurrence. The king passed through the town no fewer than three

times ; distinguished military individuals and soldiers were quartered upon it, as they passed and
repassed from place to place, at no slight expense ;
bulwarks and barricades were made, trenches were
dug and watches were set, and when the soldiery
could not be had for the safety of the town, the inhabitants were obliged to arm themselves and call in
the countrymen from the surrounding villages to aid
in defence of their property and homes.

King Charles I. paid his first visit to Uttoxeter in
1642, no doubt in the course of movements occasioned
by the unsettled political state of the country, when
he stayed at Mr. Wood's Hall, which was swept for
the august occasion, and was then the principal genteel residence in Uttoxeter.[1] It was in this year that
the king, failing to give satisfaction to his parliament
by his concessions whilst he refused his assent to the
militia bill, resolved to appeal to the sword for the
maintenance of his rights, and commanded the High
Sheriff of the county of Stafford to garrison Tutbury
Castle, and levy contributions upon the county for
all requirements. From Uttoxeter, where he probably stayed one night, the king marched to Stafford,
for it appears that the sum of £1, 14s. 6d. was paid
for trained soldiers accompanying him to Uttoxeter,
and from thence to Stafford to wait upon him.

Uttoxeter has generally been spoken of as a royal
town, and it would appear that at some period of this
unsettled time there was a predominent leaning to

---

[1] A further account of the hall will be found further on.

the Stuart dynasty. At the beginning of the war, however, whatever opposite compulsion had been forced upon it, it is evident the people of Uttoxeter inclined to the side of the parliament. There was no welcome to the king pealed from the church bells when he stayed at Uttoxeter Hall, and the ruin threatened to the town in the Star Chamber, was in remembrance against him being favourably received. This is also further evident. When Stafford became possessed by the royalists, the moorlanders, amongst whom the people of Uttoxeter were included, and who indeed were perhaps especially intended, applied to Sir John Gell, then at Derby, for his assistance.[1] According to the Parliamentary narrative, " Sir John Gell asked what assistance they would have, they said two-hundred musquetters and one saccer, not doubting but that they had men enough with that assistance to regaine the towne—doubtless that of Stafford—and save themselves. Hee commanded his major Mollanus immediately with two-hundred foot and one saccer to march towards their appointed rendezvous att Uttoxeter. His major being there two or three dayes, and nobody coming to assist him, and hearing that the enemy increased, was forced to retreat in the night to Derby." Sir John Gell, himself, joining his force with that of Sir William Brereton, soon after marched upon Stafford, and at Hopton Heath, near that town, came up with the enemy, " Whereupon hee sett his ffoot in order of battalis,

[1] Hobson's History of Ashbourne and Valley of the Dove.

and Sir William his horse, the enemy advancing in a full body with above one thousand two hundred horse, whereof the Earl of Northampton was general, and soe setting upon their horse, Sir William's horse presently ran away, and left Sir John Gell alone with the ffoot. The enemy drew his horse into a body againe, and charged his ffoot, but hee gave them such a salute, that the enemy in a disorderd manner drew off and marched away towards Stafford, but left many dead bodies behind them, whereof my Lord Northampton was one, Captayne Middleton, and many other brave commanders of horse, and at least one hundred dragoones; and on our side three carters and two souldyers were slayne; wee lost two casks of drakes, which the dragoones had drawne a greate distance from the ffoot, under the hedges to save themselves, and soe Colonel Gell retreated with my lord's dead body towards Uttoxeter, with his fforces, and Sir William Brereton with his fforces towards Cheshire. And att Uttoxeter Colonel Gell remayned three dayes, and set Staffordshire in as good posture as hee could; within the said three dayes there came a trumpetter to him from my younge Lord of Northampton, for his father's dead body, whereupon hee answered, if hee would send him the drakes which they had gotten from their dragoones, and pay the chirurgeons for embalming it, hee should have it; but he (the Earl of Northampton) returned him an answer, that hee would do nither th' one nor th' other, and soe Colonel Gell caused him to be carried in his company to Derby, and buried him in the Earle of Devonshire's sepulcher, in All Hallowe's Church."

About this stage of civil commotion, Uttoxeter presented all the features of a place in a state of siege. Various defensive works were raised about the town, especially on its west and south sides. One man, a John Sherret, led clods for five days to the bulwarks; carpenters and other day labourers were paid the sum of £5, 13s. 2d. for their services in the erection of similar works, in the construction of which timber (of which a large quantity could be had for a little money) and other articles were required, costing the sum of £1, 6s. 8d. Besides the expense of these works, which were intended for a vigorous defence, there were also coal, and the war-like materials of powder and bullets, for the town ends, amounting to about £4 in value. In an apprehension of an advance from Stafford way, trenches were dug in the Picknals, at which men from Loxley and other places were employed. That the town at this period was actually attacked there is not the slightest doubt. Wortley with a force of men, came against it, but they were repulsed and a number of them taken prisoners. On this occasion the town was assisted by men who had been previously called in from most of the villages and hamlets about—as Tean, Loxley, Marchington, Crakemarsh, and Creighton. Lord Stanhope and his son were also this year in custody at the Crown, one of the two inns of that name then in the market place, and were kept there under the strictest watch of a guard.

In 1643, King Charles I. was again at Uttoxeter, but where he was passing to does not appear. This time he was honoured by a peal from the church bells. The bulwarks were this year pulled down, although there was still great cause for apprehension, for a strict watch had to be kept upon the neighbourhood from the church tower, which commands a view of most of the approaches to the town, for the safety of which other precautions were taken by the employment of guards and sentinels. One of the bulwarks, thus taken away, had been at the church gates, and the fact clearly intimates that the church would have been occupied as a defensive position, and perhaps, as a last resort for the defenders of the town if much pressed. Colonel Gell this year took Wootton Lodge, to the defenders of which Uttoxeter had sent a cart load of bread. The expenses occasioned to Uttoxeter by the war during these two years amounted to about £68, but they afterwards became excessive year by year for twenty years, and it is really a wonder how the town survived so fearful a crisis.

The levies upon Uttoxeter, in provisions and money, amounted, during the succeeding year, 1644, to no less a sum than £608, 13s. 2d., whilst the hamlet of Loxley, for the same period, furnished the sum of £85, 8s. 6d. There was, however, considerable warmth amongst the two political parties in Uttoxeter at this time, and there can be little surprise if there was a ringing clash of wordy controversy, and sometimes of violent rancorous contention, and it

must have been owing to some strife in the difference
of parties, that one Mr. John Scott, who belonged to
a family of respectability and property in Uttoxeter,[1]
was killed. The person who committed the guilty
deed was soon discovered and seized, and the manner
in which he was dealt with was amazingly summary,
apparently without judge or jury, for a rope and cords
were speedily procured, with which he was pinioned
and hanged, and then hastily buried in the church
yard; the sum of eightpence being paid for taking
him there. Mr. William Fish, one of the constables,
was also taken prisoner this year by Lord Goring,
who lay in the town with his foot guards on the
4th of May. This worthy man, probably under the
influence of his political leanings, either neglected
or positively refused to supply provisions to Lord
Goring, which was sufficient excuse for his imprisonment. The matter is referred to in the following
entry by his brother official in the constables' accounts, " Charges and martial fees expended by my
fellow constable being kept prisoner three weeks concerning provisions, £1, 6s. 4d."

On the 24th of May, 1645, it being Whitsunday,
the king arrived for the third and last time at Uttoxeter, from Stone. He was accompanied by Prince
Rupert, son of Frederic V., elector of Palatine, by
Elizabeth, daughter of James I., a rash and impetuous
individual, but possessed of varied abilities, and well
skilled in most matters, from engraving a picture to

[1] Lightfoot's Survey.

commanding an army. The king and prince were
at the head of a large force of horse, numbering about
5520.[1] On the succeeding day they proceeded to
Tutbury, and from thence to Ashby-de-la-Zouch and
Leicester, which latter place they took by storm, on
the 14th of June.

On the king arriving at Uttoxeter on May 24th,
his Majesty was again saluted with peals from the
church bells, and the records of the town fully confirm the traditionary account that he slept at Sir
Thomas Milward's, judge, at Eaton. A hogshead of
beer, costing Uttoxeter £1, 6s. 8d., was conveyed to
Eaton for his Majesty's use by one Edward Ball. A
family of this name appear to have had some property
in Uttoxeter, but the only source which could, fails to
show what public-house he occupied.[2] The account
of King Charles sleeping at Eaton is also confirmed
by a notice in Captain Symond's diary. Prince
Rupert, and another prince, whose name is not given,
lay at Uttoxeter, and their quarters for one night
only cost the town £5, 12s., whilst his cook, who accompanied him, claimed and had paid to him a fee
of 5s. The town was not capable of accommodating
the whole of the king's troops, and consequently some
of them lay in the villages about. The Earl of
Lichfield and others were quartered upon Marstone,
near which place a soldier, for ravishing two women,
was tied with his shoulders and breast naked to a

[1] Shaw's History of Staffordshire.
[2] Lightfoot's Survey.

tree, and every carter of the train and carriages was to lash him in passing.[1] On the army leaving Uttoxeter on the 25th, the aid of a waggon and several horses were required to accompany it, for the conveyance of luggage. Not any of them were, however, returned, the army doubtless being unwilling to part with them; and as the engagement for them had been made with their owners by the town officers, a demand was made upon the town for their value, which was paid and entered in the town accounts. During the time the army stayed at Uttoxeter, a man was slain at the same Edward Ball's who took the beer to Eaton. Under what circumstances the deed was committed, is left entirely to conjecture. It seems the town had no power to interfere with the man who was the slayer, as if it had, and had carried it out as in a previous case, there would have been entries in the town accounts, specifying expenses attending his trial or punishment. But there are not any. It may therefore be presumed he was one of the soldiers belonging to the army who had encountered a man of the opposite faction, and both probably being in liquor, an affray naturally took place, in which the man lost his life. The man who met with his death belonged to Draycot-in-the-Clay, and the sum of 6s. was given for the conveyance of his body to that village. During the remaining part of the year, bodies of soldiers were either constantly in the town for its protection, or

(1) Captain Symond's Diary.

quartered upon it in the course of their movements. In June, soldiers were drawn up in Balance Close, which is land, then known by that name, overlooking the town at the south-east side of the New Bridge, at the Hockley. A number of soldiers were also quartered at Blunt's Hall, where they were supplied with provisions from Uttoxeter. Again, on the 20th of July, soldiers were drawn up in some place called " in the field," and before the close of the month, the men of Colonels Ashenhurst and Watson, appear to have been encamped in the Broad Meadow, where they were supplied with provisions. Uttoxeter is specially mentioned as being guarded in August, when the parliamentary forces went against Tutbury Castle for three nights, on each of which nights scouts were sent out from the town with guides, probably to Tutbury, to take account of the enemies' actions, or perhaps more likely to report any danger apprehended to the town itself. At all events Uttoxeter was in considerable trepidation, and a messenger was despatched to Alton for Colonel Bowyer, at the same time that Colonel Jackson's soldiers had their rendezvous on Uttoxeter Heath, having previously had their quarters at Somersall. In September, Sir William Vaughan had a guard at Uttoxeter, and for a fortnight in October General Poyns had Uttoxeter in his protection. The town ends and street ends were barricaded and blocked up by the soldiers, who were in the town under him. All this seems to have presaged something more serious, and it did in reality happen that a soldier was slain in the public streets. This incident is somewhat difficult to account for, but as barricades were made and the town ends were blocked up, evidently in full expectation of an attack upon it, it may very reasonably be supposed that a detachment of the enemy actually succeeded in breaking through the impediments, although doubtless defended, and so a conflict ensued in the midst of the town, in which the individual referred to was cut down. Indeed if he had been killed in the same unwarrantable manner as John Scott, the murderer would have met with the same summary retribution which we have just described. The body of the unfortunate soldier was wrapped in its winding sheet, and for "making the grave, ringing," beer, and for burying it in so slim a protection from the crushing earth, a sum of "4s. was expended." The accounts for the year ending in October, as disbursed for the war, although not passed till February 5th, following, amounted to the sum of £975, 7s. 1d.

The battle of Naseby decided in effect the fate of the unfortunate monarch; but even then, despairing as the royal cause had become, the beleagured and trusty garrison at Tutbury boldly held out in his favour. But the difficulty of retaining it after this crisis was, of course, proportionably increased. The disposal of the troops of the Parliamentarians contracted the already limited district from which the garrison of Tutbury had to draw its subsistance,[1] and rendered it impossible for provisions to be con-

(1) Mosley's History of Tutbury.

veyed to the castle without a strong escort to protect those who furnished them. But even then, as might be expected, repeated encounters took place with the Parliamentarian horse, and two occurred so near Uttoxeter as the High Wood;—Uttoxeter furnishing a great portion of the provisions to the castle. An account of two of these is preserved in the " Gesta Britaniorum," by Sir George Warton, in the following, notices: " Feby. 15th, 1645. A sharp encounter between a party of the king's troops from Tutbury Castle, and a party of the Parliament's from Barton House in Derbyshire." On February 18th he also says, " A party of the Parliament's forces routed by the king's forces near Uttoxeter." These occurrences are not mentioned in the constable's account, but on the 22nd of the same month it appears that two soldiers, who had been maimed by Tutbury soldiers in the High Wood, were conveyed to Carswall (no doubt Caverswall) at an of expense 2s. 6d., which leaves no doubt of their being in the engagement, and of belonging to the Parliament's forces. By these accounts, which are probably the only sources of information about the conflicts, we are not told whether any of either party were slain, although Sir Oswald Mosley seems to think such was the case. There were, doubtless, many other similar incidents occuring near Uttoxeter, and one in March of a less serious kind was that of the cavaliers carrying off a bay mare and a quantity of oats which were going from Uttoxeter to Tutbury. It appears probable, also, that Mr. Gilbert Gerrard lost six horses in th way, for at the same time he was paid the sum of £21, in lieu of that number and their furniture. The pressure of the times were now very much felt in Uttoxeter; arrears due to the army through Commissiary Ward drew upon it, and they were only obtained by the force of a warrant It is possible, at the same time, that the tide of affairs had also something to do with it, by disinclining the town to support the hopeless cause of an already fallen monarch.

If up to this time Uttoxeter had supplied chiefly the requirements of the Royalists, and now especially the besieged Royalists at Tutbury Castle who were in great want, the claims, also, of the Parliamentarians were required to be entertained and promptly met now that in full vigour they were investing the castle, determining upon its surrender, and producing thereby the utmost interest in its vicinity. On the 30th of March, 1646, stores were sent from Uttoxeter to the " Leaguer" as he is called in the parochial statements, Sir William Brereton, costing £7, 4s. 6d., and also again on the 8th of April, to the value of £11, 2s. 9d ; and the occupiers of the castle, who had made repeated sallies with varied success, capitulated to the honourable terms proposed, on the 20th of April of the same year. On the 21st a number of Leek soldiers, who had aided either in taking or defending Tutbury Castle, though the former is the more probable, arrived at Uttoxeter, on their return, where they were entertained with " bread, cheese, and drink," and just coming hot from the scene of conflict, smeared with the blood, and aching with the

tussle of war, had no doubt a great deal to tell to
eager listeners of what they had done and seen.
From Tutbury the " Leaguer," Sir William Brereton, marched to Lichfield, where on the 29th of
April, he was supplied by Uttoxeter with sixty strikes
of oats, and for having gained Tutbury Castle, and
for going against Dudley he was paid by demand on
the 5th of May, the sum of £16. On April 21st and
29th, and again on May 17th and 20th, many of the
great guns which had been employed with such success against the Castle at Tutbury, and very likely
others which had been used in defending it, arrived
at Uttoxeter on their way of transport to Eccleshall
and Lichfield. It is also to be observed that the
quartering of General Fairfax's soldiers in October
upon the town cost it £20, and on the 13th Colonel
Cromwell's, £20. The latter took a number of
horses with them when leaving for Tamworth, but
two were killed. The other remaining noticable
matter at the close of 1646, is that of Colonel Oakley's men having their quarters upon Uttoxeter at a
cost of £13, 6s. 2d. The Colonel himself stayed at
the Crown in the Market-place, and his expenses
amounted to the moderate sum of 3s. 6d. The accounts for the year ending October 1646, which, however, were not examined till the 28th of April, 1651,
amounted to the tolerable sum of £796, 2s., the whole
of which was the fruit of the war with the exception
of a few pounds.

The disbursements by the constables of Uttoxeter
from October, 1646, to May, 1647, amounted to

£97, 17s. 5d. At the beginning of 1647 Uttoxeter
paid £2, 10s. 4d. to fifteen men, to aid in pulling
down Tutbury Castle, it having previously, in the
month of May, 1646, contributed £3, to a Captain
Cloyd for [pulling down the bulwarks at Tutbury.
After this period Uttoxeter was greatly relieved from
the oppressive demands made upon it whilst Tutbury
Castle was occupied; still the sums required by the
British army, to which payments had commenced
some time before, were of considerable amount and
frequency. By the town accounts it does not seem
whether Uttoxeter was now in a defensive position;
but in the church book of Mavesyn Ridware of
August 27th, three or four months after the seige
at Tutbury was over, it is noticed that the sum of
10s. 10d. was paid to twenty soldiers who had come
from Uttoxeter from the seige. It should not be
passed over, that in 1647 forty-six Egyptians, with a
pass from Parliament to travel for the space of six
successive months for relief, arrived at Uttoxeter, and
were given the sum of 4s. Their number and appearance must have excited considerable interest and
proved a novelty.

At the commencement of 1648 the constables lost
£1, 1s. 7d. by exchanging £3, 4s. 4d. of *clipped*
money for £2, 2s. 9d. in good money; but what this
money was, and how they had received it, no record
is left. In May there was great fear of an insur-
rection in the town, and two men were placed in
the church steeple, secretly, it is likely, to watch
any risings of it. This seems to intimate how

strongly and dangerously party feeling and opinion
manifested themselves, although it does not appear
that any more alarming evidence of it took place.
At this time, and for several years, the town paid
every three months to the British army £13, and upwards. In June of 1648 the demolition of Tutbury
Castle was still proceeded with, and a demand was
made upon Uttoxeter for men to assist in the barbarous work, but there was great reluctance in the town
to agree to it, and to free it from so undesirable an
alternative the sum of £4 was given, and the work
of spoliation left to less reluctant hands. In August
of this year the church was desecrated in the way
many other churches were at this time. A number
of Scotch prisoners arrived at Uttoxeter, as others ôn
several subsequent periods did, and they were lodged
in the church. They were a violent set of fellows,
and a proper guard could not have been had upon
them. They broke up the planks of the church floor,
broke many of the windows, and left the sacred
edifice in a state of perfect filth. The windows cost
nearly £1 in repairing, and so detestable a state was
the church in, that the cleaning of it amounted to
nearly half as much. The accounts were next passed
October 20th, 1648, but the amount is not given, and
the items entered, which amount to about £44, do
not contain the whole of the payments made by the
constables. Only the more remarkable items, on account of which payments were made, appear to be
preserved.

In 1649 the accounts were taken on the 7th No-

vember, and were £225, 11s. 5d., cheifly in pay to
" the army," but from then till the time of passing
the accounts again on March 3rd, 1651, there is little
to notice except that in August of 1650 there was a
thanksgiving-day when a person named Percival was
paid for " warding," at which time there was a guard
of sixteen soldiers at the Cock, belonging to Mr.
Thomas Gilbert, the publichouse which remained till
lately, where the brewery premises are. The three
month's pay to the army, which had increased to £20,
ceased in August of 1650, The accounts, when passed, appear to have been about £44.

The opening of 1651 found Uttoxeter in a state of
internal danger, but the constables were determined
to suppress any popular manifestation, and a warrant
was carried into effect for searching and seizing
Papist's and delinquent's arms. It seems that in
April monthly pay to the army was renewed, when
£20 was paid to it, and in June another monthly
payment was made to it of upwards of £30. In
August the magazine of the army was at Uttoxeter,
and a number of teams were required, some of which
were obtained by warrant in the night from Doveridge, intimating the necessity of great despatch in
the case, to convey them to Tamworth. One of the
teams belonged to Mr. Peter Lightfoot, who was
paid £1, 4s. for its use. In August a number of
Uttoxeter men were pressed for the militia, their
names being John Clark, Fran. Allen, Phil. Nead-
ham, Richard Wilkinson, and Thomas Vernon.
They were each provided with a horse and a saddle

and 7s. 6d. The militia horse were called in again
in September, but in November the militia horse
and foot soldiers were summoned for some purpose
to Cheadle, where they remained three days. Several
lots of Scotch prisoners were at Uttoxeter during
the year, in custody, one lot of which was being
taken from Chesterfield to Stafford. The accounts
were not audited till May 3rd, 1651, and given as
£304, 3s. 2d., and must comprise many more items
than those which have been preserved.

By this time the entries in the town accounts had
become much rarer, and only a few items of interest
appear in the course of several years. Several of
them are, however, of real interest. In 1652 one
entry is very curious, especially as there are no
circumstances recorded as attending it to afford
any clue as to its meaning. It is a notice of public warning in Uttoxeter to set water at every door.
On April 14th one Robert Adin was prosecuted as a
traiter; and in February, 1653, some excited individual disturbed the congregation in the church and
was conveyed to Stafford for trial. At this time the
town paid year by year to the army the sum of
£67, 10s. The proclamation of the Lord Protecter
was duly observed, and on May 29th, 1660 a similar
demonstration was made on the advent to the throne
of King Charles the II. On his coronation day the
spirit of royalty had thoroughly regained its ascend-
ancy in the town. Whilst only 1s. was spent over the
proclamation of Cromwell, 5s. was spent in ringing
on the proclamation of the king, and 8s. when he was

crowned; besides which the town went to the expense
of " painting the royal arms and four tribes." The
expenses occasioned by the political necessities of the
times had now dwindled down to comparatively small
amounts, except in 1667, when two sums of £44, 1s. 1d.
each, one of £14, 13s. 8½d, and another of £29, 7s. 5d.
no trifle, it may be thought, to be levied upon the
town during the three first months of the year, were
required to be paid for royal aid.

From the year 1653 to 1660 or 1661, most of the
leaves are torn out of the constables' accounts. At a
fair calculation, however, it may be inferred that
during those seven or eight years the expenses caused
to the town by the times could not have been less
than £250 a year, making something like a total for
the whole period of at least £2000.

On June 1st, 1688, Uttoxeter presented a scene of
rejoicing such as, perhaps, had not before occurred
in it. It was occasioned by the release and acquit-
tal of the seven bishops whom King James the II.
had cast into the Tower, and brought to trial on the
charge of an alleged false and seditious libel, pretended to be grounded on a petition which they had
made to the King for not reading in the churches
the Declaration of Indulgence to all Dissenters from
the Church.[1] Bonfires were lit in High Street, at
the churchyard, and at the Market Cross; drummers
were employed to swell the acclamation, which was
national; the watchmen and populace of Uttoxeter

(1) Penny Cyclopædia, Art. James.

were treated with ale; and the more *elite* of the town both on that day and the previous one at the "Crown" (which was a day of thanksgiving for the Prince of Wales), indulged in ale and wine to the score of £2. 2s.

At the close of the old accounts in 1688 another interesting item appears, in which "an alarm" is mentioned. Coals were collected for fires, and a quantity for the same purpose was paid for by Mr. Shallcross. There was considerable excitement in the place; strangers were brought into it by the frightening notifications, the fear occasioned by which they and the towns-people did their best to allay by draughts—about a guinea's worth—of a Mrs. Norton's ale. This was the alarm produced by the men employed by the Prince of Orange, or his friends, to run or ride through every town in England in one day crying "fire and sword! the French are coming!" which filled people's minds with the utmost consternation and terror.

Uttoxeter does not furnish any particulars for the attention of the local historian from the interesting period just passed through until the rebellion of 1745, when Prince Charles Edward, called the Pretender, sought to recover the fallen fortunes of the Stuart dynasty by an appeal to arms. Previous to this he had made two unsuccessful attempts upon Scotland, but being encouraged by the zealous partizans of his house in England, and flattered by France with a promise of powerful assistance, he resolved to make one more attempt for the throne of England. The nucleus of his army consisted of one hundred men, formed by a French officer, and it was pretended they were for the East India Company's services, and they were put on board a small frigate carrying eighteen guns, which was joined by a French man-of-war, with sixty guns, arms for several thousand men, and about £400,000 sterling. He succeeded in landing in Scotland in August, where he was joined by about two thousand men. The number being shortly after increased to five thousand, he ventured with them towards the south, after having gained several minor successes, including the memorable battle of Prestonpans, and continued his course to Carlisle, and so on to Newcastle, Manchester, Macclesfield, and through Leek and Ashbourne to Derby.

The army of the Duke of Cumberland was at this time, November 28th, forming in Staffordshire. His troops lay in a line betwixt Tamworth and Stafford, with a line of cavalry in front. They consisted of 7500 veteran soldiers, 3000 newly raised solders, 1400 veteran horse, and 800 newly raised horse, the whole being 12,700 men.[1] The Duke had taken up this position, expecting that the Cavalier would have attempted to have proceeded by Birmingham to London. On receiving information that the rebels were at Derby the Duke despatched thither a gentleman of the name of Birch to ascertain their strength. This person, the better to conceal his purpose, bought a pint of peas at a shop in that town, and put them

---

[1] A History of England, published soon after.

LORD GARDNER'S HOUSE, UTTOXETER.

into a pocket; taking, however, a quantity in one hand, he dropped a single pea into an empty pocket for each file of the Pretender's army as it passed. On the whole having filed off he directly returned at an almost inconceivable speed for those days, and communicated the intelligence of the number of the enemy to the Duke.[1] The Duke thereupon started to Uttoxeter, having in the mean time sent to Parliament to know if he must proceed to Derby to attack the enemy there. He came through Abbott's Bromley with his troops, and there are those living who knew well an old woman, named Ann Buxtone, *alias* Nan Brown, who used to talk of having seen them, and of having displayed her best manners before the Duke, and received a shilling from his hands. The Duke of Cumberland remained at Uttoxeter two nights, waiting a reply to his message, and was hospitably entertained by an ancestor of Sir Allan Gardner, at Uttoxeter House, at present, and for many years past occupied by Doctor Taylor, where he slept two nights in the tapestried room. The single troop of horse with him were drawn up for review in the croft at the back of the same residence.

It was on the 4th of December that the young cavalier arrived at Derby with his followers, numbering about 7000 men, with fifteen field-pieces and fifty covered carts with ammunition. Their first act was to hold a council of war, but the only resolution

(1) This information was told to Dr. Taylor by a descendant of the same gentleman.

passed was to make a levy upon the inhabitants of about £3000 besides making a successful demand on the post-office for £100, and committing various ravages upon the town and neighbourhood. They remained at Derby two days, when they retreated from it with confused precipitation, through fear of surprise from the Duke of Cumberland's army, leaving behind them swords, pistols, targets, hot, powder, and other articles. Their loss of these was, however, made up by the plundering and robberies they committed in going back towards the north. Gentlemen's houses were entered and robbed far and near; horses were forcibly taken away; and at Hanging Bridge one Humphrey Brown was shot dead for refusing to comply with their demand for his horse. Various gentlemen's houses in Ashbourne did not escape.[1] The late Mr. Crossley of the Old Turnpike, Uttoxeter, who died in 1835 at the age of 100 years and 8 months, was then a young man at Brailsford, and he, with a horse and cart, were pressed into the service of the Pretender as he returned.[2] Indeed the Pretender's followers on retreating spread themselves as far as Foston, and the people in the neighbourhood for miles round were terrified, and drove off their horses and cattle. Even at Knypersley, near Uttoxeter, the then owner of the place,

(1) Hutton's History of Derby. History of Ashbourne. Published by Messrs. Hobson.

(2) Communicated by the Rev. J. Cooke, of whose congregation he was a member.

Mr. Minors, drove his horses and cattle into Flyer's coppice, or copy, and for safety buried various household valuables. And the curious circumstance is told that a number of females collected at Foston Bridge, with red petticoats over them, to intimidate the rebels, which gave rise to a song or ballad, which was printed, and some portions of which, relating the particulars, I have heard recited.

Some of these and other deeply interestiug reminiscences of the times I have the pleasure of giving from a communication of F. Cope, Esq., of Uttoxeter. This gentleman was born at an ancestral place in the woodlands, in 1778, and his family had melancholy recollections of this exciting period. The traditions of the neighbourhood were the frequent theme of a large household at night, as they sat round the blazing wood fire, of a large old-fashioned house, when his father, surrounded by his family, and aroused by what he felt so much interest in, would recount the traditions of the family as far back as Henry VIII., when they held only from the Crown— how at the Revolution they suffered for their loyalty, when six brothers, each standing six feet high and upwards[1] joined King Charles I. at York, and all perished except one, from whom he is descended; how the Bagots established the *Blue Coat Hunt* and Bowling-greens at the Hartshorn Inn at Lichfield, the Talbot, Rugely, and the White Hart,

---

(1) Descendants of the same family now living are equally tall and powerful men.

Uttoxeter, to keep up the loyal feeling towards
the Stuarts; how they were betrayed and a king's
messenger sent to secure their papers, and take the
chairman, secretary, and other leading men into custody; how these parts were so loyal to the Stuarts[1]
that he (the messenger) was *detained* at Lichfield for
post-horses, and finally forced to go forward with his
jaded beasts to Ridware, when he applied for assistance and information to C. Robinson, Esq., who gave
him an excellent dinner, a bait and a rest for his
horses and two guides—one to show him or his assist-
ant the way to Rugely, and the other the way to Uttoxeter, where Mr. Robinson *knew* that the whole hunt
was dining. However, while thus relieving the officer
he despatched his son on foot to Colton and Rugely,
and a faithful servant on his horse to Uttoxeter.
Leaving Ridware the messenger in time got to the
White Hart, found the room there crowded with
bachanalians, rosy, and as the Scots say, *fou*: making his way with one Copestake, a lapidary, who was
constable, to the head of the room, he seized Sir
Walter Bagot, and Mr. Daniel, the vicar of Bromley,
who was secretary. The papers on the table, however, expressed nothing but a scrawled programme
of the dinner, a rather sneering toast to King George
and the Queen, with lots of other lewd toasts and

(1) The Rebels were heard to complain at Derby that the English
promises of support were delusive; that they were extremely loyal to
the House of Stuart when warmed by a good fire and good liquor;
but the warmth of their fire, their liquor, and their loyalty evaporated
together.—HUTTON.

sentiments, and snatches of song, *purporting* to have been sung, &c. But unfortunately the fireplace told tales; evidently much paper had been recently burnt, so the messenger seized several of the party—Sir W. B. and parson Daniel, being the principal—and believing that Mr. Daniel might probably have papers at home, he despatched Copestake, who knowing a private road by Uttoxeter High Wood and through Bagot's park, proceeded that way to Bromley to search his house. Again, however, they were foiled, for one of the young Mynors was at the dinner, and had already apprised both the Mynors of Knypersley, and the Cope family; so the grandfather of my informant and the Mynors were on the alert, but *apparently* drinking and enjoying themselves only at Mr. Cope's, in front of whose house the road went. Copestake was soon seen approaching, and as they saw him turn towards the door here they waited for him jug in hand. Thus he stopped to drink, and one jug succeeded another till Copestake was incapable of proceeding. Meanwhile, my informant's (Mr. Cope's) father, then in his 'teens, had been sent to Bromley, and on getting there called on old Waltham, the thirdborough; together they went to the churchwarden, a John Wetton—all old loyalists—and proceeded from his back-door to the vicarage—getting over the rails and crossing the garden. They searched the vicarage-house and finding the vicar's desk, took the back out of it, and, abstracting the papers it contained, bundled them up and took them away. Meanwhile the messenger and his prisoners had left

H

Uttoxeter for Colton and Rugely ; but the former re-
collecting that he had come that road in his way to
Uttoxeter, calculated that it must go either through
or just by Abbot's-Bromley ; so he began to think he
had been wilfully misled, and insisted on being first
taken to Bromley.   Thus the chaise stopped abso-
lutely at the front door of the parsonage as Mr. Cope's
father, with the thirdborough and the churchwarden,
were getting over the pailing out of the parsonage
garden with the papers.   So the affair ended.   Copestake was taken up and slightly punished for drunk-
enness.   He afterwards rejoiced that he had not been
the means of any one being sacrificed through his
attention to duty, and he left his halbert at the house
in token thereof, where it remained many years, and
where it may even now be preserved.   Wetton and
Waltham had each a grant of land on a long lease,
which is now about half expired, from Sir Walter
Bagot.   Mr. Cope's father, who was always considered
the head tenant of this part of the estate, had done
his duty, and was, to his death, looked upon with
great favour.

After this the feeling in favour of the Stuarts became much cooled ; small bands of pretended or
licentious partizans ravaged the country ; and the
treachery and mistrust which existed caused the
stocks and pillory at Uttoxeter to be in frequent
requisition.   The patience of those who were faithful
begun to wear out, so that when the Scots entered
Derby a general mistrust of them pervaded the whole
country, and serving-men and labourers hid them-

selves for fear of been pressed into the king's service. Thus, for instance, the present Mr. Cope's grandfather was, at the time of the occupation of Derby, left for days together with one of his sons, a servant-boy, and an old man. Maids and women there were in abundance, but the men had fled. It being in so wooded and secluded a situation, everyone who could claim acquaintance fled to Knypersley, or the Forest Banks, to be out of harm's way. Many an hour Mr. Cope says he has wandered, when a boy, through the deep ravines which penetrate the Forest Banks, the cliffs of Bagot's Park, or Buttermilk and Dixon's Hills, sauntering in a moody way among the places where horses had been picketed day by day; and where silver and pewter ware, and other utensils, then considered valuable, had been deposited. Thus in the narrow ravine which runs up into the park called Frane Coppice Bank, Mr. Cope's father and the old servant man stood sentinel day by day alternately, and watched at night while the cattle grazed in the fields, and which were taken up again before daylight—his grandfather and the women attending to the cows and dairy, and occasionally making excursions across the Dove to Sudbury and Scropton to hear the news. Thus, according to an old song, it was narrated that the rebels penetrated as far as Scropton; and were frightened away by the woodland lasses, who, peering over Draycott Bridge, were told to return, as the Highlanders were plundering the houses. This song, as far as can be recollected, was very rude, and not particularly delicate in its allusions. It was, as such rude productions frequentlly are, coarsely but keenly satirical, and it enumerated the names of owners whose houses were ravaged, many of whose families remained to Mr. Cope's time, and some—as Steel, Greatorex, Smith, Manlove, and Taverner—even to the present. Thus:

> " Manlove was a cudgel player
> Of courage and renown,
> Who beat the Gilly from his house,
> And fairly cracked his crown."

Again the old women of the Woodlands volunteered to look what was doing at Scropton, and, it raining, they pulled off their red flannel petticoats, putting them as cloaks over their shoulders, and skulking under the hedges in large numbers, so alarmed the Scots that a panic seized them, and they fled with their booty. The chorus had for its substance the following particulars. From one house they took a pig (which the owners had killed to hide conveniently) and put it across a horse. They remained however to run the links of the pig-puddings, just made and hot, upon a pole, that they might carry them away more safely. In the mean time some of the red petticoats neared the village, whom the Scots who remained perceiving, took for soldiers of the Royal army, and they fled, struck with alarm. The song leads us to believe that the pig-pudding stealers escaped through the back door of a cow-house, and, jumping from a heap of manure, fell up to the neck in a cesspool. The lines were something like this—

> " With the puddings strung upon a pole
> They jumped from the muck-hill into the muck-hole."

However, they never crossed over into Stafford-shire.

In connection with these particulars of the commotion occasioned by the Pretender's army the following anecdote, copied from "The Reliquary," [1] will be read with interest :—" A Relic of ' 1745'—I have now before me an old stone bottle, some eight inches high, light in colour, and bearing upon it the words, ' SACK, 1640.' Insignificant as it is it possesses some little interest, and claims connection with the stirring times of the ' Rebellion of '45.' On the rumoured approach of the insurgents at that memorable period, a worthy farmer, then living near Leek, deemed it prudent to conceal his valuables, and had for that purpose raised a flagstone in the stable. At the suggestion, however, of an old woman who was standing by, he changed his plan, and buried his treasure in a heap of manure in the farmyard. Amongst other articles so buried were forty-eight ' sack bottles' full of home-brewed ale ; and when the storm was blown over the owner coming to examine his deposit, found the liquor exceedingly ripe and good. Bottle after bottle, on being handed out, met the admiring gaze of an aged (and perhaps expectant) looker on, who, being astonished at their apparently great number, exclaimed to the farmer, ' Mester, dun you think they'ne bred i' th' hole ? ' One of these is the bottle before alluded to, which is still possessed by the descendant of the worthy yeoman of 1745."

(1) "The Reliquary ;" Quarterly Journal, Edited by Ll. Jewitt, F.S.A.

The Duke of Cumberland receiving whilst at Uttoxeter an intimation not to proceed to Derby, and doubtless learning that the Cavalier had hastily left that town, departed from Uttoxeter and rejoined his army.

From Ashbourne Prince Charles continued his retreat through Yorkshire to Carlisle, his progress to the heart of the kingdom and back with about 7000 men having been effected in the presence of two regular armies under Marshal Wade and the Duke of Cumberland, in the depth of winter. After crossing into Scotland he attempted the seige of Stirling Castle, and Lord Murray gained a complete victory over General Hawley at Falkirk. The siege of Stirling Castle was raised, and on the 15th of April Prince Charles resolved to make a night attack upon the Duke's army, which had followed him ; but it being two o'clock in the morning when they had yet three miles to march to where the Duke lay, and being weary and dispirited, they retraced their steps to Culloden, where they had previously been drawn up in order of battle. The Duke of Cumberland had heard of the attempt. About eight o'clock his forces were observed on their march, and about one o'clock the king's troops opened a heavy cannonade, which was but feebly returned. The Highlanders suffered severely and became impatient; the Mackintosh regiment broke from the line and drove back the king's troops sword in hand, but were brought to the ground by a terrible fire. The Macdonald and other Highland regiments, being thus deprived of the post of

honour which they had possessed from time imme-
morial, retired, and it was in vain any attempts were
made to rally them. The Prince himself became
hesitating when urged to make a final attempt or
die like one worthy of a crown; and Lord Elcho,
who had sacrificed everything for him, left him with
execrations, and swore never to see his face again.
Prince Charles[1] had a reward of £30,000 set upon
his person, and for many weeks he wandered about
with fatigue and hunger; and finally, after many
escapes and much trouble, safely arrived in France.
After all hopes of recovering the crown of Britain
were lost, he assumed the title of Count of Albany,
and died at Rome, January 31st, 1788. [2]

For many years there was a party of Prince
Charles Edward's adherents in Uttoxeter and its
neighbourhood, who met annually at the White
Hart; and there is a cup which was used at this
celebration, out of which the Prince had drank, preserved by a gentleman living not far from Uttoxeter.
I believe, also, there is a secret correspondence or collection of papers, which had a narrow escape of being
seized at the time, having reference to plans which
were devised by these partizans for the Prince's elevation to the throne of England, all still in preservation in Staffordshire. T. C. S. Kynnersly, Esq.,
stipendiary magistrate of Birmingham, has a mina-

(1) He was accompanied by a single person, who wrote an account of
their sufferings during these anxious weeks. This MS. has just come
to light, and is being printed.

(2) Penny Encyclopædia.

ture likeness of him, given to a member of his family by the Prince, as a mark of gratitude for hospitality shown to him.

After a lapse of 39 years Uttoxeter became the scene of an incident all the more remarkable because it is associated with so distinguished a name and person as Dr. Samuel Johnson. It is the act of penance by the celebrated Doctor which he self-inflicted for refusing to obey a request of his father's when a boy at home. It forms a striking feature in his biography, and has been celebrated in no less direct a way in papers, some of an ephemeral and others of a lasting character. Some have written of it philosophically, as Thomas Carlyle; others poetically, as Walter Thornbury; whilst others have tried to draw lessons from it for the young, or cautions to the Christian in matters of faith. Thomas Carlyle says, "The picture of Samuel Johnson standing bareheaded in the Market-place there is one of the grandest and saddest we can paint." [1] As it is a matter of so much interest I will give the fullest particulars of it I am enabled to do.

The father of Doctor Johnson was Michael Johnson, a native of Cubley, in Derbyshire, a place not many miles from Uttoxeter. After some vicissitudes he became established as a bookseller at Lichfield, and amongst other places he was in the habit of attending Uttoxeter on Market days with books for sale. Doctor Johnson, his son, spent two years when

---

(1) Thomas Carlyle's Works, vol. iii. p. 89.

verging upon his twentieth year, in learning his father's business; and a few years back there were books in existence in Lichfield said to have been bound by his own hands. It was during this period when his father, being unwell, requested him to go to Uttoxeter to attend the book-stall, a desire which, probably in a fit of pride, he refused to obey. In contrition for this act of disobedience, towards the close of his life, in 1784, he repaired to the spot where the book-stall had stood in Uttoxeter Market-place, and there remained for a considerable time bareheaded in the rain by way of expiatory penance.[1]

At the time this took place Doctor Johnson was on a visit at Miss Seward's and his other friends at Lichfield. During his stay he was missed one morning from the breakfast table, and on an inquiry being made of the servants, they stated that they understood that he had set off from Lichfield at a very early hour without mentioning to any of the family whither he was going. The day passed without the return of the illustrious guest, and the party began to be very uneasy on his account, when, just before the supper hour the door opened and the Doctor stalked into the room. A solemn silence ensued of a few minutes, nobody daring to inquire the cause of his absence, which was at length relieved by Johnson addressing the lady of the house in the following manner:—" Madam, I beg your pardon for the abruptness of my departure from your house this morn-

(1) A Short Account of Lichfield, 1819.

ing, but I was constrained to it by my conscience. *Fifty years ago*, madam, *on this day*, I committed a breach of filial piety which has ever since lain heavy on my mind, and has not till this day been expiated. My father, you recollect, was a bookseller, and had long been in the habit of attending Uttoxeter market, and opening a stall of his books during that day. Confined to his bed by indisposition he requested me, this time fifty years ago, to visit the market and attend the market in his place.   But, madam, my pride prevented me from doing my duty, and I gave my father a refusal.   To do away the sin of this disobedience, I this day went in a post-chaise to Uttoxeter, and going into the market at the time of high business, uncovered my head, and stood with it bare an hour before the stall which my father formerly used, exposed to the sneers of the standers by, and the inclemency of the weather—a penance by which I trust I have propitiated heaven for this only instance of my contumely to my father."[1]   A confession and contrition more touching never fell from the lips of a great and venerable man.

Is it then any wonder that distinguished writers should so frequently notice the circumstance? or that any one should even visit Uttoxeter to try to see the spot consecrated by Johnson's tears?   Scarcely, however, would one think that a gentleman who lived three thousand miles away, although happening

[1] Johnsoniana and Warner's tour through the Northern Counties of England.

to be in England, would come to Uttoxeter for such a purpose. Yet, so it has been. No less noted a person than Nathaniel Hawthorn, of America, author of " Twice told Tales," and " Transformation," visited Uttoxeter in 1857, to see the spot where this remarkable incident took place. It appears nearly all concern, locally, about the place had passed out of people's minds, until this eminent foreigner, after seeing Uttoxeter for the intention stated, wrote a description of his visit for one of the annuals, and which was copied into the local papers, and perused with great eagerness. The production, as might be expected from so vivid a pen, was the occasion of several letters appearing in a local paper,[1] but without finding out, as they were intended to do, the place where the Doctor stood.

The paper is so pleasing in its style, and so interesting as proceeding from such an author, and relating in the manner it does to such a subject, that any thing but an apology is required for giving it in this place. Mr. Hawthorn proceeds—" At Lichfield, in St. Mary's Square, I saw a statue of Doctor Johnson, elevated some ten or twelve feet high. The statue is colossal, though not more so than the mountainous Doctor, who sits in a chair with a pile of big books underneath it, looking down upon the spectators with a broad, heavy, benignant countenance, very like Johnson's portraits. The figure is immensely massive, a vast ponderosity of stone, not

(1) The Era.

finely spiritualized, nor indeed fully humanized, but
rather resembling a great boulder than a man.   On
the pedestal are three bas-reliefs.   In the first Johnson is represented as a mere baby, seated on an old
man's shoulders, resting his chin on the bald head
which he embraces with his arms, and listening to
Doctor Sacheverel.   In the second table he is seen
riding to school on the backs of two of his comrades,
while a third boy supports him in the rear.   *The
third bas-relief possesses to my mind a good deal of
pathos.* It shows Johnson in the Market-place of
Uttoxeter doing penance for an act of disobedience
to his father fifty years before.   He stands bareheaded, very sad and woe-be-gone, with the wind and
rain driving against him, whilst some market-people
and children gaze awe-stricken into his face, and an
aged man and woman with clasped hands are praying
for him.   These latter personages, I fancy (though
in close proximity there are living ducks and dead
poultry), represent the spirit of Johnson's father and
mother, lending what aid they can to lighten his half
century's burden of remorse.   I never heard of this
statue.   It seems to have no reputation as a work of
art, and very possibly may deserve none.   Yet I
found it somewhat touching and effective, perhaps
because my interest in the sturdiest of Englishmen
has always been peculiarly strong; and especially the
above-described bas-relief freshened my sense of a
*wonderful beauty and pathos in the incident it com-
memorates.*   So the next day I left Lichfield for Uttoxeter on a purely sentimental pilgrimage (by rail-

way, however) to see the spot where Johnson performed his penance. Boswell, I think, speaks of the town as being about nine miles from Lichfield, but the map would indicate a much greater distance, and by rail, passing from one to another, as much as seventeen or eighteen miles.

" I have always had an idea of old Michael Johnson's journey thither on foot on the morning of the market-days, selling books through the busy hours, and returning home at night. This cannot well have been.

" Arriving at Uttoxeter station, the first thing I saw in a convenient vicinity was the tower and tall grey spire of a church. It is but a very short walk from the station up to the town. It had been my previous impression that the market-place of Uttoxeter lay immediately round about the church; and if I remember the narration aright, Johnson describes his father's book-stall as standing in the market-place, close beside the sacred edifice. But the church has merely a street of ordinary width passing round it, whilst the market-place, though near at hand, is not really contiguous, nor would its throng and bustle be apt to overflow their bounds and surge against the churchyard and old grey tower. Nevertheless, a walk of a minute or two would bring a person from the centre of the market-place to the church door, and Michael Johnson might very well have placed his stall, and laid out his literary ware, in the corner at the tower's base; better there perhaps than in the busy centre of an agricultural market. But the pic-

turesqueness and full impressiveness of the story require that Johnson doing his penance should have
been the very neucleus of the crowd—the midmost
man of the market-place—the centre figure of memory and remorse—contrasting with, and overawing
the sultry materialism around him.   I am resolved,
therefore, that the true site of his penance was in the
market-place.   This is a pretty spacious and irregular vacuity, surrounded by houses and shops, some of
them old, with red tiled roofs ; others wearing a pre-
tence of newness, but probably as old as the rest.

" The only other thing that impressed me in Uttoxeter was the abundance of publichouses—one at
every step or two—' Red Lions,' ' White Harts,'
' Bulls Heads,' ' Blue Bells,' ' Cross Keys.' These are
probaby for the accommodation of the agricultural
visitors on market days.   At any rate, I appeared
to be the only guest in Uttoxeter on the day of my
visit, and had but an infintessimal portion of patronage to distribute amongst so many inns.

" I stepped into one of these rustic hostelries and
got my dinner—bacon and greens, a chop, and a
gooseberry pudding, enough for six yeomen, besides
ale, all for a shilling and sixpence.   This hospitable
inn, miscalled the ' Nag's Head,' and standing besides the market-place, was as likely as any other to
have contained old Michael Johnson in the days when
he used to come thither to sell books.   He perhaps
had eaten his bacon and greens, and drank his ale,
and smoked his pipe in the very room where I now
sat—a low, ancient room, with a red brick floor

and whitwashed ceiling, traversed by rough beams,
the whole in the rudest fashion, but extremely neat.
Neither did the room lack ornament, the walls being
hung with engravings of prize oxen and other pretty
prints, and the mantelpiece adorned with earthenware
figures of shepherdesses. But still as I sipped my
ale I glanced through the window into the sunny
market-place, and wished I could honestly fix on one
spot more than another as likely to have been the
spot where Johnson stood to do his penance. How
strange and stupid it is that tradition should not
have marked and kept in mind the very place! How
shameful! — nothing less than that — that there
should be no local memorial of this incident, as
beautiful and as touching a passage as can be cited
out of any human life—no inscription of it, as sacred
as a verse of scripture, on the walls of the church!
no statue of the venerable and illustrious penitent in
the market-place to throw a wholesome awe over its
traffic, its earthliness, its selfishness. Such a statue,
if the piety of man did not raise it, might almost
have been expected to grow up out of the pavement
of its own accord on the spot that had been watered
by Johnson's remorseless tears, and by the rain that
dropped from him.

 "Well, my pilgrimage had not turned out a very
successful one. There being no train till late in the
afternoon I spent I know not how many hours in
Uttoxeter, and, to say the truth, was heartily tired
of it, my penance being a great deal longer than
Doctor Johnson's. Moreover, I forgot, until it was

too late, to snatch the opportunity to repent of some
sins.   Whilst waiting at the station I asked a boy
who sat near me—a school-boy of some twelve or
thirteen years old, whom I should take to be a clergyman's son—I asked him whether he had ever heard
the story of Doctor Johnson ; how he stood an hour
doing penance beside that church whose spire rose
before us ?   The boy stared and answered ' No !'   I
inquired if no such story was known or talked about
in Uttoxeter ?   ' No !' said the boy, ' that I ever
heard of."   Just think of the absurd little town
knowing nothing of its one memorable incident which
sanctifies it to the heart of a stranger from three
thousand miles over the sea !   Just think of the
fathers and mothers of Uttoxeter never telling their
children the sad and lovely story which might have
such a blessed influence on their young days, and
spare them many a pang hereafter."

   This sketch by a foreigner about Johnson's penance is very touching and beautiful.   It has been
mentioned that it gave rise to inquiry at the time,
about the place where the Doctor did penance, but
without being found out.   I made inquiries myself
amongst old people then, which resulted, about two
years afterwards, in the place being discovered.
Amongst others of whom I inquired was Joseph
Twigg.   He had then no recollection of any such
occurrence; but about a year and a half, or two years,
afterwards, when he was no longer able to get out of
the house, on going to see him (he being at that
time in his eighty-sixth year), asked me " if I had

not once asked him whether some one, when he was a lad, had done penance in the Market-place?" I told him I most probably had, and that a very great man had once done penance thereabout. He then related that he had a recollection of something of the kind. He said that, when he was a lad, his father, one *market day*, came into the house late, to dinner, and his mother asked him why he had not come sooner? To which he answered, "*that he had been looking at a man standing in the Market-place, at the pillory*, without his hat, doing penance." The pillory, to which the stocks were connected at that date, stood, he informed me, in the centre of Bear Hill, the open space at the east end of the Market-place. This is a considerable distance from the conduit and weighing machine, where the stocks stood in recent years, and where it was supposed the Doctor imposed upon himself the penance. Twigg also told me that what his father stated so struck him for its singularity, that either that day or early the next morning, he went to Bear Hill himself, and although he did not see the renowned penitent, he saw the rubbish and stones which had been cast at him in derision by children. My informant was then about eight years of age, and was therefore quite old enough to have the recollection of so strange an affair—particularly as he visited the spot himself where it took place—impressed upon his memory.

That the circumstance thus related by the old man, who fixes the site at Bear Hill, is identical with the so-called expiatory act of Dr. Johnson, there is

scarcely a doubt. By an attentive look at the bas-
relief on his monument at Lichfield, it will be perceived that the figures confirm the attempt to show
that Bear Hill is the spot where "the one memorable
incident" in the life of Johnson was carried out.
Besides the representation of the aged persons in the
group, the nose of a pig obtrudes itself; also dead
fowls are observed to hang over the old-fashiohed
rails. The designer of the cartoon could not have
gained his ideas from the Market-place, strictly
so-called—particularly not from anything near the
conduit, but from Bear Hill. There the pig market
used to be held, and besides the space allotted to
the pillory and stocks, there was a square portion
railed out for the protection of a sort of reser-
voir, which had an immensely large iron grate
over it, swelling upwards half a yard, [1] and these
must have been the rails which the designer of the
monument had seen the dead fowls hanging over.
Fixing, then, the centre of Bear Hill as the place of
this singular incident, there is no necessity any longer
to contend with the paradox of its happening at the
conduit, where the view of the church is obstructed,
and yet in sight of the church at the same time. At
Bear Hill the church is quite conspicuous, and both
are only a few yards from each other, and it was also
then an invariable feature of the market that it extended a considerable way into each street, so that

---

(1) A gentleman is living who recollects that this was the cucking
hole, the cucking-stool projecting from the pillory (to which it was
fastened) over it.

there is no doubt it "surged" quite round the old church-yard wall.[1] Adding, therefore, these views to the statements of Joseph Twigg, any doubt as to the actual spot where Dr. Johnson relieved his mind of the burdening sense of his guilt, for refusing to comply with a lawful requirement of his father, when a boy, may be considered at an end. The supposed circumstances and features of the market day when the penance was performed have been made the subject of the following pathetic lines, by Walter Thornbury, which appeared in "Once a Week," for 1861 :—

A country road on market-day
  (Is what I fee arife),
Crowded with farmers, ruddy men,
  Muffled up to the eyes ;
For cold and bitter rain beats faft
  From the grey cheerlefs fkies.

Paft carts, with white tilts flagging wet,
  Paft knots of wrangling hinds,
A burly man with deep-lined face,
  Chafed by the' churlifh winds,
Strides on like dreary packman who
  His galling burden binds.

He wears no ruffles round his wrifts,
  His wig is fcorch'd and worn ;
His flouching coat flaps loose and long—
  Its buttons but of horn ;
The little lace upon its cuffs
  Is frayed and foil'd, and torn.

(1) Tour through Great Britain, by a gentleman, 4 vols. 1760.

It is a day of fullen cloud,
  Of fhrinking leaf and flower —
A day the fun to fhine or warm
  Has neither wifh nor power ;
So fitful falls the wavering vail
  Of the cold bitter fhower.

The blackbirds from the hedges break
  In chattering difmay,
Like wicked thoughts in finners' minds
  When they kneel down to pray ;
He fees them not, for darknefs deep
  Bars out for him the day.

Before him black and open graves
  Seem yawning in the way ;
The fun, a mere vaft globe of jet,
  Bodes God's great wrath alway ;
He hears ftrange voices on his track
  That fill him with difmay.

The black rooks o'er the fallows whirl
  Like demons in the fky,
Watching to do fome hurt to man,
  But for the fleeplefs eye
Of God that, whether day or night,
  Still baffles them from high.

The miller's waggon, dripping flour,
  Toils on, clofe covered in ;
The pedlar, fpite of cloak and pack,
  Is drenched unto the fkin ;
The road to U'xeter is thronged
  With cattle crowding in.

With butting heads againſt the wind
　　The farmers canter on,
(Sure, corn that morning has gone down,
　　They look ſo woe-begone) ;
Till now ſhone out the ſteeple vane
　　The ſun has flaſhed upon.

'Tween ſtrings of horſes dripping wet
　　The burly man ſtrides faſt ;
On market-ſtalls and crowded pens
　　No eager look he caſt ;
He thought not of the wrangling fair,
　　But of a day long paſt.

He comes to where the market croſs
　　Stands towering o'er the ſtalls,
Where on the awnings brown and ſoak'd
　　The rain unceaſing falls ;
Where loud the vagrant auctioneer
　　With noiſy clamour bawls.

He heeds not yonder rocking-ſwings
　　That laughing ruſtics fill,
But gazes on one ſtall where ſits
　　A ſtripling, quiet and ſtill,
Selling his books, although the rain
　　Falls ceaſeleſsly and chill.

There, in the well-remember'd place,
　　He ſtands, head low and bare,
Heedleſs of all the ſcoffing crowd
　　Who joſtle round and ſtare,
Crying, " Why, lads here's a preacher man
　　Come to this April Fair."

" Here's th' April Fool ! " a farmer cries,
   Holding his fwollen fide ;
Another clacks his whip, a third
   Begins to rail and chide,
While falefmen cried their prices out,
   And with each other vied.

Yet when he filent ftood, nor moved
   For one long hour at leaft,
The market women leering said
   " This is fome crazy prieft
Doing his penance — pelt him boys —
   Pump on the Popifh thief ! "

Some, counting money, turned to fneer ;
   One with raifed hammer there
Kept it still poifed, to fee the man ;
   The buyers paufed to ftare ;
The farmer had to hold his dog,
   Longing to bite and tear.

As the old clock beats out the time,
   The ftranger ftrides away,
Paft deafening groups of flocks and carts
   And many a drunken fray ;
The fin of fifty years agone,
   That penance purged away.

Call it not fuperftition, friends,
   Or foolifh weak regret ;
He was a great good man, whofe eyes
   With tears that day were wet ;
It was a brave act to crufh his pride —
   Worthy of memory yet.

Mr. Norris, stationer, possesses a pen and ink sketch of Dr. Johnson and Captain Astle (or rather the Rev. Thomas Astle), which is supposed to be a representation of the Doctor as he stood doing penance, and was probably executed by Captain Astle himself, who was acquainted with him. By Mr. Norris's permission a reduced fac-simile is here engraved.

As to the inn where old Michael Johnson staid when he came to Uttoxeter with books, it is perhaps more likely to have been the Red Lion Inn than the Nag's Head, which I believe was not then in existence. But of course nothing but conjecture can be given as to any place he made his calling house for refreshment. When Johnson did his pen-

ance there was another inn at Bear Hill, close to the
Red Lion, and as it was a posting house, it is not at
all improbable that the chaise which brought him to
Uttoxeter in 1784 was drawn up there. The following
copy of a card, printed in 1793, by the late Mr.
Richards, announces the amalgamation of the two
Inns :—

" Red Lion Inn (opposite the church). W. Garle
takes the liberty of acquainting his friends and the
public, that, having taken and laid to his house
the assembly room, stables, and other conveniences
lately belonging to the ' New Star ' Inn, and made
various other alterations and enlargements, he has
very complete and desirable accommodation for gentlemen travellers and others who will honour him
with their company. He begs leave to observe that
he has laid in ample stock of the very best port and
other wines, and also spirits of the best quality.
☞ W. Garle continues the malting business as
usual. May 14th, 1793."

It does not appear that there was any other bookseller in Uttoxeter at the period when Michael Johnson brought books for sale, or for some time afterwards.
He must consequently be regarded not only as the earliest medium by which books got disseminated in the
neighbourhood, but as the earliest pioneer in intel-
lectual and moral improvement of whom Uttoxeter
can boast, and of whose name, therefore, it ought
to be proud. Not till at least, sixty years after
Michael Johnson, is there any account of Uttoxeter
having the advantage of a second bookseller, as re-

membered by one of "the oldest inhabitants." About that distance of time after, one Mr. Sanders, of Derby, opened a shop in the Market-place, at the north side, for the sale of books and stationery. Railway travelling not then being thought of, this worthy and plodding tradesman brought his books and the *et ceteras* to Uttoxeter in a couple of saddle-bags over a horse. [1]

There are no notable events after the penance of Dr. Johnson to be recorded as having taken place in Uttoxeter at the close of the last century; but the treaty of peace entered into between England, France, Spain, and Holland, in the year 1802, was celebrated in that town with accompanying festivities. The town was illuminated, and Mr. Samuel Bently, then in his 80th year, appeared as the personification of Peace at his house door, with a laurel wreath on his head, and he also gave memory to the event by the following invocation :—

"INVOCATION TO PEACE,
By Mr. Samuel Bentley, of Uttoxeter,
March 30th, 1802.

All hail, ſweet peace ! hail, thou treaſure !
Brighteſt ſource of real pleaſure :

---

(1) It does not lie within the range of this book to give a life of Dr. Johnson, but the following particulars, which I conceive are original, and have never before been published, I have much pleasure in adding here in form of a note. They are observations in the handwriting of the late Lord St Helen's, in the margin of his lordship's copy of Murphy's Life of Johnson. The copy is in the possession of Sir William Fitzherbert, Bart., Tissington Hall, who kindly offered the use of it to me. On page 44, Mr. Pitt's speech is

Come, lovely peace, triumphant come,
Deign to fix here thy laſting dome.
England ſhall then loud peans ſing ;
Fortiſſemo the bells ſhall ring :
Goddeſs, deſcend, nor make delay ;
Hither, O hither, wing thy way.
Infants ſhall liſp thy pleaſing name ;
Joyous all ranks thy worth proclaim ;
Kings, Lords, and Commons, all ſhall join,
Loud to proclaim thee, Peace, divine :
Muſic ſhall all its graces lend,
No note of diſcord ſhall offend ;
Organs ſhall ſwell each ſolemn ſound,
Prieſts, poet's chorus hymning round ;
Quite round our iſle, on every ſhore,
Rejoicing, deathleſs cannons roar :
Shepperds ſhall pipe with open reeds ;
Light nymphs and ſwains dance round our meads,
Unbleſt wars ravages, no more
Virgins and matrons ſhall deplore ;
Wiſe kings, adored, O peace, thy grace ;
Xerxes ne'er viewed thy ſmiling face ;

referred to in the text, on which Lord St. Helen's has the following remarks :—" According to Dr. Brockleſby, who was also present at the conversation, the speech particularly mentioned was Lord Chatham's celebrated invective against Horace Walpole; such a specimen (said one of the company) of the superiority of that great statesman, as to afford a sure prognostic of his future eminence." " Yes," replied Johnson, " I composed every syllable of that speech, and many others, in a garret in Exeter-Street, at the price of 3s. 6d. per sheet of very close writing." The other has reference to what is on page 101, and is this—" Foote knew the intrepidity of his antagonist, and abandoned his design, yet it can hardly be doubted that the character of ' Grace' in Tooke's Commissary was introduced for Johnson."

Yearly to thee we 'll homage pay,
Zealous to guard thee night and day.
CHORUS ——
Tyrants of old ufurped the laurel bough.
Laurels with olive wreathed, fhall grace thy brow ;
Peace, plenty, liberty, we will adore
Eternally —— till time fhall be no more.

Richards, Printer."

It will not be thought uninteresting and unworthy of notice that the Queen of these realms, whose husband, "Albert the Good," has been so mysteriously and suddenly snatched from the nation and from his family, passed through Uttoxeter when a young Princess, when, as might be expected, a crowd of people filled the streets to have a glance at one so high in society as to have the prospect of the British crown before her. About twenty years ago, the Queen Dowager also passed through Uttoxeter to Alton Towers. A halt was made at the White Hart Hotel, Carter-street, where the Yeomanry Cavalry were drawn up to protect with military formality her carriage, and escort her to Alton.

About this period there was also a matter before the inhabitants of Uttoxeter in which they were deeply interested. Reference is made to the circumstances attending the birth of William John Fox, Esq., which, with his majority and marriage, have an historical importance in the estimation of the local chronicler. These circumstances were attendant upon a course of litigation which was instituted about

1835, and continued through several years, having issue to the question who was the legal inheritor of considerable landed estates and other property which had belonged to Mr. Fox, an old and exceedingly wealthy inhabitant of Uttoxeter, then recently deceased. Amongst the legal proceedings arising out of this question, was the consignment of Mrs. Fox, who had been married to the deceased gentleman a very short time before his death, to the care of a jury of matrons, of Uttoxeter, until the birth of a posthumous child of which she declared herself pregnant, and who it was contended, on her behalf, would be the heir or heiress to Mr. Fox's estates. The novelty of this proceeding, taken by direction of the Court, excited considerable interest at the time, and has since been referred to in several works on medical jurisprudence. In due time the child (the present Mr. W. J. Fox) was born, and when, after protracted litigation, involving trials at *nisi prius* at Stafford, Chester, and Gloucester Court of Appeal, the joy of the people of Uttoxeter, who all along had been faithful to the cause of the widow and fatherless, found expression in every conceivable way.[1]

It was to be expected that the attainment of his majority by a young gentleman, the circumstances surrounding whose birth were so peculiar, would not be permitted to pass by unnoticed. On this event, which took place on Thursday, October 14th, 1856, he was invited to a public dinner by the gentlemen

---

[1] "Staffordshire Advertiser."

of the town and neighbourhood, which was held under the presidency of the late Joseph Bladon, Esq., at the Town Hall, Uttoxeter. A very full assembly did honour to the occasion. On the same day Mr. Fox himself gave to the poor of Uttoxeter a substantial quantity of coal and beef, and during the excessively severe winter of 1860–61, he again generously bestowed upon the poor of the parish about thirty-five tons·of coal.

The marriage of W. J. Fox, Esq., with Ellen Elizabeth, eldest daughter of Thomas Bladon, Esq., of Uttoxeter, took place on the 7th October, 1858. The marriage ceremony was solemnized by the late Mr. Dashwood, grandfather of the bride. There was quite a demonstration of public enthusiasm on the occasion.

Preceding this event by two years, the peace rejoicings in Uttoxeter, following upon the proclamation of peace between the Allied Powers and Russia, were of a character to be remembered. After such an holocaust of victims to the lust of despotism and war as that which had been made in the Crimea, causing bleeding hearts and desolated homes in almost every town and village throughout several nations of Europe, it was sufficient to cause rejoicing in any town when the message of peace was sent forth. The rejoicings in Uttoxeter took place in the usual form, resulting chiefly in good doings to the poor, on the 1st of June, 1856. This is a somewhat strange and peculiar feature amongst the English people, but it is owing, I presume, to the excessive unselfishness and benevolence of the upper classes. The sum of £75 was collected in the town, and collected, too, in the short space of two or three days, and was laid out, in providing for the festivity, 1200 lbs. of the best cuts of beef, 110 stones of flour for bread, and in the purchase of numerous barrels of ale. The distribution was made in the centre of the Market-place, where arrangements had been previously made, to about 450 families by ticket. The National Anthem, however, was first sung, and three cheers given for the Queen. The committee of management consisted of Messrs. R. Bagshaw, J. B. Johnson, J. Dunnicliffe, Joseph Wood, C. Turner, Joseph Clarke, and James Cook.

There was also a whole sheep roasted at Tinker's-lane End, and cut up for the people in that part of the town. There were besides numerous public tea meetings in the town in the afternoon. In Carter-street there were three; in Balance-street one; in Smithy-lane one; and in Silver-street one; besides one in the Market-place, at which about 300 persons gathered. The teetotallers also had one, and the people of the workhouse were handsomely provided for in the same manner.

The streets were profusely decorated during the day with evergreens, wreaths, garlands and mottos, and at night a display of fireworks and an illumination by gas were made in the Market-place. The day passed off most pleasantly, and everything showed that if the terms of peace were not all that could be

desired, the inhabitants of Uttoxeter yet valued peace
as a blessing and a fact worth rejoicing for.

> " Were half the power that fills the world with terror ;
>   Were half the wealth bestowed on camps and courts,
>   Given to redeem the human mind from error,
>   There were no need of arsenals and forts."
>
> LONGFELLOW.

THE SHREWSBURY PEERAGE CASE.

WE have only to pass along a few more years, in
the interim of which nothing occurred in Uttoxeter
to merit particular notice, to be brought to the most
important local event of the century—one in which
Uttoxeter and the neighbourhood took a particular and
lively interest. Indeed the part which Uttoxeter
took on the occasion makes it almost historically its
own. It need scarcely be said that it is the occasion
of Lord Shrewsbury and Talbot taking possession of
Alton Towers and the other Shrewsbury estates. Such ·
an outburst of good feeling and popular enthusiasm
could not, however, have been owing merely to a great
legal achievement in the right of property. Nothing
short of the noble qualities inherent in his lordship,
than whom there " is no more brave, generous, and
open-hearted Englishman amongst the subjects of
Queen Victoria," [1] and the estimable Lady Shrewsbury herself, in connection with the just decision,
after a most trying struggle, in his Lordship's favour,
could have produced such a spontaneous demonstration, unequalled probably in any similar case, as
that which took place at Uttoxeter on the 13th of

(1) Staffordshire " Advertiser," April 14th, 1861.

May, 1861. As, however, the history of the Shrewsbury peerage, and an account of the struggle which
terminated in favour of the Earl of Shrewsbury,
seem an important preliminary to a description of
the festivities at Uttoxeter, which were held to inau-
gurate the taking formal possession of Alton Towers
and estates, the following accurate summary will prove
not uninteresting :—

"We learn from 'Burke's Peerage,' and other
equally reliable sources of information, that the emi-
ment family of Talbot is one of ancient celebrity
and almost unequalled historic interest. It deduces
its descent from a period antecedent to the conquest;
but Richard de Talbot, who came over to England
with William I., may be considered its founder.
From him the Shrewsbury branch in England, and
the Talbots of Malahide, in Ireland, as well as the
untitled but elder branch of Talbots of Bashall, Yorkshire (now extinct in the direct male line), can trace
their pedigree through nearly eight centuries by direct descent to the present day. From the second son
Hugh, Governor of the Castle of Plessy, in Essex,
who afterwards assumed the monastic habit, like so
many warriors of his time, six generations bring us
down to Sir George Talbot, Lord Chamberlain to
King Edward III., by whom he was summoned to
Parliament as a baron in A.D., 1331. His son, Sir
Richard, Lord of Goderich Castle, and second baron,
distinguished himself in the French wars of Edward
III., and became great-grandfather of Sir John Talbot, sixth baron, summoned to Parliament, in 1409

J

as Lord de Furnivall.   In 1412 the latter illustrious
warrior was appointed Lord Justice of Ireland of
which he became Lord Lieutenant in A.D., 1414.
He subsequently rendered good service to his country
in the French wars of Henry V., but his highest
renown was gained under Henry VI., upon the same
field under the Regent Plantagenet Duke of Bedford.
It is said that his character became far and wide so
formidable to the French, owing to the constant success which attended his expeditions, that mothers
used to hush their children into silence by pro-
nouncing the name of the ' Great Dogge Talbot.'
He was attacked however by Joan of Arc, the Maid
of Orleans, at Patay, in 1429, when his army was
routed and he was himself taken prisoner.   Being
subsequently exchanged, and having gained for himself fresh laurels, he was created Earl of Shrewsbury
by King Edward IV. in 1442.   Again resuming the
Lord Lieutenancy of Ireland, which at that day was
rather a military than a civil post, and having been
appointed Lord High Steward of that country,
he was raised to the earldom of Wexford and Waterford in A.D. 1446, and thus became Premier Earl in
the Irish as well as the English peerage.   Again engaging in foreign warfare, though in the 80th year
of his age, the Earl advanced with a British force to
the relief of the Castle of Chatillon, in France, beneath the walls of which he was mortally wounded,
and died July 20th, 1453, with the reputation of
having been victorious in above forty different battles.
His younger son, Lord Lisle, fell dead upon the same

field. John, the second Earl of Shrewsbury, K.G.,
Lord Treasurer, first of Ireland and afterwards of
England, was killed at the battle of Northampton,
in A.D. 1460, while fighting under the Red Rose.
He was succeeded by his eldest son, from whom the
title descended regularly to the fifth earl, the most
consistent statesman of Queen Mary's reign, and the
only nobleman except Viscount Montague, who, on
Elizabeth's accession, opposed the repeal of the act of
submission of the Houses of Lords and Commons to
the authority of the See of Rome, which had been
carried into effect in the preceding reign. Though
thus strongly attached to the religion of his forefathers Queen Elizabeth retained him in her service,
and even admitted him to her privy council. His
son, the sixth earl, is known to history as the most
wealthy and powerful peer of the realm, and the
guardian to whose custody the person of Mary Queen
of Scots was intrusted by Elizabeth. On the death
of the eighth earl in 1617 the title reverted to a distant cousin, Mr. George Talbot, of Grafton, as great-
grandson of second earl ; and from him it descended
regularly to Charles, twelfth earl, who, having con-
formed to the Established Church, became a promi-
nent statesman in the reigns of William III., Mary,
Anne, and George I., under whom he held the highest offices, and by whom he was rewarded with the
the Dukedom of Shrewsbury, the Marquisate of
Alton, and the Knighthood of the Garter. At his
death in 1717 the dukedom and marquisate expired,
and it is not a little singular that from that day to

this the earldom has never passed directly from a
father to a son.   The thirteenth earl, being a Jesuit
priest, of course did not assume the title, which accordingly passed to the son of his brother George, as
fourteenth earl, and the last of his male descendants
is now deceased.   It would be alike tedious and profitless to trace the exact pedigree for the last century,
which merely exhibits a series of nephews and cou-
sins inheriting in succession: we will therefore only
mention that the son and the nephew of John, sixteenth earl, having died during their minority, Bertram Arthur Talbot, in 1846, became heir presump-
tive to the Shrewsbury title and estates, to which he
succeeded as seventeenth earl towards the close of
the year 1852.   His lordship was the only son of the
late Lieutenant-Colonel Charles Thomas Talbot,
nephew of Charles, fifteenth earl, by Julia, third
daughter of Sir Henry Tichborne, Bart.   He was
born December 11th, 1832, and died without issue
at Lisbon, August 10th, 1856.

" The kindred of the Earl of Shrewsbury and Talbot to Bertram, seventeenth Earl of Shrewsbury,
consists in his lineal descent from the famous Sir
Gilbert Talbot, of Grafton (third son of the second
earl of Shrewsbury), who was High Sheriff of Shropshire in the time of King Richard III., but a staunch
adherent of the Earl of Richmond, the right wing of
whose army he commanded at the battle of Bosworth.
The victorious prince showed his gratitude by bestowing upon Gilbert the honour of knighthood, with
the grant of the manor of Grafton, in Worcester-

shire, and other lands. Two years afterwards Sir Gilbert had a command at the battle of Stoke, when the Earl of Lincoln and Lambert Simnel were defeated, and for this service he was made a knight-banneret. The most noble member of this branch of the Talbot family was Charles Talbot, who was bred to the bar, attained to the summit of his profession, and established the highest legal reputation. On the 31st of May, 1717, Mr. Talbot was appointed Solicitor-General to the Prince of Wales, which office he continued to hold until 1733, when he was constituted Lord High Chancellor of England, sworn of the Privy Council, and elevated to the peerage December 5th, by the title of Baron Talbot, of Hensol, Glamorganshire. His lordship married Cecil, daughter and heiress of Charles Mathews, Esq., of Castley-Menich, Glamorganshire, and was at his death (February 14th, 1736-7) succeeded by his eldest son, William, who was appointed Lord-Steward of the Household, sworn of the Privy Council in 1761, and advanced to the earldom as Earl Talbot, March 10th in the same year. His lordship dying without male issue the earldom expired, the barony of Dynevor (which title had been conferred upon him with special remainder to his daughter and her male issue) descended as limited, and the barony of Talbot of Hensol reverted to his nephew, John Chetwynd Talbot, who was advanced to the viscountcy and earldom July 3rd, 1784, by the title of Vicount Ingestre and Earl Talbot. He died May 19th, 1793, and was succeeded by his son Charles Chetwynd Chetwynd-Talbot, who was constituted Viceroy of Ireland on the retirement of the late Duke of Richmond, and executed the duties of that important government until the appointment of the Marquis Wellesley in 1821. His lordship was also Lord-Lieutenant of the county of Stafford.   At his death, which occurred on the 10th January, 1849, he was succeeded by his second son, the present Earl of Shrewsbury and Talbot.

" The present representative of the two great branches of this famous house has not, however, without a protracted struggle, succeeded in uniting in his own person the time-honoured titles.   Within a few days of the death of the late Earl of Shrewsbury an earnest was given of the serious intentions of the Ingestre branch to assert the claim of Earl Talbot to that title, for on the 18th of August, 1856, Viscount Ingestre (on behalf of his father, who was abroad), accompanied by Mr. Hand, his solicitor, formally demanded at Alton Towers possession of that mansion, and the estates of the late earl, alleging that Earl Talbot was the legal heir.   Lord Ingestre was informed that the trustees under the will of the deceased earl had taken possession, and he was refused admission into the house.   Earl Talbot at once resolved upon appealing to the highest tribunal in the land to decide the question of the title to the premier earldom of England ; but partly in consequence of the autumnal and winter recesses, and partly from the dissolution of Parliament in the Spring of 1857, it was the 11th of May of that year before Earl Talbot's claim was formerly brought be-

fore the House of Lords. On that day the petition
of his lordship to Her Majesty, praying Her Majesty
that the title, dignity, and peerage, or honors, of the
Earl of Shrewsbury might be declared and adjudged
to belong to him, together with Her Majesty's reference thereof to the House, and the report of the
Attorney-General thereof was presented, by command to the House. The petition, reference, and
report were read, and were subsequently referred to
the Committee of Privileges to consider and report
thereupon. The opponents to his lordship's claims
were three in number—first, the Duke of Norfolk, as
guardian of the interests of his infant son, to whom
the late earl bequeathed his magnificent property at
Alton Towers; secondly, the Princess Doria Pamphili, of Rome, as only surviving child of John, 16th
earl; and thirdly, Major Talbot, of Talbot, county
of Wexford, who traced his pedigree up to William,
fourth son of George, fourth earl, who was made a
Knight of the Garter for his valiant conduct at the
battle of Stoke, June 16th, 1487. The Committee
of Privileges met for the first time on the 13th of
the following July, when Sir Frederick Thesiger
opened the case on behalf of Earl Talbot, and on the
same day Mr. Sergeant Byles, who represented Lord
Edward Howard, admitted that the determination of
the claim to the title determined the title to the estates. On the 27th of the same month Mr. Sergeant
Byles opened the case for Lord Edward Howard, and
several subsequent days were occupied with the production of evidence against Earl Talbot's claim. On

the 14th of the following month the Attorney-General replied on behalf the Crown, and said that he proposed instituting further inquiries before asking the Committee to come to any resolution on the question at issue. The Committee unanimously approved of this course being pursued, and they then adjourned *sine die.* It is not until the 20th of April in the following year that we again find the Committee of Privileges engaged in this important investigation. The Attorney-General then stated the nature of the additional evidence which he intended to produce. This was cheifly of a documentary character, but its reception occupied their lordships during two days. On the 4th of May Sir R. Bethell addressed the committee on behalf of Earl Talbot's opponents. Two or three days were then devoted to the production of evidence on this side, after which Mr. Roundell Palmer pleaded on behalf of the appellants against the claim, and the Attorney-General, during the greater part of three days, summed up Earl Talbot's case. The Solicitor-General was then appealed to for his opinion on behalf of the Crown, and he stated his conviction to be " that the noble claimant had made out his case, and was entitled to the earldom of Shrewsbury." On the 1st of June the final sitting of the committee was held, and their lordships proceeded to give judgment. Lord Cranworth addressed the committee, and after going over the leading points of the case submitted on behalf of Earl Talbot, concluded by moving, " that their lordships report that the claimant has made out his title." Lord St. Leonards,

" having come to the clear and satisfactory conclusion
that the claimant's title admitted of no doubt," se-
conded the motion. Lords Wensleydale and Brough-
ham also expressed themselves to the same effect,
after which, Lord Redesdale, chairman of the committee, put the question, whether the claimant had
made out his title, and it was unanimously carried in
the affirmative. We read in the journals of the day
that the galleries of the house were crowded whenever
their lordship met, and that the Earl and Countess
of Shrewsbury and Talbot were warmly congratu-
lated by a large number of their friends immediately
after their lordships had come to the above resolution.

Those who anticipated (if any such there were),
from the admission made by Mr. Sergeant Byles at
the opening of the proceedings in the House of Lords
with respect to the title, that the right to the estates
of the deceased earl would be quietly conceded to
the succesful claimant for the title, were undeceived
at the earliest possible opportunity. On the 6th of
December, 1858, in the Court of Common Pleas,
before Mr. Chief Justice Cockburn and a special jury,
the cause of the Earl of Shrewsbury, *v.* Hope Scott
and others first came on for hearing. The action
was brought to recover the mansion-house of Alton
Towers and the annexed estates, and defendants, who
represented the infant son of the Duke of Norfolk,
defended as to all the property claimed. The Attorney-General opened the plaintiff's case, and produced
certain documentary evidence. On the same day Mr.
Sergeant Shee addressed the jury for the defendants,

and evidence on the same side having been produced,
it was agreed that a verdict should be entered for the
plaintiff, subject to leave to the defendants to move
to enter a verdict for them, or subject to a special
case if the parties should so agree. On the 21st of
January in the following year, in the Court of Common Pleas, Mr. Sergeant Shee obtained a rule upon
all the points of law raised by him on behalf of his
clients, and on the 31st of May the cause was again
called on. The Attorney-General, on behalf of the
noble plaintiff, appeared to show cause against the
rule, and Mr. Rolt, Q.C., Mr. Manisty, Q.C., and Mr.
Baddeley also addressed the Court on the same side.
Mr. Sergeant Shee and Sir R. Bethell replied on behalf of the defendants, and on the 8th of June the
Lord Chief Justice, and his learned brethren, Mr.
Justice Williams, Mr. Justice Willes, and Mr. Justice Byles, unanimously gave judgment to the effect
that the rule to set aside the verdict for the plaintiff
must be discharged. Undeterred by this defeat the
defendants at once resolved upon carrying the case to
the court of error. Little progress was, however,
made during the next term, but on the 1st of February in the present year the writ of error was
brought from the Court below, and came on for hearing, both sides being represented by counsel of the
highest eminence. The proceedings having lasted
three days, the Lord Chief Baron said the Court had
considered the very learned, elaborate, and ingenious
arguments urged by the Attorney-General (Sir R.
Bethell) on behalf of the defendants, but desired to

give them still further consideration before delivering judgment. The court would not then call upon the other side to reply, but would announce their conclusion as early as possible. This was naturally enough considered as virtually a victory on the part of the plaintiff, and all doubt was removed on the 18th February, when the Court gave judgment against the defendants. Notice of appeal to the House of Lords was given to the other side, but, doubtless, believing that they had no chance of obtaining a reversal of the decision of the Court of Exchequer, the defendants from this time abandoned all idea of carrying on the litigation, and on the 25th of the same month the Earl of Shrewsbury and Talbot took possession of Alton Towers.

" As a record we may mention that the counsel who appeared in the causes were—for the peerage, Lord Chelmsford (then Sir F. Thesiger), Sir Fitzroy Kelly, Mr. T. F. Ellis (Recorder of Leeds), and Mr. J. Hannen, of the Home Circuit. Mr. R. Nicholson, Earl Shrewsbury's London solicitor, had charge of the proceedings. In the action of ejectment—Sir Fitzroy Kelly, Mr. Rolt, Q.C., Mr. Manisty, Q.C., Mr. T. F. Ellis, and Mr. Hannen.

" The premier earldom of England having been thus adjudged to belong by right to Earl Talbot, his lordship delayed not in asserting his claim to those vast estates, which even his antagonists had admitted would legitimately pass to the successful competitor for the title of the deceased earl. These estates, the annual value of which is upwards of £40,000, lie in

the counties of Stafford, Salop, Chester, Oxford,
Berks, and Worcester.   The Oxfordshire estate comprises the site and ruins of a magnificent seat called
Heythorp, burnt down in the time of earl Charles;
and the Worcestershire estate an old family manor
house, at Grafton, the remains of a mansion which
is supposed to have been one of more than ordinary
size and magnificence in the time of Sir Gilbert Talbot, of Grafton, K.G. (knighted for his valour in the
field), who died in 1517.   The estates are all old
family properties; the Oxfordshire, Berkshire, and
Worcestershire belonged to Sir Gilbert, while the
Cheshire estates came into the family on the marriage
of Mr. John Talbot, of Albrighton, son of Sir Gilbert, with Miss Troutbeck, a Cheshire heiress.   The
Cheshire estate comprises very nearly the whole township of Oxton, near Birkenhead.   The greatest interest attaches, however, to the Staffordshire estates,
chiefly on account of the magnificent mansion which
the 15th earl erected at Alton, and which has from
that time been the principal seat of the house of
Talbot."[1]

As already stated the day for taking formal possession was Friday, the 13th of April, 1861, for
which such great preparation had been made in Uttoxeter.   Earl Talbot's tenantry, friends, and the
Staffordshire Yeomanry Cavalry, resolved to attend
his Lordship to Alton.   The procession was formed
at Blount's Green, about three parts of a mile to the

[1] " Staffordshire Advertiser," April 14th, 1860.

west of Uttoxeter, where by ten o'clock the Queen's Own Yeomanry Cavalry, under Captain Levett, the Uttoxeter and Blythfield troop, under the command of Captain Meynell Ingram, the Cheadle and Alton troods under Lieutenant Heywood, and the Leek troop, under Captain Sneyd, took up their respective positions in the field at the junction of the Stafford and Lichfield roads. The number was betwixt two and three hundred men and officers. At eleven o'clock the approach from Ingestre Hall was announced by outriders, and was met by a burst of cheers from the vast multitude of persons assembled. On its subsidence the procession was arranged in the following order :—

The High-Sheriff's carriage, drawn by four horses,
with outriders preceding;

R. H. Haywood, Esq, High Sheriff;	Howard Heywood, Esq.,
R. W. Hand, Esq., High Sheriff;	Major Fulford,

Break drawn by four horses,

Mr. Edward Talbot,	Right Hon. W. Berisford,
Mr. A. Talbot,	
Dr. Berisford,	Hon. W. North,
Mr. Denis W. Pack,	Lord Ralph Kerr,
Mr. Cockerell,	Lord Walter Kerr,

Barouche, drawn by four horses,

Dowager Marchioness of Lothian,	Countess of Erne,
Lady Alice Kerr,	Lady Louisa Crichton,

Carriage, drawn by four horses,

The Hon. and Rev. C. A. Talbot,	Dr. Talbot,
The Hon. and Rev. Gustave Talbot,	Hon. Col. Talbot,
The Hon. and Rev. Wm. Talbot,	Hon. Gerald Talbot,

The post-boys for each carriage wearing blue jackets.
Omnibus, drawn by four horses, the post-boys
wearing yellow jackets.

Hon. Mrs. Gustavus Talbot,	Miss Emily Talbot,
	Mr. John Talbot,
Hon. Mrs. Wm. Talbot,	Mr. Hervey Talbot,
Hon. Mrs. Gerald Talbot,	Mr. George Talbot,
	Mr. Adelbert Talbot,
Miss Jessie Talbot,	Mr. Charles Talbot,

Carriage, drawn by four grey horses, and the
post-boys wearing red jackets, and scarlet
hunting caps.

Marquis of Lothian,	Viscount Ingestre,
Marchioness of Lothian,	Viscountess Ingestre,
Marquis of Waterford,	Earl of Eglingtoun,
Marchioness of Waterford,	Countess of Eglingtoun,

Ten members of the Stafford troop of Yeomanry
formed a guard to this carriage, which was preceded
by that troop. It was followed by the Talbot tenantry on horse-back, three a-breast, numbering
about sixty. Next followed the Leek troop, and
after them the Alton tenantry on horse-back, three
a-breast, and fully equal in number to those of the
Talbot estates. The Uttoxeter troop of Yeomanry
succeeded them. Then came the standards of the

Yeomanry, with the trumpeters and outriders, Chief
Superintendent of Police Sweeting, and Super-
intendents Cole and Povey. Following these was
the carriage of the Earl of Shrewsbury, containing

Earl of Shrewsbury,	Lady Adelaide Talbot,
Countess of Shrewsbury,	Hon. Walter Talbot,
Lady Gertude Talbot,	Hon. Reginald Talbot.

Captain Meynel Ingram and Lieutenant Heywood
rode on opposite sides of the noble earl's carriage; at
the rear rode Captain Thorneycroft and Lieutenants
Perry and Carser, of the Wolverhampton troop of
Yeomanry, and Lieutenant Campbell, of the Newcastle troop. The Cheadle and Alton troops formed
the rear guard of honour, and closed the long cor-
tege. The procession stretched upwards of a quarter
of a mile, and proceeded at a smart space on the
road to Uttoxeter, large numbers of persons lining its
sides, and cheering as the Earl of Shrewsbury and
his friends passed.

As the procession left Blount's Green the merry
peals of the church bells were heard, the flags on the
battlements of the church were plainly seen in the
distance, and the lively strains of the band proclaimed
the hearty welcome awaiting the procession. The
aspect of the town was of a very animating and exciting description. The townspeople and hundreds
of strangers took up positions at every available
place—at doors, windows, and on the causeways—
along the line of route through Uttoxeter. Almost
every house had some kind of decoration; and in
High Street the sky was almost hid by numberless

wreathes of evergreens, and by banners, garlands, flags, and devices so profusely displayed.

There was a triumphal arch of evergreens, surmounted by a flag, at the entrance of Carter Street, against the Far Talbot, with the inscription in the centre, " Welcome, Premier Earl." The principal decoration, however, was a triumphal arch in the front of the Town Hall, designed by Mr. Fradgley, architect. The piers consisted of two spruce firs, transplanted from the Alton estates, the branches of which were cut off, except at the top, the trunks being thickly surrounded by sprays of fir, yew, and other evergreens, tied on and festooned by ribbons. The arch was made in a similar way. On the right-hand column was a shield charged with the ancient arms which the family bore when it came over with William the Conqueror, bendy of six *argent* and *gules*, under which was placed the word Talebote, the original way of spelling the family name. At the crown of the arch were the present arms of Talbot, *gules*, a lion rampant, within an engrailed bordure, *or* (being the arms the family took on the marriage of a Talbot with Gwendylline ap Rhess, a Princess of Wales), over which stood an earl's coronet, and underneath the motto, " Prest d'accomplir." On the left hand pier of the arch were the arms of the Earl's eldest son, Lord Ingestre, which were distinguished by a label for difference.

At the front of the Town Hall a platform was erected, where a deputation, consisting of the Rev. H. Abud, M.A., vicar; Herbert Taylor, Esq., M.D.;

Rev. R. Howard, Mr. W. J. Fox, Mr. Thomas Bladon, Mr. A. A. Flint, and Mr. R. Bagshaw, waited to present the Earl of Shrewsbury and Talbot with an address. On arriving at the platform Viscount and Viscountess Ingestre halted a moment, and W. J. Fox, Esq., presented a splendid bouquet to the Viscountess, and shortly afterwards, on the arrival of the carriage containing the Earl and Countess of Shrewsbury, Dr. Taylor presented the Viscountess of Shrewsbury with a beautiful bouquet. Thomas Bladon, Esq., then presented an address to the Earl of Shrewsbury, from the inhabitants of Uttoxeter. The address was written on parchment, having a deep gold border, and enclosed in a walnut wood box with mediæval mountings, and lined with silk. The following is a copy :—

" TO THE RIGHT HONOURABLE THE EARL OF SHREWSBURY AND TALBOT, PREMIER EARL OF ENGLAND.

" May it please your lordship,—We, the inhabitants of the town of Uttoxeter, in the immediate neighbourhood of the princely estate of Alton Towers, beg to offer your lordship our public respects and congratulations on the auspicious occasion of your progress through our ancient town, to take formal possession of a property and title now happily settled upon your lordship's branch of the house of Talbot, by the decision of the highest authority of these realms.

K

" We heartily congratulate your lordship on the successful issue of an anxious series of costly and arduous litigations, by which this influential estate has been finally, and, we trust, for ever, vested in a Protestant line of inheritance.

" Connected with your lordship as one of the lords of the manor of Uttoxeter, we, its inhabitants, cordially welcome the event of your lordships occupation of Alton Towers ; and we beg most sincerely and respectfully to sympathize with your lordship's triumph over the formidable difficulties so gallantly encountered by your lordship and family, so skilfully disentangled by your lordship's eminent counsel, and at length, by the Divine blessing, so happily surmounted by the legal recognition of your lordship's title to the patrimony of the house of Talbot.

" We hail as a happy omen the coincidence of your lordship's first act of public impropriation of the estate with the anniversary of the birthday of Viscount Ingestre, your lordship's eldest son, and heir to the united earldoms of Shrewsbury and Talbot.

" We cannot better express our felicitations to the Viscount Ingestre, than by the earnest prayer that he may prove as justly popular and esteemed a successor to the Earldom of Shrewsbury and Talbot as his lordship's father inherited, without impairing the honours of the noble earl, the late Lord-Lieutenant of this county.

" The example of the late Earl Talbot's administration of the vice-regal government of Ireland, so as to secure the satisfaction of all parties in that difficult position, will encourage your lordship's Alton tenantry of every shade of sentiment to repose confidence in the successor of a nobleman so universally revered as your lordship's father. We are assured no well advised suggestions of the late noble proprietor of Alton Towers, for the social and benevolent interests of the neighbourhood, will fail of your lordship's candid consideration.

" Most heartily and respectfuly entreating the noble lady, the Countess of Shrewsbury and Talbot, and the other members of your lordship's family, to permit us to include them in our fervent prayer for the long life, health, and uninterrupted peace and happiness of your lordship, and all the noble family, we respectfully present to the Premier Earl of England, and to the now united house of Shrewsbury and Talbot, the public and unanimous congratulations of Uttoxeter."

The noble earl, on receiving the address, said— " Gentlemen, I beg leave to thank you most warmly and most cordially for the honour you have done me in so kindly presenting me with this excellent address. You will forgive me for not saying more now than to briefly thank you, which I do from the bottom of my heart." His lordship having thus briefly acknowledged the address, the carriage moved away amid loud cheers, which continued for some time. The High Street just then was crowded from end to end.

Before reaching Alton the procession must have increased to more than a mile in length. The scene at Alton, only that it was bloodless, reminded one of the days of chivalry, when some powerful lord was taking possession of some feudal castle, and at the blast of trumpet and with flashing sword was leading his knights and hosts of mounted retainers triumphant through its no longer defended entrances. It was calculated that some 35,000 or 40,000 persons assembled on the ground to witness the proceedings, or rather from their deep sympathy with Lord and Lady Shrewsbury and family on the occasion. Addresses were presented at Alton to Lord Shrewsbury from his Alton and Ingestre tenantry, by the Rev. W. Fraser, and the late Mr. Hartshorne, as well as from his lordships tenantry in Wales. About 4000 persons were entertained at the Towers at the expense of his lordship. Lord Shrewsbury and family returned through Uttoxeter to Ingestre at night.

At Uttoxeter during the afternoon of the day the poor were made to enjoy the occasion by having given amongst 500 families of them, numbering several thousand persons, about 600 lbs. of beef, 600 loaves, and upwards of 300 gallons of ale. A band played at the Town Hall during the same period, and a cannon, planted on the new cemetery ground, was occasionally fired.

The most recent event worthy of being kept in memory, is the share Uttoxeter took in the national rejoicings on the occasion of the marriage of the Prince of Wales with the Princess Alexandra of Denmark, on March 10th, 1863. Business was entirely suspended; the church bells were merrily rung all day ; the principal houses were decorated with flags ; the band played in the front of the Town Hall ; a cannon was planted in the Smithfield, and frequently discharged, and every one heartily joined in the rejoicings. A committee of gentlemen was formed, and about £60 collected and expended in bread, beef and ale, for the families of the poor; for the schools for tea ; for the bell-ringers, and for the band. At twelve o'clock at noon, or soon after, the Rev. H. Abud, vicar, amid an assemblage of persons and bursts of cheers, proposed the health of the newly wedded Prince and Princess. A procession, consisting of a band of music, school children of all denominations, and a large number of people paraded the principal streets, and added much to the appearance of the town. In the forenoon, however, an event took place which has no precedent in Uttoxeter, so loyal was everybody, and so utterly forgotten were all sectarian prejudices. This was the assembling in the Parish Church, for the recital of pieces to be sung in the Market-place in the afternoon, of the children of all denominations—Church, Wesleyan, Independent, and Primitive Methodist. In the afternoon, after perambulating the streets, headed by the band, the children accordingly, numbering 700, were assembled with their teachers in the Market-place, being formed in a circle of some seven deep, the space round being crowded with people, and the windows of the houses round glistening with the faces of ladies. Numerous pieces were sung, including the National Anthem, and loud cheers rose for the Prince and Princess of Wales, and for the Queen. Illuminations and transparencies took place at night, and so closed a day long to be remembered in Uttoxeter.

The rejoicings on this happy occasion were not confined to the town of Uttoxeter only, but were general throughout the neighbouring villages, which seemed to vie with each other in the hearty demonstrations of joy on the auspicious event.

HISTORY OF CHRISTIANITY IN UTTOXETER.

CHURCH MATTERS, CHURCHES, ALTER-TOMBS, INSCRIPTIONS, CHURCH REGISTER, &c.

THE early history of Christianity in Uttoxeter lies in complete obscurity.—Doomsday Book is silent as to whether it had a church and priest at the time of the Conquest. It is nevertheless probable that Uttoxeter had a church even in Anglo-Saxon times, from the fact of the gate forming the south entrance to the church yard being still called, as already mentioned, " Light Gate," an expression, the former part of which is corrupted from the Saxon word " Lich," meaning a dead body. Lichgate, therefore, signified the entrance (amongst the Saxons) through which corpses were conveyed to their burial place. This, of course, could only have been after christianity had been received amongst them, as before then they practised the heathenish mode of burial in barrows. Uttoxeter is mentioned as having a church in 1251, which is about 171 years after Doomsday Book was written, and its rector at that time was Thomas, one of the witnesses to the charter of William de Ferrars. In 1297 it was held, however,

by one Nicholas Butler, when its advowson was
£66, 13s. 4d., at that period a large sum of money.[1]
About 34 years afterwards, viz.—in 1331, probably
the date of the consecration of the old destroyed
church, the vicarage of Uttoxeter was ordained at
Islington, in the month of February, and confirmed
by the chapter of Coventry to the vicar of Uttoxeter
in the calends of March, 1333.[2] It was during
this century, between 1307 and 1377, which is called the " Decorated Period" of ecclesiastical architecture, that the late church, of which the tower
and spire connected with the present one are remains, was erected. If the church which was superseded by the one which was built in the time of
Edward III. had stood nearly as long as it, the
date of its erection would not be later than the
eighth century. But, of course, if there is any validity in this inference, it rests only upon the supposition that the earliest church in Uttoxeter was erected
of equally durable materials, a supposition not un-
reasonable, from the known substantial character of
Saxon church architecture. However, when prepara-
tions were being made for the erection of the nave of
the present church, remains were discovered of some
kind which fixed the existence of a church at Uttoxeter more than a thousand years before that date.[3]

(1) History of Tutbury Castle, by Sir Oswald Mosley, Bart.

(2) Lightfoot's MS. Survey of Uttoxeter, 1668.

(3) Information from the widow (an intelligent person) of the sexton.

The church at Uttoxeter is mentioned by Leland, who wrote in the sixteenth century, in the words, " Uttockcester has one paroch chirch."

In the reign of Mary, daughter of Henry VIII., the antagonism of religious parties appears to have been carried, in Uttoxeter, to a violent extreme, ending in the death of a person of the town. The outrage occurred at the time of those sanguinary persecutions of the adherents of the reformed faith, about 1555, when 280 victims, including Hooper, Bishop of Gloucester; Farrar, of St. David's; Latimer, of Worcester; Ridley, of London; and Cranmer, Archbishop of Canterbury, perished at the stake.[1] The victim at Uttoxeter was a Thomas Flier,[2] a gentleman belonging to an ancient family of property in Uttoxeter, who was slain by a desperate Papist. The persecutions in the See of Lichfield which led to this tragedy were instigated by Dr. Bane, bishop of the diocese. Besides the compulsion of many in the see to do penance, several others had to pay with their lives the penalty of their adherance to the reformed doctrines, one of whom was Joane Waste, who was burnt at Derby in 1555. Dr. Bane was suceessor to Richard Sampson in the See of Lichfield, and his character will be seen by the following notice:—He was a Doctor of Divinity of St. John's College, Cambridge, and was a great proficient in the Hebrew tongue, which he taught some years

(1) Penny Cyclopædia.

(2) Martyrologia, by Samuel Clarke, 3rd edition, folio, 1677.

at Paris. He returned to England in 1554, about
the time of Bishop Sampson's death, and was promoted to the See of Lichfield and Coventry the same
year. His persecutions grew out of his endeavour to
restore the See to what it was before the Reformation,
and in trying to recover its possessions. He did not
hold the bishopric long. Being appointed by Act of
Parliament to give the sacrament to Queen Elizabeth
he refused to administer it to her, and was *ipso facto*
deprived of his See. He returned to Islington, and
died and was buried there in 1559.

The celebrated and pious Bishop Hackett, who restored Lichfield Cathedral after the damage it had
sustained during the Civil War by the Parliamentarians, preached in Uttoxeter Church, and held a confirmation in 1664. A brief memorandum of the fact
is preserved on the inside of the cover of the early
register of Uttoxeter Church, and is this—" Bishop
Hackett came to this town the second day of July
and preacht and confirmed the third, 1664." This
prelate was a man of great fortitude. When great
penalties had been enacted to prevent it, he continued
to read the Liturgy regularly at his church at St.
Andrews, Holborn. In consequence of this a sergeant, with a file of men, entered the church and
threatened him with instant death if he did not de-
sist. " Soldier," said the intrepid Hackett, " I am
doing my duty ; you do yours," and with a more
audible voice proceeded with the service. The soldier, astonished at his undaunted composure, left the
church without doing him the slightest injury.

An augmention to the church was obtained in the year 1646, and Peter Lightfoot was delegated by the parish of Uttoxeter to apply for the same; and his journey to London for the purpose, at the instance of parish, lay in about £5.[1]   After this the Bounty of Queen Anne was also obtained for the church living at Uttoxeter by the Rev. Mr. Ledgould.   With this sum a piece of land was purchased, called Monk's Field, belonging now to the vicar,[2] and the following case, which unquestionably had respect to it, and in which is shown what monastic lands were freed from the payment of tithes, was heard in the Exchequer Chamber sometime before 1685.   That eminent lawyer, Sir Symon Degg, in " Parsons' Counseller," page 271, part second, published 1685, remarks, " Now the reader must observe once for all, that all monastries under £200 a year were to have been dissolved by the Statute of 27 Henry VIII., and are usually called the Smaller Abbeys; and those of £200 a year and upwards were not dissolved till the 31st year of Henry VIII. and are commonly called the Greater Abbeys.   And upon these two statutes the case lately happened in the Exchequer Chamber between Walklate, farmer of the rectory of Uttoxeter, in the county of Stafford, to the Dean of Windsor, and Wiltshaw, owner of the farm in that parish, that was part of the possessions of the Abbey of Croxden, in the same county, and was one of the

(1) Parochial Account.

(2) Shaw's Staffordshire.

Cisterian Order, which order was freed from the payment of tithes, as shall be shown hereafter ; and this abbey was discovered by the defendant Wiltshaw, to be continued by letters patent under the Great Seal of England, and so not dissolved till the statute of 31st, Henry VIII., whereupon the defendant was dismissed, and the court clearly held the lands discharged of payment of tithes by the statute 31st of Henry VIII."

About the year 1649, during the ministry of the Rev. Thomas Lightfoot, who was then at a venerable age, a theological controversy was rife in Uttoxeter, and threatened very much the peace of the church. It originated in attacks upon the ordinances of the church by a Mr. Heming, who appears to have occupied a pulpit in Uttoxeter, although it is not stated to what religious persuasion he belonged, though probably he was an Anabaptist. He had indiscretely, in the pulpit, called the sacrament as administered in the church, " a communion of dogs and devils; a rotten twopenny communion," and bragging to prove to all men " that Judas did not receive the sacrament ;" and telling the congregation " that if they did believe that if Judas did receive the sacrament they might do as Judas did ; that is, go and receive, and then go and hang themselves." This kind of teaching appeared exceedingly bitter to some of the church people, particularly to Peter Lightfoot, physician, who drew up notes upon the points for his own and the satisfaction of a few friends ; and, although it was not intended they

should, they fell in their manuscript form into the
hands of Mr. Heming. The latter thereupon put
his declarations into print in a pamphlet entitled
" Judas Excommunicated ; or a Vindication of the
Communion of Saints," in which he made Mr. Lightfoot the especial object of his abuse. Whether he
makes out his point as to whether Judas did not receive the sacrament, or whether it is not scriptural
for persons indifferently to receive it in the church,
it would not do any particular good here to go
through his arguments to show. But some of the pas-
sages of abuse are so strongly expressed, particularly
against Mr. Lightfoot, that it can be little wondered
at if they produced a strong and bitter sensation
in the Rev. Mr. Lightfoot's congregation, and indeed
through the town. Some of them are thus given :—
" Mr. Lightfoot and his unholy communicants ;"
" Mr. Lightfoot and his unholy crew ;" " his profane
fellow-members ;" " I should superabundantly wrong
him if I should not rank him with the vilest in the
kingdom ; for with them he will have communion as
a member of the same external, visible body, by virtue of which relation they are all his brethren and
sisters ; so that he hath his brother drunkard, brother
thief, brother murderer, brother liar, &c. ; sister
whore, sister witch, &c. ; yea, all that have been
hanged at Tyburn, and all other gallows in England,
ever since he was born and baptised into that fellowship he pleads for, have been his brethren and sisters, and this I dare say I can prove against all the
devils in hell."

Peter Lightfoot replied to the pamphlet of Mr. Joseph Heming in a lengthy and curious tract of fifty-two pages, entitled, " A Battle with a Wasp's Nest," London, 1649. He accuses his opponent chiefly of spleen, virulence, and scandal, and points out that such arguments as he had used he had cooked up from a Scotch writer—Mr. Gillespie, in " Aaron's Rod Blossoming." Mr. Lightfoot goes through his antagonist's strokes of spleen as well as his arguments, and both with logical wit and acumen proves himself an able controversalist.

Mr. Heming appears to have looked upon Uttoxeter as a place of Babylonish darkness, stating that " what he had done was for their souls who came out of Babylon, out of Egypt, the other day." Mr. Lightfoot looked upon this expression as a reflection upon the ministry of his father, and in a dignified appeal respecting it, he writes—" The reader, if he were of Mr. Heming's charity, and no higher, might be induced to think that poor Uttoxeter is the veriest Sodom and Gomorrah upon earth ; and that till he came hither, it had been led and lived in the deepest superstition and darkness that ever Babylon and Egypt did. It is not for me to speak what ministry this town hath had ever since before Mr. Heming was born. The relation I stand in to him that hath been their minister so long does stop my mouth. But let all in the countries hereabout—Cheshire, Shropshire, Staffordshire, Derbyshire, &c., let any in England that ever heard of old Mr. Lightfoot, minister of Uttoxeter, what he hath

been, what his ministry and conversation hath been;
nay let Mr. Heming's own saints be witnesses what
his pains, doctrine, life, and ministry hath been
among them for above these thirty years. If they
have not dissembled, the day hath been when 'some
of them have acknowledged and taken upon them to
think this town, in a happy ministry, hath gone
in equal pace and degree with most towns in
England. And the case is so altered that till Mr.
Heming came amongst them, poor Uttoxeter is said
to be in darkness, and in Babylon and Egypt, and
he proved a Moses and a Zorobabel to bring it out."

Lightfoot gives the following picture of the condition of Uttoxeter produced by Mr. Heming:—" It
seems Mr. Heming hath a singular faculty of recon-
ciling dead men; and I wish he would let the evange-
lists alone, who are at sacred peace among themselves,
and that he would reconcile poor Uttoxeter, which is
torn in pieces with dissensions since he came among
us. I know not whether Tenterton steeple was the
cause of the stopping up of the haven two or three
miles of it; this I know, that till Uttoxeter knew
Mr. Heming, peace, amity, and charity, dwelt
amongst us, in few towns more; but now nothing
but dissension, biting, and backbiting, in no town
the like." This is, no doubt, a tolerably fair representation; and it would be a natural result of Mr.
Heming's violent language. Mr. Lightfoot finishes
with his opponent thus—" A wisp or a cuckstool, the
reward of scolds, had been a fitter return for your
railing than patience and reason, but you see I have
waited upon you with salt and spoons," &c.

Mr. Heming appears also to have been the author of another work, entitled, " Queries touching the rise and observation of Christmas Day," which Mr. Lightfoot accuses him of having filched out of Mr. Prynne's " Histriomastic," and the " Scripture Almanack." This was answered, according to a bibliographical work, in 1655, and the answer's were printed with Fresher's " Christian Covenant."

In 1814 the spire of Uttoxeter Church sustained a serious accident by lightening. On the 6th of February of that year it was struck by the electric fluid, by which a stone, about half way down was forced out. It passed through the belfry, and finally penetrated the wall of the chancel, on the north side of the window. The damage which the spire sustained by the shock, made it necessary for a part of it to be taken down. When it was re-built, and the gilt cross, globe, and vane, had been placed at its apex, two incidents occurred, which, as they show the daring spirit of two females, deserve to be perpetuated in their remembrance, as well as on account of their amusing nature. When, as stated, the whole was finished, Mary Allport, a chamber-maid at the Red Lion Inn, ascended, stood upon the ornamental stone-work under the globe, and kissed a young man named Henry Smith, of Uttoxeter Heath, who was one of the masons, and who stood on the opposite side. Sarah Adams, a fellow servant of Mary Allport, also accomplished the intrepid feat, to win a kiss from another workman, whose name was Henry Adams. A crowd of spectators, some of whom are still living, thronged round the church at the time. Both the

OLD CHURCH, UTTOXETER, NOW TAKEN DOWN.

male adventurers descended safely, and subsequently became the wives of the young men. Henry Smith, with Mary Allport for his wife, settled down at Wetley Rocks, as parish clerk, but what became of the others is not to be learned.

The Old Church, the date of whose erection has been mentioned, was built of stone, and has been described as (when in existence) being very much out of repair on the exterior parts.[1] The churchyard was then enclosed by an ancient low stone wall. The church consisted of a nave, two side aisles, and a chancel, and it was covered with lead. Where the present vestry-room is, at the south side of the present church, the family of Mynors, formerly of great distinction at Uttoxeter, had a chapel where a mass priest was appointed to say mass for the family.[2] It was also their burying place. This chapel was one of those private religious foundations called a chantry, of which it is stated the family of Kynnersley also had one. There has been as much as 46a. 1r 16p. of chantry land in Uttoxeter parish ;[3] but it does not appear by whom the land was left, or whether by one or more persons.

Chantries were established for the purpose of keeping up a perpetual succession of prayers for some particular family whilst living, and for the repose of their souls when dead, particularly of the founder, and

(1) Pitt's Staffordshire.

(2) Gentleman's Magazine, 1788.

(3) Mr. P. Lightfoot's Survey.

L

other persons specially named in the deed of foundation.   Chantries were first founded in the twelfth
century, on the decline of the taste for monasteries.
They were usually founded in churches already exist-
ng, all that was required being an altar with an area
before it, and a few appendages ; and places were easily
found in churches of even small dimensions, in which
such an altar could be raised without interfering
inconveniently with the more public and general
purposes for which the churches were erected.   An
attentive observation of the fabrics of the parish
churches of England will often detect where these
chantries have been, sometimes in remains of the altar
which was removed perhaps at the Reformation,
but more frequently in one of those ornamental niches
called piscinas, which were always placed in proximity to the altars.   Sometimes there are remains
of painted glass which it is easy to see has once been
the ornament of one of these private foundations,
and more frequently one of those arched recesses in
the wall which are called " Founder's Tombs," and
which in many instances, no doubt, were actually the
tombs of persons to whose memory chantries had
been instituted.   When the fabric of a church afforded of itself no more space for the introduction of
chantries, it was usual for the founders to attach
little chapels to the edifice.   It is these chantry
chapels, the use and occasion of which are now so
generally forgotten, which occasion so much of the
irregularity of design which is apparent in the parish
churches of England.   Erected as they generally

were in the style of architecture which prevailed at the time, and not in accommodation to the style in which the original fabric was built, they are a principal cause of that want of congruity which is perceived in the architecture of different parts of the parish churches.[1]

The same family of Mynors had likewise a private gallery at the south side of the interior of the old church, and it was reached by stone steps from the outside. The steps are represented in the engraving of the old church almost at the junction of the nave of the church, and the chapel of that family built at the south side of the chancel. They had also some very ancient monuments in the former church. Previous to his entering upon the laborious undertaking of compiling a history of Staffordshire, the Rev. Simeon Shaw first visited most of the places in the county, both for church inscriptions, sketches of churches, and sepulchral monuments and family records. In a communication, giving an account of his success, to the " Gentleman's Magazine" in 1794, he mentions that the fine old spire of Uttoxeter Church afforded him a good subject for a drawing, and the inside some curious monuments of the Mynors, an ancient family in the parish, and of the Kynnersley's of Loxley, very ancient. All the monuments of the former family have disappeared; two of the latter remain, but have been placed within iron rails under the stairs leading to the gallery in the north west

(1) Penny Cyclopædia, vol. vi.

entrance. These monuments are of the altar-tomb description, a kind which was introduced about the thirteenth or fourteenth century, having on them effigies in alabaster, or incised slabs with engraved outlines of persons and arms, or engraved plates of brass, the latter of which were particularly prevalent towards the close of the fifteenth century. Both the altar-tombs of the Kynnersley's have been much mutilated. They are both of the sixteenth century, and are in alabaster. One is of Thomas Kynnersley de Loxley, whose name is legible in the letters of the period, although but little more can be made out of the inscription to him. On the top is an engraved figure of the deceased, but the border to it next to the wall, which is nearly one-fifth the width of the slab, has been cut off the whole length, and the surface of the remainder is so much cut with dates, initials, and other senseless markings, that many parts of the figure and ornamented border are effaced. The engraving has been filled with pitch or some other bituminous substance. The remaining side of this monument—for the opposite one has evidently been cut away with the border to the engraved figure at the top—contains shields of arms, and several figures of persons in bas-relief, with intervening foliated columns, supporting three canopies. There is great irregularity in the foliated sculpture, particularly at the corners of the canopies. The central figure represents Christ on the cross ; the figure with arms upon it is most likely a female child of the deceased ; the others are probably nuns. The latter

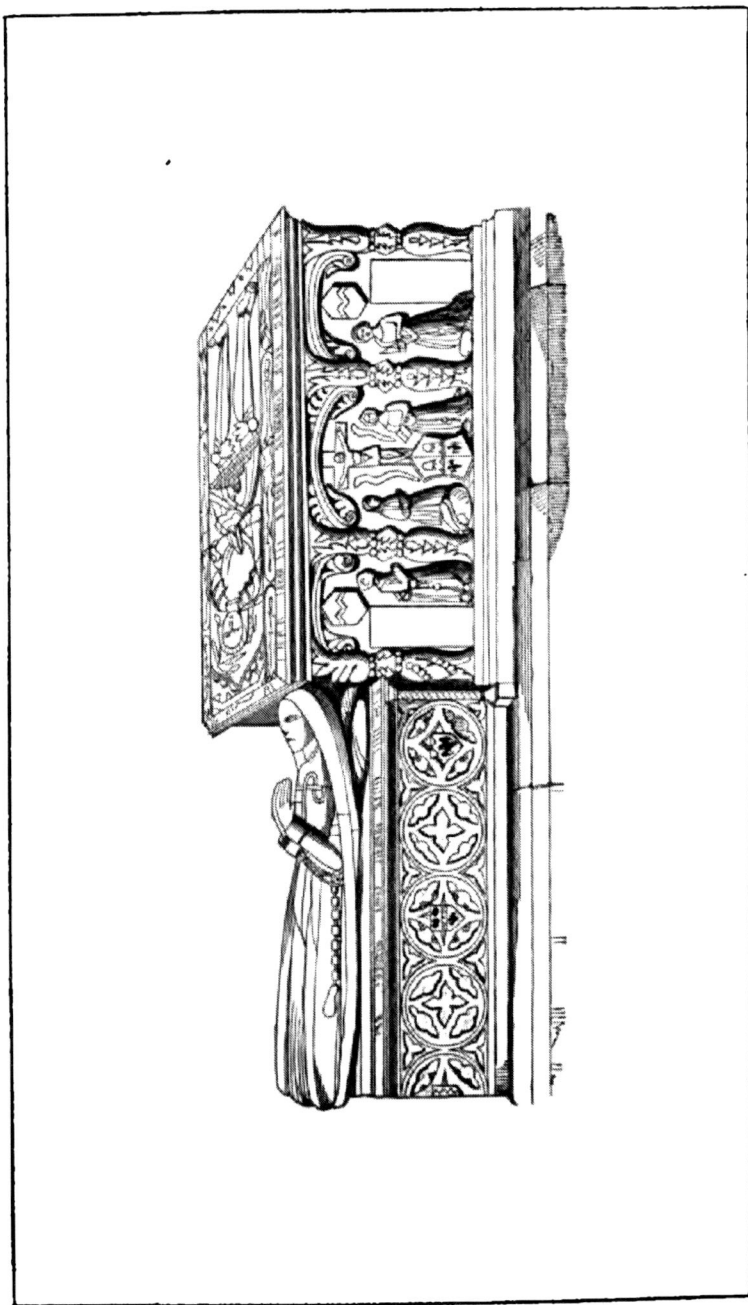

ALTAR-TOMBS, UTTOXETER CHURCH.

are all represented in the reticulated head-dress of the time, and the folds of their robes appear to be very gracefully and naturally given by the artist.

The other altar-tomb has a more recently sculptured effigy lying upon it, in the habit of a *religieuse*, and from the execution would seem to represent a lady of the same ancient house, who at a very early date, appears, from her arms, to have come into the possession of Loxley by marriage with the noble family of Ferrars.[1] One end of this tomb has been sawn off, including the feet of the effigy, to make it fit in the place where it is. Except the three first letters the name of Kynnersley is observable, but very little more of the remaining inscription, if any, can been made out.

There is an interesting legend respecting this effigy, to which rise has probably been given by some lingering tradition of what possibly occurred at the dispersion of the nuns at Hanbury by the Danes. It is said, and also firmly believed by many, that the effigy represents an abbess who had been lost in the woods below the town, many centuries ago,—an idea which has been embodied in "Wood Leighton" with the addition of such imaginary circumstances as give the story an air of truthfulness. The following is the account of the discovery of the effigy, made at the time the church was destroyed, as related to me by an eye witness. At that time the altar-tombs and effigies had been walled, or boarded, over, for a

(1) Natural History of the County of Stafford, by T. Garner, Esq., F.L.S.

period of sixty years, for the purpose of making pew room, and when the pews were being removed, the covering, which hid the effigy and altar-tomb, fell, none of the workmen present being aware that there was such a piece of exquisite art behind it. When the tombs and effigy so suddenly and unexpectedly appeared, the people present started back in fright, thinking the effigy, which was quite black with dust, was the corpse of some one long hidden there. Recovering themselves, they approached it, and on brushing off the dust, lo! a most beautiful alabaster female figure revealed itself. She had a fine Roman nose; a chain hung round her neck and reached down to her abdomen; over her breast she had a handsome stomacher; there were four coats of arms round the figure, with an inscription, and the date of 1555.

A knowledge of this discovery soon spread through the town, and numbers of persons crowded to see the interesting objects. Amongst them were the late Mrs. Hart, and an aged female of the name of Reeves. The latter, on going to the effigy, was at once excited with remembrances of former days, and giving vent to her feelings, clapped her hands and exclaimed "Oh! it is my lady Tansley; I am glad to see her again." "Oh! Mrs. Reeves," said Mrs. Hart, "what do you mean; did you know her? Tell us all about it." "Why, madam," replied Mrs. Reeves with great simplicity, "I used to play round it when I was a girl. She was a lady abbess, and being driven away with a single attendant from Tutbury, she came for Uttoxeter, and was lost at night in Uttoxeter woods; but hearing the curfew bell ring she was enabled to direct her course to Uttoxeter by its sound. She was very much wearied by anxiety and rambling about, and when she reached the town she left a bell full of money for the bell to be perpetually rung." " And did you see the bell full of money?" interrogated Mrs. Hart. Oh! no; it is so long since, *but it used to be said so.*" So far was the tradition believed that till a new sexton was appointed about ten years since, three tangs for the lady abbess were invariably given before the curfew bell was rung night and morning; and it is said that a daring individual on once willingly omitting to give the tangs was alarmed by the sudden appearance of the abbess in person, who ascended the bell-rope and vanished out of sight.

Besides these tombs the former church had a skeleton effigy, still preserved out of sight over the door of the west entrance. Such effigies are supposed to represent the buried corpse of a person of high ecclesiastical rank, contrasting with the gorgeous effigy of the deceased in his robes in such a manner as to convey a wholesome lesson of the transitory nature of human greatness to persons destitute of learning, and to whose feelings a highly coloured representation of the fate of all flesh would appeal in a startling manner.[1]

The nave and chancel of Uttoxeter church were re-built in the year 1828, in the style called

(1) Vestiges of the Antiquities of Derbyshire.

" Decorated English." The roof is supported by two rows of six arches, betwixt the side and middle aisles. The cost of rebuilding this part was £6061, 1s. 11d., of which £1632 was raised by subscription, £1779 by rate, £2249 by the sale of the pews, and £400 by the society for building churches. The pews are of oak, and the number of sittings are about 1414. Of these 422 are free. During the re-building of the church the worship of the members of the Church of England in the town was conducted in the Wesleyan Chapel, with the approbation of the bishop of the diocese.

Since the enlargement of the church the spire has been touched, in 1849, by William Critchlow, and the dangerous task was accomplished without an accident. More recently, in 1858, a new final stone was put on, and the vane re-gilt and replaced by men in the em-employ of Mr. Evans, builder. A many people ventured to the top when the work was finished, although the spire ascends to the height of 179 feet.

The living of Uttoxeter church is a discharged vicarage, in the Archdeaconry of Stafford, and in the patronage of the deans and canons of Windsor. The tithes were commuted in 1839, and produce to the lay impropriator[1] about £725 annually. The Rev. Henry Abud is the present vicar.

The church contains a large number of mural tablets, all of beautiful design, in marked alabaster, and some of really elaborate character and high

(1) Till lately the late Joseph Bladon, Esq.

UTTOXETER CHURCH.

artistic workmanship. In the chancel, besides the costly stained glass window in the east end, the gift of the late Thomas Hart, Esq., and Sir T. Cotton Sheppard, Bart., representing the apostles of Christ, there are two memorial windows to Thomas Sneyd Kynnersley, Esq., who died in 1844, aged 70 years. The oldest of the memorials on tablets in the chancel is to the Rev. George Malbon, the friend of Samuel Bentley, who has perpetuated his memory in his poem on the river Dove—

> " The cell where the bank slow doth bend
>   Was Malbon's, the learned and the sage ;
> My teacher, Mecænas and friend,
>   With pleasantry tempered with age.
> Flow tears the dear urn to bedew ;
>   Flow elegy mournfully tuned ;
> Oh ! could I those chords wake anew,
>   When Milton his Lycidas mourned."

The inscription to Malbon, which is in Latin, is as follows :—

D.   O.   M.

GEORGIUS MALBON, A. M.
Hujus Parochiæ Vicarius:
Ex Vico de Bradeley, in Agro
Cestrensi,
Antiqua Stripe Oriundus.
In matrimonium duxit
Mariam,
Johannes Alleyne, de Greseley,

In Com. Derb.. Armig.,
Filiam Natu Maximam
Hoc Monumentum
Optimæ Conjugi Ponen-
dum Mandavit
Et Sibi
1768.

The others are to the following persons :—

" In memory of Joseph Mallaby, Esq., of Loxley Park, a Justice of the Peace of this County, who died at Lugano, Switzerland, September 15th, 1855, aged 50 years."

" Sacred to the memory of Jonathan Stubbs, A.M., who died November 27th, 1810, aged 57 years. In grateful testimony of his faithful and laborious exertions while curate of this parish, the inhabitants, by voluntary contribution, have caused this stone to be erected."

The Rev. Mr. Stubbs was greatly beloved in the parish, and his death, from the circumstances under which it happened, was most acutely felt. On the 13th of November, 1810, he had an overturn in a carriage, occasioning a compound fracture of the leg, which eventually produced a delirious fever, and terminated his short career on the 27th of the same month. His remains were deposited in the chancel of the Parish Church of Tutbury, near which place the accident occurred. Mr. Stubbs was the son of the Rev. Jonathan Stubbs, rector of Overton Longueville, Buckingamshire. He received the early part of his education at

Hitchin, in Hertfordshire, under the Rev. Thomas Evans, and was successively a Scholar of Winchester College, Pensioner of Emmanuel College, Cambridge, and was afterwards elected on the foundation of New College, Oxford, and in course of time succeeded to a fellowship of that college. In 1789 he became curate of St. Alkmund's Parish, Derby, in which he continued till 1803, when he had the care of the churches of Scropton and Broughton, in Derbyshire. He undertook the curacy of Uttoxeter in 1804, and in 1807 married Miss Kirk, of Derby. He left one son of the age of sixteen months. There is an inscription to Mrs. Stubbs, who died March 12th, 1846, in the 73rd year of her age.

Another is to the memory of Lieutenant-Colonel John Herring, C.B., (son of the late Rev. A. Herring, vicar of Uttoxeter[1]) who died at Hyderkhail, September 3rd, 1839, in his 50th year, when he was in command of the 37th regiment, Bengal, No. 7, on his march with the army of the Indus. He was interred in the Armenian burial ground at Cabool. He had been with the regiment 34 years.

Another memorial bears the following inscription :—

"Sacred to the memory of Joseph Bladon, of Old-field House, who departed this life January 12th, 1862, aged 75."

On the north side of the church are these memorials :—

1 The Entries in the Church Register by Mr. Herring are beautifully written.

" In beloved memory of James Campbell Bell, who entered into rest March 1st, 1859, aged 10 years and 5 months."

" This marble is erected by Thomas Kynnersley, Esq., in memory of his beloved wife, Barbara Kynnersley, eldest daughter of Sir Gilbert Clarke, in the County of Derby, Knt. She left two sons, Craven and Thomas, and three daughters, Barbara, Mary, and Dorothy. She departed this life, ye 6th of July, 1717."

"Sacred to the memory of Dame Margaret, second wife of Sir Thomas Shephard, of Thornton Hall, in the County of Buckingham, Bart., who departd this life, on the 26th of December, MDCCCXIII., in the LXIII. year of her age. Her remains were deposited near this place."

" Near this place lieth interred the body of Miss Dorothy Kynnersley, daughter of Thomas Kynnersley, Esq., of Loxley, who departed this life, June the 23rd, 1759, aged 52 years.

At the west end of the church are the following inscriptions:—

" Sacred to the memory of Humphrey Oldfield, Esq., of the Marines, who died, whilst on Service in America, A. D. 1776, ætat 54. John Nicholas Oldfield, Esq., late of the Marines, who died at Portsmouth, April 9th, A. D. 1793, ætat 41. Thomas Oldfield, Esq., Major in the Marines, who fell during the memorable defence of St. Jean D'Acre, in Syria, by Sir Sydney Smith, against General Buonaparte and the army of Egypt, whilst leading a sortie made by the garrison, on the 7th of April, 1799, for the purpose of destroying the enemies approaches ; ætat, 45.   And Elizabeth, daughter of William Hammond, Esq., Lieut. in the Royal Navy, and widow of J. N. Oldfield, Esq., obiit November 30th, A.D. 1808, ætat 51. "

The above are all on one oval tablet of black marble—a group of names of Uttoxeter men whose lives have been spent in the service of their country.

One very ornamental tablet on this wall is to the memory of Edward John Smith, late of the borough of Stafford, son of Edward Smith, and Sarah his wife, who died 4th July, 1753, aged 20 years.   He had a sister, Sarah, and two brothers, John and Paul, who died in their minority.

On a neat tablet, erected by his widow, is an inscription to Thomas Gardiner, architect, who departed this life October the 8th, 1804, aged 67.   Near to this is another tablet, to the memory of his widow, erected by their son, William George Maxwell.   She died September 1st, 1806.

On this wall also is fixed the old black-letter memorial, in latin, to the Rev. John Lightfoot, father of Dr. John Lightfoot, the distinguished Hebrew scholar. It was written by his son, Peter Lightfoot, of Uttoxeter, physician :—

M.   S.

Huc Oculos et Lachrymas, O viator
Qui veteri studes veritati, pietati, charitati,
Huc : ubi teipsum es olim celaturus,

THOMAS LIGHTFOOTE,

Verbi Divini per Annos 56 fidelissimus minister.
Ecclesiæ hujus per Annos 36 vigilantissimus pastor
Vir antiquorum morum, et primævæ sanctitatis,
Coruscantis zeli, doctrinæ, virtutis, exempli,
Vir verum exscribens virum : Pastor pastorum :
Sudore semper squalidus, at formosus pastorali :
Salutem suam inhelans semper et aliorum,
Gloriam magni pastoris ambiendo indefessus,
Annis Satur tandem et bonis operibus,
Confectus studendo, docendo, faciendo, patiendo,
Onustus spolii de Satana triumphatis,
Idemque improborum odiis bene oneratus,
     Hic suaviter in Christo obdormit
     Abstersis lachrymis et sudoribus,
     Vivacissimus resurrecturus,
Unaque ELIZABETHA tori consors et pietatis,
     Digno Conjuge Conjux digna.
     Obiit ille Julii 2, 1653, Ætat 81.
     Obiit illa Januarii 24, 1636, Ætat 71.

The following is a translation of this beautiful and touching inscription :—

On this bestow a glance and tears, O passer by ;
Who car'st for ancient truth, for piety and love,
On this: for here thou soon thyself shalt buried be.
THOMAS LIGHTFOOTE,
For 56 years a most faithful minister of God's Word ;
For 36 years a most watchful pastor of this church ;
A man of antiquated habits and primitive sanctity,
Of distinguished zeal, learning, virtue, example;

A very pattern of a true man, pastor of pastors.

Always bedewed with sweat and exemplary in dis-
    charge of his duties,

Always anxious for his own salvation and that of
    others,

Unwearied in seeking the glory of a true pastor ;

At length, full of years and good works,

Worn out with study, teaching, labour and patience ;

Loaded with spoils recovered from Satan,

And also well laden with the hatreds of the wicked,

       He placidly sleeps in Christ,

       Tears and sweat being wiped away,

       To rise again to life.

And also Elizabeth, his spouse and pious consort ;

    A worthy husband and a worthy wife.

    He died July 2, 1653, aged 81.

    She died January 24, 1636, aged 71.

From this memorial it appears that the Rev. Thomas Lightfoot was vicar of Uttoxeter for the long period of 36 years, and that he lived to the advanced age of 81 years.

According to the Church Register, one Richard Taylor was clerk to Mr. Lightfoot, during the whole period of his ministry—

"Richard Taylor, who served 44 years Clark of this church in Uttoxeter, and died at the age of 88, and was buried on the 24th day, (of January) 1656."

The entry of the burial of the Rev. Mr. Lightfoot is as follows—

"Thomas Lightfoot, Vicar of Uttoxeter, was buried
the 2nd day of July, 1653."

The south side of Uttoxeter church contains a memorial window erected by T. Osborne Bateman, Esq.,
to Hugh Athelstan Bateman, who died May 23rd,
1857.

There is also a monument to the memory of Joyce
Osborne Bateman, daughter of Richard and Eliza
Bateman, who died, at the age of 15 years, on the
13th of May, 1808.

Another tablet, on this side of the church, records
the death of the Rev. Thomas Keeling, who died
February 20th, 1804, aged 75 years, and Mary, his
wife, who died the 17th of January, 1799, aged 62
years; and John their son, aged 2 years.

Also there is a mural tablet to Miss Grace Copestake, second daughter of Henry Copestake and
Mary, his wife. She died January the 3rd, 1808,
aged 56. Miss Copestake is mentioned in "My Own
Story."

There is also a memorial with the following inscription :—

• Sacred to the memory of John Hawthorn, surgeon, late of this town, who died March 14th, 1843,
aged 71 years. And Mary Ann Hawthorn, wife of
the above, who died Sept. 4th, 1861, aged 79 years."

Likewise on the south wall of the church, the
family of Kynnersley have several tablets, with inscriptions, as follows:—

" In memory of Clement John Sneyd Kynnersley,
eldest son of Thomas Sneyd Kynnersley, of Loxley

Park, who died at the age of 4 years. Also to Harriet Berthe, who died Dec. 5th, 1839, aged 9 months. To Mary, wife of the Rev. Henry Sneyd, Curate of Stone, who died March 13th, 1838, aged 23 years. And to John Clement Kynnersley, who died February 12th, 1836, aged 28 years.

There are also tablets commemorating the names, as follows, of members of the family of Bladon, on the same side of the church. To Thomas Bladon, who died March 30th, 1819, aged 87 years ; to the wife of Mr. Bladon, who died March 30th, 1812, aged 57 years ; also to Thomas Bladon, who died the 18th of March, 1841, aged 83, and to Mary his wife, who died the 11th of March, 1839, aged 53 years ; to Charles, their eldest son, who died the 26th day of July, 1832, aged 20 years; and to Ann, wife of Joseph Haigh, eldest daughter of the late Thomas Bladon, who died January 25th, 1845. Likewise to Francis Blagg, Esq., who died in 1853, at the age of 50 years and to Elizabeth his wife, daughter of Thomas Bladon, Esq., who died February 4th, 1860, aged 75 years.

In the west entrance to the church, are two long monuments bearing inscriptions in old English letters. That at the right-hand side has a Latin inscription and verses to Sir William Milward, of Eaton, with his shield, bearing *ermine* on a fess *gules* three plates, for Milward, impaling his wife's arms party per pale nebulée *or* and *sable*, six martlets, counterchanged.

His age, the date of his death, and other particulars have been erased, and the places painted over

M

again, with black paint. It is of the 17th century,
Sir William dying in 1630.

Carmina in commemoratione reverendi
Viri GULIELMI MILWARDE de Eton,
In Comitatu Derbiæ Armigi,
nuper defuncti.

Ut ceter antiqui memor esto insignis amici,
    Qui tibi vicinus pervenerandus erat,
Nomine Milwardus Gulielmus sit sibi junctus,
    Eton quem coluit villa propinqua tibi,
Armiger inque gradu quoque ter venerabilis inde,
    Ac semper patriæ pater amansque suæ,
Ut spargit rivus vicinis partibus undas,
    Vicinis Milwarde sparsit opesque suas,
Quæ pars in patria non ejus sensit amorem,
    Pauper enim quisnam non sapuisset eum,
Non apud humanos erat his generosior heros,
    Promtior auxiliis gratior autve suis.
Quo sibi dum vixit meruit sic laudis honorem,
    Ut sua posteritas laudet abinde deum,
Hei mihi quot vivunt vixisset mortuus ardent
    Nestoris ætatem ter magis atque suam.
Sed fera dum rapidæ tenuere hunc vincula mortis
    Mors ipsum laqueis vinciit atra suis
Quo quæ mortis erant solvit cupidissimus inde
    Atque deum petiit qui fuit ante dei.
Ossa sepulta manent quia sic rata terra reposcit
    Spiritus in cælo est luce perenne vigens.
Heu mors infelix patriæ cur tollis amantem ;
    Vulturiosque viros vivere posse sinis.
Vivit edax vultur ducitque per aera gyros,

Milvius ac pluviæ graculus author aquæ.
Vivit et armiferæ comes invisa Minervæ,
   Illa quidem seclis vix moritura novem.
Dulcis avis philomela suis citius cadit odis
   Quo felix avium gloria nempe jacet.
Sic apud humanum genus est modo cursus in orbem
   Vivit ut indignus dignior ipse cadit
Sed tamen haud doleat quisquam quod terra re-
     condit
   Quem deus in tabulam scripserat ante suam.

This inscription may be thus translated—

Strains to the memory of that worshipful man,
   WILLIAM MILWARDE, of Eton,
     in the County of Derby, lately deceased.
Be mindful, Utceter, of an old friend renowned,
Who was to thee a neighbour and with right worship
     crowned ;
Sir William Milwarde to thyself associate,
Whom Eton reared, a village near to thee ;
A knight he was, and in degree a truly noble man,
And ever to his country a father and a friend.
As spreads a stream fertility o'er plains that skirt her
     bounds,
So Milwarde's wealth was lavished on all who dwelt
     around.
No portion of his country but experienced his love,
And never poor man failed relief from him to move.
Throughout the human race was worthier hero none
More ready to assist or more benignant to his friends,
By which the whiles he lived he earned his meed of
     praise,

So great they'd fain exaggerate the honour due to man.
Ah me ! how many living men would welcome back
　　　　the dead,
That three long lives of Nestor he here below might
　　　　live.
But since, alas ! fierce chains of rapid death do bind,
Him gloomy death hath vanquished with its snares.
His bones lie buried underground ; earth hath her
　　　　perquisite ;
His spirit breathes free air in realms of everlasting
　　　　light.
How sad that death should carry off a patriot so
　　　　sincere,
And men less well-disposed permit to live on year by
　　　　year.
The rude, rapacious vulture lives and wheels in cir-
　　　　cling flight ;
The jackdaw which does bring the rain in torrents
　　　　down ; the kite ;
The crow whom wise Minerva doth in deep abhor-
　　　　rence hold,
Nine lives of mortal men doth live ere it becometh
　　　　old ;
The sweet, melodious bird, doth fall more quickly
　　　　than its songs,
A greater glory hence to it than other birds belongs.
So fares it with the human race, and man in his
　　　　career
What though in life unhonoured, in death men him
　　　　revere.
Yet may we cease to mourn for them, their sorrows
　　　　overlook,

Whose names a just Divinity hath written in His
    Book.

The other ancient monument is at the left-hand
side of the next entrance, and is to the memory of
John Archibold, who appears to have been acquainted with ancient writers, and to have written in imitation of them. It is in old English letter, a good
deal faded. At each side of the long inscription are
representations of death, with the accompaniment of
spades; and in the middle of it a tomb, and a mourner
at each end are pictured. At the bottom is an escut-
cheon, with the arms and crest of Archibold. He
died in 1629, aged 103.

Epitaphium JO. ARCHEBOLDI,
generi philomeli in sepulchrum suum.

Hic jacet Archboldus generosus dummodo vixit,
    Redditus in cineres, qui fuit ante cinis.
Hunc fera quem rapidæ retinent sua vincula mortis
    Mors ipsum laqueis vinciit atra suis.
Bis tamen ipse decem lustris prius antea vixit
    Bis quoque, sex annis plus erat orbe manens.
Opsimathes didicit (res nota est pluribus) artes
    Octoginta annis præteritisque prius
Edidit ipse librum quem fert sua musa libellum
    Dedita sacricolis, qui sua jura canit.
Laus datur inde deo et reverentia scā ministris
    Quos deus obsequiis jusserit esse suis.
Plura senex senio seruoque studendo peregit
    Credite, quam vix est tot pepigisse senex.
        Carmina quoad mortem.

Aspice mortalis quam formam mors tibi format
　　Quamque jubet nullo sit varianda modo,
Mandat ipsa locum tibi quem dedit esse tenendum,
　　Dum deus ipse domum vult tibi ferre novam.
　　　　Carmina de insignibus authoris
Author ab antiquis tulit hic insignia avorum,
　　Arma per antiquum munera nata sibi.
Si genus excutias satis hoc ab origine longâ
　　Usque per innumeros invenietur avos.
Nos non degeneres proavis succedimus illis,
　　Terra manens genitis, nomine cumque meo.
Seono pri antiquos vatum vestigia gressus,
　　Ac feror hinc uti quod cecinere patres.
Fecit hoc Ovidius permulti aliique poetæ,
　　Cur imitans veteres hoc tulit author opus.

The following is a translation of this curious inscription :—

　　　Epitaph on JOHN ARCHBOLD,
　　　on his tomb, by his poetical son-in-law.

Here lies Archbold, in life a liberal man,
Ashes before, returned to ashes now.
Him whom fierce chains of rapid death do bind,
Death, gloomy death, hath conquered with its snares.
But full the space of five score years he lived,
And well-nigh six years more he lingered still.
Late on in life (the legend's widely known)
He learnt the arts when past his eightieth year.
He published a book, which his muse calls small,
Dedicated to the priests and treating of their rules.
There praise to God is given and reverence to the
　　　　　ministers

Whom God has commanded to engage in his service.
The old man, full of years, by study hath done much,
Believe me, how hard it is at such an age so much to
      achieve.
      Strains on occasion of his death—
Look, O mortal, what form death leaves to thee,
And how she wills it should be varied in no wise.
She chooses out a place and gives it thee to keep
Whilst God himself prepares a new abode for thee.
      On the author's armorial bearings—
This author brought his armorial bearings from the
      ancients,
His arms from antiquity at his birth bestowed on him.
If you trace out your pedigree from sufficiently re-
      mote origin
It will be found continuously through innumerable
      ancestors.
We, not degenerate, our fathers do succeed,
Our land remaining to our children with our name.
The poets I have followed and in their steps I've trod,
Which has led me to refer to the tales my fathers told ;
Ovid has done the same, and many poets more,
So imitating them the author published this.

THE CHURCH BELLS.

NOTICE must not be omitted of the church bells—
those reminders of so many joyous, and also of so
many sad events to us all ; whose tones so constantly
welcome the gladsome Sabbath morn ; announce and
celebrate the nuptials of early love ; and peal forth
the tidings of great national events.

Bells, we are told, were first used to drive away evil spirits, and keep away storms, and were formerly tolled to call upon the good to pray for some soul as it was fluttering to take its departure, and not as now to tell us that it has passed the inevitable bourn. The present peal of six bells was cast in 1729, on each of which is an inscription, which I here give in the order of their scale—

1ST BELL.—ABR. RUDHALL, OF GLOUCESTER, CAST VS ALL. 1729.

2ND BELL.—" PROSPERITY TO THIS TOWN AND PARISH." A. R., 1729.

3RD BELL.—" PEACE AND GOOD NEIGHBOURHOOD." A. R., 1729.

4TH BELL.—HENRY COTTON, VICAR, A. R., 1729.

5TH BELL.—EDWARD BALL AND THOMAS MARRET, CHURCHWARDENS, 1729.

6TH BELL.—" I TO THE CHURCH THE LIVING CALL, AND TO THE GRAVE DO SUMMON ALL.

1729."

It does not appear whether this set was cast from the metal of the old bells or whether it was entirely new.   In the previous century, however, four of the bells were recast, each at a different date, and most probably all at Nottingham, and I am in possession of particulars about them.   In 1640 the great bell was recast at Nottingham and cost £10, 13s.   The fourth bell was cast at the same place in 1641, and, with an extra amount of metal, came to £17, 4s. 9d.   In 1648 another bell was recast, having 28 pounds of metal put to it, which incurred a charge of, the account states, £7, 8s.; but looking at it in comparison with the other statements it is more probable it was £17, 8s. Again, in 1671, the great bell was cast a second time at Nottingham, and cost £19.

Uttoxeter is one of the few places where the curfew bell is still rung. This custom was in existence at the Conquest, and was intended to warn people to put out their fires and lights at eight o'clock in the evening as a precaution against fires, which were frequent and fatal, owing to many houses being built of wood.

CHURCHYARD INSCRIPTIONS.

Uttoxeter churchyard possesses very little either for the notice of the antiquary or of the curious. Its tombstones are modern; many of the older ones having been broken up and laid in the foundation of the present church when rebuilt. The principal epitaph is that, perhaps, on the tomb of Colonel Gardner— " In memory of Colonel Gardner, late of his majesty's eleventh regiment of Dragoons, in which he served with honour from a cornet, and died lamented, August 1st, 1762, aged 91 years. The widow for the sincere affection for him, caused this stone to be erected."[1]

According to Mr. Samuel Bentley, who was his contemporary, " Colonel Gardner, who at the same time that he was the polite and agreeable gentleman,

[1] This tomb is falling to pieces, and should have the speedy attention of the descendants of the family.

was the truly worthy veteran. He was of signal service to his country at the battle of Culloden, and served several campaigns abroad in the last war,[1] with honour to himself and his king. He sold out of the army a little while before his death, but had some time before settled his family at Uttoxeter."

There is a tombstone over the remains of a lady, about whom an interesting story is told, but it has no inscription upon it, further than the lady's initials. She had arrived, as is well remembered by several aged persons, in a post-chaise at the White Hart Hotel in a dangerous state of illness, accompanied by a gentleman. Medical aid was procured, but was unavailing, and she died the next day. The gentleman was rent with distress, and he interred her in a most costly manner, but refused to tell who either himself or deceased were, and had no communication with any persons except the clergyman and undertaker. All was mystery. The stone is said to be a little below the church on the right hand side of the walk, and laid on bricks. The Rev. Clement Madely preached an affecting funeral sermon, which was handed about the town in MS..[2]

The following tombstone inscriptions in the church-yard will, perhaps, be found curious and amusing enough for preservation :—

" To three brothers of the name of Crosby, of Stramshall—Thomas, who died in 1808, aged 43 ;

[1] This refers to a period previous to 1774.
[2] See also " My Own Story," by Mary Howitt.

Phillip, who died in 1816, aged 54; and George, who
died in 1815, aged 48, a bachelor, are these lines—

" Three loving brothers doth lie sleeping here,
   That lov'd each other from their cradle dear,
   But found this world a city full of crooked streets,
   And death a market-place where all men meets;
   If life was merchandise that men could buy,
   The rich would live for ever and the poor must die."

The next is in memory of Joseph Slater, a clock
and watch-maker, who died November 21st, 1822,
aged 49.

" Here lies one who strove to equal time,
   A task too hard, each power too sublime;
   Time stopt his motion, o'erthrew his balance-wheel,
   Wore off his pivots tho' made of hardened steel;
   Broke all his springs, the verge of life decayed,
   And now he is as though he'd ne'er been made.
   Such frail machine till time's no more shall rust,
   And the archangel wakes our sleeping dust;
   Then in assembled worlds in glory join,
   And sing—" the hand that made us is divine."

This epitaph is in memory of Elizabeth, wife of
George Cook, who died in 1822—

" Oh dear, blest woman, partner of my life,
   Thou tender mother and thou faithful wife,
   Heaven thy virtue could no longer spare,
   But left thy children to a father's care.
   Resigned, he places this memorial here,
   And sighing consecrates it with a tear."

Another is in memory of Jane Aston, who is not mentioned as either the daughter or wife of anybody, though she had friends loving enough to write her this epitaph. She died in 1841.

> " Dear as thou wast, and justly dear,
>   We will not weep for thee ;
>   One thought shall check the starting tear,
>   It is—that thou art free."

Another original epitaph is to John Ash, of Lea Mills, Derbyshire, who died in 1841, aged 49—

> " A pale consumption gave the fatal blow ;
>   The stroke was certain, but the effect was slow ;
>   With lingering pain, Heaven saw me sore oppress'd,
>   Pitied my sighs, and kindly gave me rest."

To Thomas Hartshorn, who died in 1659, is this union of new and old rhyme, by his widow—

> " Here lies the only comfort of my life,
>   The best of husbands to a wife ;
>   Great was my loss for his eternal gain ;
>   I hope with Christ we both shall meet again."

Many interesting incidents are related respecting the conspicuous monument, surmounted by a flame typical of love, which stands at the south of the church, and is surrounded by massive iron railings—how deep and unexhausted in its sorrow after their death was the affection of the mother whose two children had been entombed underneath—how bitterly she wept at the tomb long after their death, and who also kissed its very stones, consecrated as they were by

containing the ashes of those she so deeply loved—
how she frequently had the sepulchre opened to see
the mere but sacred dust of all that she esteemed
precious¡in¡this¡world, and so showing how hard it is
to part with dear ones, even when Providence calls
them to a better sphere. Let such love be an example to mothers, and a rebuke to those callous people who can say ·when a child dies, " it is only a
child." If Christ loved children so much, and if the
inhabitants of heaven are to be like them, how much,
with so much that is tender, innocent, and loving in
them, should they be loved by a mother ! One of
these was a son, and the other a daughter, and the
following are the inscriptions to each respectively :—

" Sacred to John Fox Croker, son of John and
Mary Croker, of Newcastle, born May 10th, 1801,
died July 12th, 1807.

" Sweet interesting boy, how ardent
    Thy wish to live, veiling thy sufferings
    In cheerful smiles, and as nature ebb'd,
    In melody of song the bright ethereal spark evane-
            scent."

" Sacred to Elizabeth Fox Croker, daughter of
John and Mary Croker, of Newcastle, born January
28th, 1806, died July 12th, 1822.

" Most beauteous she was, and gifted
    With every charm the muses could inspire ;
    In song, in music, and in eloquence
    She formed a star ; and when she fled
    Within her tomb, Nature made her bower
    To shed the sorrowing tear."

There is a headstone to Elizabeth Powell, who died January 1st, 1812, aged 132 years. It is in the new part of the churchyard.

The most elaborately carved headstone of slate is of the date 1763, to James Bradbury. It is truly beautiful.

On the south side of the old church, close by the old chancel wall, there was formerly a vault and tomb of the Musgrove family; and it is said that when the last of the family was buried therein, the key of the oaken door admitting into the vault was thrown into Dove-hole. This tomb was destroyed when the old church was taken down, when seventeen leaden coffins which it contained were cut in halves and sold. The buyer, however, it is said, could not rest with his purchase; and it is affirmed that a supernatural being haunted him until he took the coffins back to the churchyard. He was glad to get rid of them, and to ease his mind, although at the loss of their cost. They were again buried at the east end of the church. The old tomb of the family of Degge was destroyed at the same time. It is well remembered for its old appearance, standing as it did at the south side of the church. Such desecration of human dust is enough to make one repeat the epitaph to the immortal Shakespeare—

" Good friend, for Jesus' sake forbear
   To dig the dust enclosed here ;
   Blest be the man that spares these stones,
   And CURST be he that moves my bones."

THE PARISH REGISTER.

THE Register of Uttoxeter Church commences in the year 1596, from which date it is complete to the present time. It is consequently very voluminous, filling a large iron safe in the robing-room. From a cursory glance at its contents, it does not appear that the vicars have been in the habit of making many remarks with their entries, so that the register does not contain much to interest the public. I have looked through several of the early books, and was disappointed by not finding the christening of Sir Symon Degge, nor the burial of John Archbold, who died in 1629, aged 103 years; nor the burial of Mr. John Scott, who was slain in Uttoxeter streets in 1644. The name of Degge, at an early date, is, however, of frequent occurrence. The signature of the first vicar whose name occurs in the register is that of Thomas Barns. It runs through the first book, and far on in the second, beginning in 1596, and continuing over a period of twenty-one years till 1617.[1] He had born to him and christened in Uttoxeter seven children—four sons, and three daughters. Their names are as follows :—John, Thomas, James, William, Jones, Mary, and Anne. I do not find the burial of this vicar in the register, so that he very probably resigned. He was succeeded by the Rev. Thomas Lightfoot, who was vicar from

---

(1) A remark on the cover of this book proves, however, two things —that the Register of Uttoxeter Church extended further back; and that Mr. Barns was minister prior to 1596. It is—" Thomas Barns hath been vicar of this parish ―― years."

1617 until 1653. The next registrar's name is William Roiston. Laurence Dawson is minister in 1657, and the Rev. Mr. Edge, a correspondent of the Rev. Thomas Lightfoot, becomes vicar in 1658, and in 1677 he is succeeded [by Richard Jackson, whose signature continues till 1689, although in 1688 that of Joshua Robinson occurs. A few extracts are used in connection with the persons or subjects they relate to in this volume. The following may be acceptable here, a few of which will show that there was poverty, crime, and pity in Uttoxeter more than 200 years back. 1624.—John Degg, son of Thomas Degg and Dorothy, his wife, was buried the 4th day of November. Thomas and Dorothy, here mentioned, appear in Degg's pedigree. Although there is not an entry of the burial of John Scott, in 1644, there is this of a christening—John, son of Thomas Scott, and——, his wife, christened the 2nd day of June. 1644—Robert Clark Barker (or Barber), surgeon, buried 23rd April. 1645—*Mr. Walter Mynors* was buried the 3rd day of August. Eliza Burton, a poor, low woman, buried the 5th March. William Spragg, buried at Lichfield the 2nd day of May. Henry Porter, a poor man, buried the 10th day of November. 1650—Edward Oudfield and Joane Taylor were married ye 6th d. Sept. An Edward Oudfield subsequently marries a Katherine *Aston.* 1656— John Blount was buried 18th day of January. Richard Taylor, who served 44 years clerk of this church in Uttoxetor, and died at the age of 88, 1658—John Barlow, a soldier, buried the 23rd July.

1660—John Wood and Ellen Lightfoot weere married the seconde day of August. 1671—Mr. Peter Lightfoot buried ye 18th day of Auguste. John Harding, a poor boy, buried ye 9th day October.

These names appear in the Uttoxeter Survey as owners of property—Callingwood Lightfoot, Anne Lightfoot, Elizabeth Lightfoot, and Mary Lightfoot.

COMMUNION PLATE.

ON the Paten, or receptacle for the consecrated bread, is the following inscription, " The gift of Lettice Pratt, daughter of Thomas Degge, Gent., of Stronchall." On one of the chalices, or cups, is engraved, " In 1637, Mr. Wm. & Mrs. Ann Hart gave a cup, 10 ounces and a quarter. In 1716 added to it p E., a private person, 40." While on the base of the flagon there is inscribed, " The gift of Mrs. Sarah Smith to the Parish Church of Uttoxeter, 1752," emblazoned with the monogram I.H.S., Jesus Hominum Salvator (Jesus the Saviour of mankind).

CEMETERY.

Owing to urgent requirements a new cemetery was provided for Uttoxeter in 1861. The ground selected is a few hundred yards to the west of the town by the side of the Stafford road. The chapels and the elegant spire are in the Ornamental Gothic style, from designs by Mr. B. Wilson, architect, Derby. The extent of the ground is three acres and thirteen perches, and cost £671, 17s. 2d. The contract for the chapels and entrance lodge was £1333. The

N

sum of £3000 was lent for the purpose from the
Public Works Loan Commission.   The Lord Bishop
of the diocese consecrated the cemetery on June
25th, 1861.   For some reason or other the spire was
taken down and reerected the succeeding year.

HISTORY OF DISSENT IN UTTOXETER.

QUAKERISM was introduced into Uttoxeter previous to any other form of dissent; but what is known of its history in that town may be told in a short space. The earliest mention occurs in the old parish records of 1662, when a warrant for the apprehension of a number of Quakers cost the constables the sum of one shilling. The item plainly indicates that the act of persecution proceeded from the civil authorities in Uttoxeter, but it leaves to conjecture the cause which led to the warrant for their arrest being issued. It is likely, however, that as they were otherwise unexceptionable in the sight of the law, it was for the simple attempt at promulgating their peculiar religious opinions, a proceeding which was about that time very common in many parts of the kingdom, where the magistracy were not very liberal and tolerant.

The meeting-house of the Society of Friends stands secluded in Carter Street, down a yard, at the south side. It is a small brick building, but is very comfortably fitted up. The principal attendants at this place of worship now are members of Mr. Ship-

ley's family. The attendants at the chapel used to
comprise several respectable families, amongst whom
were the ancestors of Mary Howitt, the authoress.
This lady was one of the number in her earlier days.
The Quaker's burying-place at Uttoxeter is a small
enclosure at the south side of the chapel. It contains—

> " Many a mouldering heap ;
> Each in his narrow cell forgotten laid."

CONGREGATIONALISM was introduced into Uttoxeter about the year 1788. The ministers who first
preached there in connection with this body were
the Rev. James Boden, of Hanley, and the Rev.
Mr. Whitridge, of Newcastle. The first meeting-
house of the Congregationalists in Uttoxeter was
at the west end of Carter Street, in a building which
has since served as a hoopmaker's shop. They worshipped at this place about four years, when they
erected a more suitable building for the purpose at
Bear Hill in 1792. The same at present forms a
portion of Messrs. Lasbrey's premises. This meeting-
house or chapel was opened by the Rev. Jonathan
Scott, minister of a chapel at Matlock Bath, which
had been purchased by Lady Glenorchy for the use
of the Independants and Presbyterians. The opening of it was attended by a degree and kind of persecution to make the occasion memorable. A number
of riotous persons met in the street, near the meeting-
house, who, besides disturbing the congregation,
made a bonfire at the pillory, in which they fixed
the effigy of a minister, afterwards committing it to

the flames. At night the rioters threw fire-brands at the people as they returned from the meeting, but fortunately no one was materially injured.[1]

The first pastor over the congregation at Bear Hill was the Rev. Mr. Cole, who was intended to be represented by the figure which was burnt at the pillory. Mr. Cole was succeeded in 1796 by the Rev. Stephen Chester, at which time there were but six church members and twenty others for a congregation. Mr. Chester was followed by the Rev. J. Johnson, who has since joined the Church of England, and become the travelling secretary of the Church of England Missionary Society. He, however, remained but a short time. The Rev. John Cooke, who was educated at Lancashire College, entered upon his ministerial labours at the same place in 1825, and at the present period has been pastor of the Congregationalists in Uttoxeter about thirty-eight years. The congregation increased under the ministry of Mr. Cooke, and a more suitable building than the meeting-house at Bear Hill became requisite, so that in 1827 the chapel in Carter Street was erected. The foundation stone of the edifice was laid by the Rev. John Cooke, who also delivered an address during the ceremony. The chapel was finished by, and opened on, the 15th of April, 1828, the sermons being preached by the late Dr. Raffles, of Liverpool. The school-rooms adjoining the chapel were built in 1842, and the sermons on the occasion of opening

(1) Evangelical Magazine.

them were preached by the late John Angell James
of Birmingham, and the Rev. James Galloway. The
minister's house was erected in 1848, and was the
gift of the late John Vernon, Esq.

The Rev. John Cooke is held in the highest esteem
by persons of all denominations in Uttoxeter; his
help has always been freely given when required for
the promotion of the religious, educational, and social
welfare of the town generally. On completing the
thirty-second year of his ministry, on February 3rd,
1857, he was presented with a handsome token of the
esteem in which he was held by the members of his
church. The gift consisted of a silver salver, and a
purse containing eighty sovereigns, the salver bearing
a suitable inscription. The presentation was made,
at a social meeting, by Mr. John Vernon, junior.
The rev. gentleman in acknowledging the gift read
the names of those members of his church who had
died during his ministry. The reading of this list
produced considerable emotion in the assembly.

METHODISM was introduced into Uttoxeter during
the life of its founder, the Rev. John Wesley. It is
related on good authority that the house in which
Mr. Godbehere resides, opposite Balance Street, was
the first preaching-house in Uttoxeter of the Wesleyans, and that they worshipped in it from about
1775 to 1790. The itinerant preachers at that time,
in whose district lay Uttoxeter, were the Rev. Samuel
Bardsley, a man of great popularity; the Rev. Robert
Costerdine, the Rev. Robert Swan, and the Rev.

Joseph Taylor. The house was occupied by a family attached to Methodism; and an apprentice they had to the shoe-making business was in the habit of cleaning the preachers' shoes—a not very pleasant employment, from the amount of dirty walking the preachers had to perform at that time—and for which he, no doubt, expected to be recompensed. One of the preachers appears to have been possessed either of a not very generous disposition, or of a purse not too full of money—a circumstance not unfrequent among Wesleyan preachers—or of a forgetful mind, for he omitted to give the lad any thing for cleaning his shoes. The omission became known to one of the other preachers, Joseph Taylor, who, in trying his wit to correct the fault of his brother preacher, perpetrated the following rhyme upon paper, and stuck it upon the chimney-piece of the room they slept in :—

" Pray give Jack a penny for cleaning your leather,
    Your boots are so long, so dirty the weather;
    You know that the lad has a sad nasty job,
    And if he cleans them for nothing he must be a hob."

Joseph Taylor preached in the chapel in High Street in 1828, after he had been in the ministry forty years.

At an early date the Rev. Mr. Davenport, curate of Uttoxeter church, opened his house for the public prayer-meetings of the Wesleyans; and his house was also opened for the preachers after he was promoted to the vicarage of Radcliffe.[1] The time

---

[1] History of Methodism in the Leek Circuit.

when this liberal-minded clergyman countenanced
the small and probably despised society of Methodists
in Uttoxeter, was certainly before 1780, and very
likely previous to 1775. He was an intimate friend
of John Wesley, and their correspondence appears in
the " Armenian Magazine."

It used to be related by a person living at this
period, that he remembered John Wesley once preach-
ng in Uttoxeter market-place. It is also confidently
stated that he passed through Uttoxeter on another
occasion, and whilst staying at the White Hart and
Old Star in the market-place for a change of post-
horses, he was met by the members of the society in
the town. At another time, when there was a dispute amongst them, he addressed them a letter which
had the desired effect of producing a reconciliation.

It appears that when the Wesleyans discontinued
preaching at the house in the Sheep Market, a house
was open for their reception on Uttoxeter Heath,
which was shortly after exchanged for the building
in Carter Street, previously used by the Independents. This they occupied ¦till the close of the century. The Rev. John Hampson, a preacher of some
eminence, once preached in this meeting-house, and
met with no little annoyance from a number of young
men who had met to persecute and disturb the assembly. The preacher was a powerful man, and was
no doubt pretty well used to riotous interference
when preaching, and had no fear of them. The way
in which he treated one of the number reminds one
of the rough handling David Cartwright, of Ameri-

can backwoods celebrity, frequently gave to some of his tormenters when on his errand of preaching. He took him by a leg and an arm and flung him into a cesspool, or some similar place, in the back-yard—an unpleasant and unexpected result to his annoyance of the congregation. The preacher resumed his duties, and no one again attempted to molest him. A son of Mr. Hampson wrote a life of Mr. Wesley in three volumes.

At the beginning of the present century Methodism in Uttoxeter had almost become extinct; preaching was discontinued, and only one or two persons remained clinging to the Wesleyan form of worship. A person of the name of Cartwright, and a family named Seckerson—whose ancestors existed in Uttoxeter two centuries before—were all the Methodists that remained in the town, and these went weekly to Doveridge chapel, which was then attended by the family of the late Michael Thomas Saddler, M.P. for Leeds. About 1805 a house was opened at the wharf, and was thronged by persons; but it appears they were not permitted to worship there without molestation. There were to be found persons who annoyed them by blowing the fumes of assafoetida through the key-hole in the door; and on one occasion when the people were assembled, a number of the rabble forced open the door and pushed a donkey into the house. Yet Methodism got a broader footing in Uttoxeter, and the large room at the Old Star was taken, which, however, was no protection against the violence of disorderly intruders.

The windows were frequently broken, and the congregation disturbed. The chapel in High Street was built in 1812, and opened by the Rev. Jabez Bunting, D.D. The chapel has a spacious gallery, and a good organ has recently been introduced. The preachers at the present time are the Rev. R. Brown, and the Rev. J. F. Broughton. In the rear of the chapel is a spacious school-room.

The PRIMITIVE METHODISTS have a chapel in Carter Street, which was erected in 1842. Previous to this they had a meeting-house at the top of the Hockley.

The CATHOLIC chapel stands in Balance Street, and was erected in 1839. It is in the style of the parish churches antecedent to the sixteenth century. The Rev. Peter Holland is priest.

The taxation of Pope Nicholas at Uttoxeter in the time of Edward I., in 1291, was the sum of £12, according to the item relating to it—" Uttokestratre pter pens xviii. marc———xxivs." This tax was levied on all families possessed of thirty pence yearly rent in land, out of which they paid a penny. Peter's pence was presented from England by Ina, King of the West Saxons, towards the endowment of an English college at Rome, A.D. 725, and was so called because agreed to be paid on the feast of St. Peter. It was confirmed by Offa, 777, and claimed by the Popes till suppressed by Henry VIII.[1] Amongst

(1) Camden's Britainnia.

the Roman Catholic non-jurors who refused to take the oaths in 1745, is one Henry Alport, a yeoman, of Uttoxeter, who for refusing was fined the sum of 40s. [1]

The PLYMOUTH BRETHREN have recently introduced their tenets into Uttoxeter, and they rent the room at the Red Lion Inn to worship in.

(1) Book entitled " Names of Non-Conjurors."

LIVES OF DISTINGUISHED PERSONS EITHER NATIVES OF OR RESIDENTS IN UTTOXETER.

THOMAS ALLEN.

THIS learned and distinguished mathematician and philosopher was born at Uttoxeter on the 21st December, 1542, and according to Camden was a descendent, through six generations, of Henry Allen of Bucknall. He was admitted a scholar of Trinity College, Oxford, in 1561, became a fellow in 1565, and took his Master's Degree in 1567. He pursued his studies in this college for three years afterwards, but in consequence of his disinclination to enter into holy orders, as required by the statutes, he resigned his fellowship, and went to Gloucester Hall (now Worcester College) in the year 1570. Here he pursued the study of mathematics with great attention and success, and in consequence of his attainments, acquired a high reputation for his superior knowledge in his favourite branch of learning,

Mr. Allen was now patronized by a nobleman much devoted to mathematical science, Henry, Earl of Northumberland, who invited him to his house,

THOMAS ALLEYN.

and introduced him to those celebrated mathematicians, Thomas Harrison, John Dees, Walter Warner, and Nathaniel Thorperly. Mr. Allen enjoyed in their society the greatest gratification, by the discussion of topics most congenial to his habit of thinking; and his friends were no less pleased and instructed in their intercourse with a young philosopher whose demonstrations of science were so complete and conclusive.

Amongst other distinguished persons who respected the talents of Mr. Allen, Robert, Earl of Leicester, was emulous to patronise him, and offered to confer a bishopric upon him. He, however, declined the clerical preferment, and continued in that retirement which was so agreeable to his unostentatious character, and his simple and temperate habits of life. Devoted to the studious pursuits of science, Mr. Allen continued in the University, and availing himself of the advantages of his situation, he collected many valuable manuscripts relating to antiquities, history, philosophy, mathematics, and astronomy, a catalogue of which collection is preserved in the Ashmolean Museum. Mr. Allen published in Latin the second and third books of Ptolemy, concerning the judgment of the stars, with an exposition. He also wrote notes on many of Lilly's books, and some of the works of Bates, entitled " De Scripturibus Mag Britannia," and was doubtless misled by the belief in judicial astrology so prevalent in that age. His skill as a mathematician induced the vulgar to suspect him of practising the art of magic; and the author of a book entitled " Leicester's Commonwealth," accused him of exercising his necromanic art to promote the Earl of Leicester's ambitious schemes, and effect a match between that nobleman and Queen Elizabeth. This absurd assertion doubtless originated in the well-known confidence which existed between Mr. Allen and his patron, between whom a constant correspondence was kept up, insomuch that nothing important respecting the state was transacted without the cognizance of the philosopher, who, in return, infor.ned the earl of what passed in the university.

From the uniformity of a collegian's life few interesting incidents are to be expected; and Mr. Allen was content with the esteem of a few select friends, in preference to emolument and fame. He was highly respected by several celebrated contemporaries, particularly Mr. Camden, Sir Thomas Bodley, Sir Henry Saville,[1] Sir Robert Cotton, Sir Henry Spelman, and Mr. Sheldon.

Mr. Allen died at Gloucester Hall, September 30th, 1632, in the 90th year of his age, and was interred with great solemnity. Mr. Burton, who delivered his funeral oration, called him not only " The Coryphæus but the very soul and sun of all the mathematicians of his time;" and Mr. Sheldon, who was his intimate friend, mentioned him " as a person of most extensive learning, and consumate judgement, the brightest ornament of the University of Oxford." Camden says, " He was skilled in most of the best arts and sciences." These high panegyrics from such distin-

(1) Sir Henry Saville's rare collection of MSS. and books were sold last year.

guished men are most certainly honourable memorials of the learning of Mr. Allen, yet he does not seem to have been ambitious of transmitting his name to posterity by any literary production which might have promoted the progress of science. In fact, it has long been the practise of the learned to compliment each other hyperbolically; and in the ardour of their admiration and wish to shine as encomiasts they over-praise the abilities and attainments of men of real worth.

The following sketch of Mr. Allen is from a manuscript in the library of Trinity College, Oxford:— "He studied polite literature with great application; he was strictly tenacious of academical discipline; always highly esteemed, both by foreigners and by all of the highest stations in the Church of England and the University of Oxford." Yet, with all this boasted knowledge, it is to be regretted by the world that Mr. Allen was so secret a lover of the muses; for we have not a single scrap to illustrate his taste for polite literature, and very few articles indeed from his pen respecting even his own favourite study of mathematics.

The most substantial benefits Mr. Allen left to the world are his bequests, including the foundation and endowment of a grammar school at Uttoxeter, the particulars of which will be found enumerated in his will, given in a subsequent portion.

SIR SYMON DEGGE, KNIGHT, JUDGE AND ANTIQUARY.

SIR SYMON DEGGE, Knight, was descended from

Hugh Degge, of Stramshall, gent., who lived in the time of Richard II. Sir Symon was born at Uttoxeter, January 15th, 1612, and was educated for the law in which he was much distinguished, and practised in Doctors' Commons as a civilian. The hand-writing of Dr. Symon Degge, his son, in the copy of Dr. Plott's " Natural History of Stafford-shire," at Cambridge, unmistakeably fixes Uttoxeter as his birthplace. He says on the margin of page 313, that Sir Symon Degge died in the 92nd year of his age, and that he was born at Uttoxeter, a town remarkable for the great age of its inhabitants.

Owing to his eminent legal attainments, King Charles II. appointed Sir Symon judge of West Wales, a position which he held for a period of fourteen years; after resigning this post he be-came counsel in the war of Wales during the space of twelve years, an appointment to which he was also preferred by the same king. He received his discharge from this office on his own petition, when he entered the commission of the peace for the coun-ties of Derby and Stafford, and became at the same time Recorder of Derby. He was in the commission of the peace twelve years, but the Recordership of Derby he held for thirty-nine years. In 1675 he was High Sheriff for the county of Derby. He was the author of two distinct legal treatises, entitled, " The Parson's Counsellor," and " The Law of Tithes and Tithing," dedicated to his son-in-law, the Rev. Anthony Trollope, rector of Norbury. His legal opinions are quoted by Coke, in his ecclesiastical law these works have recently been republished under the editorship of Mr Ellis.

Sir Symon Degge is, however, principally known as an eminent antiquary. He wrote copious manuscript notes to Plott's "Natural History of Staffordshire," the copy of which is in Trinity College Library, Cambridge, and to Erdeswick's "Survey of Staffordshire," about the year 1660, in which appeared his remarkable letter on Abbey Lands.

Sir Symon Degge was twice married. His first wife was a daughter of Richard Brandon, Esq., of Shenstone Hall. She died July 2nd, 1652, aged 42 years. His second wife, whom he married December 7th, 1652, was Alice, daughter of Anthony Oldfield, Esq., of Spalding, widow of James Trollope, Esq. Sir Symon Degge died in the year 1702, at Blythe Bridge Hall, at the age of 92 years, and his remains were buried in the chapel on the north side of Kingston Church, recently destroyed.

His son, Dr. Symon Degge, was a physician at Derby, living in the parish of Allhallows, and, like his father, possessed a taste for antiquarian pursuits. He was the discoverer of Roman antiquities at Fenny Bentley, in Derbyshire, as well as antiquities in other parts of that county. He was the purchaser of the manor of Marchington and Agardsley from Charles Egerton, Esq., and the Earl of Bridgewater. Although the last male descendant of Sir Symon Degge is stated to have died in 1812, there are now persons of the name in Uttoxeter claiming descent from him.

o

The above is the fullest and most correct account of any yet given of this distinguished man.

The following are inscriptions to Sir Symon Degge and his wives, which have been carefully copied from three tablets which were in the now destroyed Church of Kingston :—

" Here lyeth the body of Sir Symon Degge, Knt., who was judge of West Wales to Civri the 2nd, xiv. years, and of the same king, Council in the War of Wales 12 years, and then upon his petition (his) discharge he was in the commission of the peace for the counties of Derby and Stafford, and Recorder of Derby above thirty-five years.   Was born Jany. Vth, MDCIXII.   Dyed February X., MDCICII."

On the right side of the slate bearing the above is another slab, with an inscription to the second wife of Sir Symon Degge.

" Here lies the body of Dame Alice Degge, daughter of Anthony Oldfield of Spalding, Lincolnshire, Esq., and second wife of Sir Symon Degge.   Was born and christened June xxvth, MDCIXIV.   Dyed March xxxth, MDCIXCVI."

The following inscription to Sir Symon Degge's first wife, and other persons, was on a stone which was fixed in the north side of the chapel :—

" Against this place, in the body of the church, was buried the bodies of William Whitehall, gent., who died 12 March, 1615, aged 83, and Elizth., his wife, formerly the wife of Thos. Degg, of Stramshall, gent., great-grandmother of Sir Symon Degg, ys built this chapel. She died 10 June, 1620, aged 94 : and Symon Whitehall, their son, gent., who died 17 May, 1630, aged 63 : and Letice, his wife, who died Octbr. 20, 1649, aged 97 : and Dame, first wife of the said Sir Symon Degg, who died 2 July, 1652, aged 42 years."

SAMUEL BENTLEY.

Mr. SAMUEL BENTLEY, "The Uttoxeter Poet," was born at Uttoxeter on the 9th of May, 1722,[1] in the third or fourth house from the corner of Church Street, and almost opposite the conduit. His grandfather had lived there before his father; and it is believed, although otherwise very well off, that they carried on the business of hair-dressers.

Mr. Bentley was well educated. His lingual acquirements embraced Latin, Greek, Italian, and some knowledge of the Hebrew, languages; and amongst his other accomplishments he had an acquaintance with music, drawing, and painting. His bass-viol, bearing his initials, is still in existence. For many years it did service at the Wesleyan chapel, in Uttoxeter.[2] His early school acquisitions were probably made at Alleyn's grammar school; but as he mentions the Rev. Mr. Malbon, vicar, as his "Macænas, teacher, and friend," which implies

(1) Bentley was evidently mistaken as to his exact age, and he stands corrected by the Church Register—" Baptism : Samuel, son of Richard Bentley, and Elizabeth, his wife, baptised the 3rd of May, 1722.. Burial : March 5th, 1803, Samuel Bentley."

(2) It is now in the possession of Mr. Henry Hudson.

something more than religious teacher and literary patron, it is not improbable that he was indebted to Mr. Malbon for some of his classical knowledge.

Mr. Bentley's first literary attempt was a rhyming description of the river Dove, entitled " The River Dove, a Pastoral Lyric," a portion of which, through the entreaties of his friends, made its appearance in 1768, in a thin quarto of twenty-eight verses, occupying fourteen pages, and was " printed and published for the author by Elizabeth Stephens, at the Bible and Crown, over against Stationers' Hall, London." His collection of poems was published at the same office in a goodly octavo volume, in 1774. The " River Dove" appears in it, in an extended form of seventy-four verses. Some of the other principal poems are entitled " An Essay on Painting," " The Bowling Green," " The Haymakers, a Pastoral ;" a poem on " The Coming of Age of William, Duke of Devonshire," with some other miscellaneous poems and translations. Mr. Bentley had subscribers for two hundred and thirty-four copies of his collection, amongst whom were most of the nobility about the neighbourhood, and many living at a great distance from it. As well as being a moderately good poet he had a taste for antiquities, and contributed occasionally to the " Gentleman's Magazine."

Unlike many who have moved in the muse of higher note, he was in independent circumstances. His happy abundance is alluded to in one of his poems not in the collection, but given at the end of this notice. He bestowed the sum of £10 upon a name-

SAMUEL BENTLEY'S HOUSE, UTTOXETER.

sake poetess at Norwich, named Elizabeth Bentley, though no relation to him. She was self-educated, and in very humble circumstances. Her poems are very favourably reviewed in the " Gentleman's Magazine" of 1829, in connection with which an interesting sketch of her life, chequered by many difficulties, is given.

Mr. Bentley was very much respected, and was on terms of intimacy with Lord Gardner, who invariably called upon him, when professional duties allowed him to visit his native place. On one of these occasions, when Mr. Bentley was almost totally blind, Lord Gardner went the back way to his house, which he entered. On Mr. Bentley hearing Lord Gardner's voice he at once recognized it, and exclaimed, " Lord Gardner, I presume." Lord Gardner's reply showed how little he esteemed mere titles of dignity for eminent services, without something more substantial. He said, " Don't call me Lord Gardner ; they have given me titles and honors, but they have not rewarded me for my services." Of the accuracy of the statement, in substance, I have not the least doubt, for it was told to me by the late Mrs. Baxter, who was his servant at the time, and remembered it well.

The blindness of Mr. Bentley was owing to a flash of lightning, which struck him in the face as he stood in the front room of his house, being at the time in his 75th year. Simultaneous with the same flash, a large oak tree, which was standing at Bull's Bank, was split to pieces. By this accident he became unable to read, and Mrs. Baxter, his servant,

(her maiden name being Jones) recollected reading
to him Homer, Virgil and Don Quixote.

He died in the year 1803, at the age of 83 years.
His death was sudden. He was taken ill on the
night of the 27th of February, and his servant sent
for Dr. Madeley, physician. He got up the next
morning, dressed his hair, and went about the house
during the day. In the afternoon he expressed his
wish for tea, which was accordingly prepared for him,
and when he had taken one bite of bread and butter,
he shook his head, bowed forward, and died.[1]

Mr. Bentley never married; but three maiden sisters, whose names were Hannah, Elizabeth, and Sally,
resided with him, all of whom died in the space of
the five last years of his life. He had an intelligent
appearance, although afflicted with squinting. He
was of low stature; he dressed in the fashion of the
day—hair curled, pigtail behind, cock and pinched
hat, and walked with a long cane staff. He left his
servant, Mrs. Baxter, who lived with him the five last
years of his life, and saw the death of himself and
sisters, a legacy of £90. Besides her regular wages
he gave her a guinea every Christmas, for her great
attention to him; and the last he gave her he accompanied with the remark, " That he hoped she might
never want one." His remains lie beneath a flat defaced stone on bricks, a little below the church on the
right hand side of the walk.

(1) Comparing this statement about his death with the entry of
his burial in the register, it strikingly shows the correctness and
retention of Mrs. Baxter's memory at the age of 86.

The following autobiographical lines by Mr. Bentley are from the original copy in my own possession. When written it will be seen that he was blind :—

LINES

Written on my birthday, the 9th of May, 1799, when
I had completed my 77th year of age.

Oh ! what avails it that in early prime,
In innocence and ease I passed my hours ?
My lesson o'er, all sportive was my time ;
My life seem'd then bespread with blooming flowers.

Oh ! what avails it when in perfect health,
Blessed with kind relatives and friends in store ?
A few paternal acres was my wealth ;
I was content—what could I wish for more ?

Oh ! what avails it that my mind was fraught
With moral precepts from the sacred page ;
From many authors ancient lore was taught,
And was well read in many a Grecian sage ?

Oh ! what avails it, that with taste and skill,
From ivory keys full harmony I drew ;
And with melodious strains my flute could fill,
And from the viol strings form concords new ?

Oh ! what avails it that I joined the dance,
Cheered by the fiddle's animating strains ;
Taught in right steps to follow and advance ;
Mixed and evolved amidst the nymphs and swains?

Oh ! what avails it that in light and shade
I could expression to bright painting give,
And in good laws and attitudes displayed,
Bid all the imaginary group to live ?

Oh ! what avails it, favoured by the muse,
 In flights poetic that I penned the lay ?
Glee both in youth and age, formed to infuse—
 No satire from my pen ere winged its way.

But oh ! the sad reverse—one fatal day,[1]
 The thunder rolling with tremendous crash ;
The vivid lightning winged its rapid way,
 Blasting my eyes with instantaneous flash.

My eyesight now aids not my pen to write ;
 Poring I guide irregular my pen ;
Nor words to words can properly unite ;
 Nor when once formed can scarce my writing ken.

Veiled almost to me 's the sacred page ;
 No more am charmed with the Horacian lyre ;
Virgil's sweet numbers now no more engage,
 Nor lofty Homer with his muse of fire.

And now, alas ! no more my flute I fill ;
 Melodious strains I now must breathe no more ;
My instrumental keys and viol still ;
 All harmony is fled—is ever o'er.

I now no more must join in festive dance,
 Or with agility again must spring ;
Nor with light steps through lengthened ranks ad-
   vance ;
 Nor hand conjoined with hand lead round the ring.

Nearly two years their destined course have run,
 While day by day my recreation fled ;
No blue expanse gives joy, nor mid-day sun,
 Nor sparkling morn, nor glowing evening red.

(1) August 1st, 1797.

My pencil now no more must lend its aid,
   The beauteous landscape glowing to display ;
No more my colours mix for light and shade ;
   And charms of beauty never more portray.

Yet not extinguished quite is yet my muse ;
   Some small faint glimmerings with me still remain;
It cheers my mind—nor will its aid refuse—
   And is my antidote 'gainst grief and pain.

Though now so full of heaviness my soul,
   I put my trust in God—his mercy sure ;
His goodness stretches forth from pole to pole ;
   Is ever present—ever will endure.

Bentley

ADMIRAL LORD GARDNER.

The distinguished Admiral, Lord Gardner, was born at Uttoxeter on the 12th of April, 1742, at the house in High Street called the Uttoxeter House, now occupied by Dr. Taylor.[1]

He was the eighth son of Lieutenant-Colonel Gardner, of the 11th regiment of dragoons. Having at an early period shown a strong bias towards

---

(1) Dr. Taylor has most benevolently for many years given medical advice gratuitously twice a-week, by which many have been greatly benefited.

the naval service, he was rated, when fourteen years old, as a mid-shipman on board the " Medway," of sixty guns, under the immediate order of Captain Sir Peter Denis, an officer of distinguished merit. In this vessel Mr. Gardner remained for two years, during which time he was present in an action, in which the " Duc D'Aquitaine," a French ship of the line, was taken. From the " Medway" he afterwards accompanied his captain, first on board the " Namur," and afterwards into the " Dorsetshire." In the former he served under Admiral Hawke during the expedition against Rochfort ; and while on board the latter, was present at the capture of " A Raisonable," on which occasion Captain Denis put in practice the plan adopted by the new school, of not firing a single ball until with a few yards of the enemies' ship. He likewise bore a share in the general engagement which took place off Belleiste, in 1769, between the British and French fleets, commanded by Sir Edward Hawke and Marshal de Covflaus. Mr. Gardner, having at this time been five years in constant service, was, at the customary examinations, appointed Lieutenant on board the " Bellona." In this station he distinguished himself at the capture of the " Courageuse," whereupon he was raised to the rank of Master and Commander, and appointed to the " Raven," of sixteen guns. After the lapse of four years he was made First in the " Preston," of fifty guns, which had been fitted out as the flag-ship of Rear-Admiral Parry, whom he accompanied to Port Royal, in Jamaica. During the whole time of his being stationed there Great Britain was at peace with all the nations of Europe; so that the only circumstance which occurred requiring notice in this sketch, was his marriage with Susannah Hyde, daughter of Francis Oale, Esq., a West India planter. This lady having brought him a numerous family, and being himself ambitious to rise in the service, he made every effort to obtain an appointment as soon as the American contest began. Accordingly he was nominated to the command of the "Maidstone" frigate, in which he sailed from the West Indies early in 1778, and in the course of that year was so fortunate as to make a rich capture on the coast of America. On the 4th of November he fell in with the "Lion," a French man-of-war, having on board fifteen hogsheads of tobacco; and after a severe action compelled her to surrender. With this prize he sailed for Antigua, and was soon after promoted by Admiral Byron to the command of the "Sultan," of seventy-four guns. In the drawn battle which was fought some time subsequently with the French fleet under Count de Estaing, off the Island of Grenada, Captain Gardner led the van, and greatly distinguished himself. His ship, however, suffered so much, that he was ordered to Jamaica, from whence he shortly afterwards sailed for England, when the "Sultan" was discharged. He did not, however, remain long out of commission, having been appointed to the "Duke" in the course of a few months, with which ship he sailed to join the fleet in the West Indies, when under the orders of Sir George

Rodney.   He was fortunate enough to arrive in time
to participate in the glorious victory of the 12th of
April, 1782.   On that memorable day his ship was
the first to break through the enemies' line of battle,
according to the new plan of attack then for the first
time put in practice.   At one period of this action,
the " Duke," in conjunction with the " Formidable"
and " Namur," had to sustain the force of eleven of
the enemy's ships.   Soon after this triumph the
American war terminated, and peace continued for
several years to shed her benignant influence over
the several nations of Europe.   For some time he
acted as commander on the Jamaica station ; and in
1790 was appointed a Lord of the Admiralty, when
he likewise obtained a seat in Parliament.   In the
year 1793, having been raised to the rank of Rear-
Admiral of the Blue, he hoisted his flag on board
the " Queen," of ninty-eight guns, in which he sailed
as Commander-in-Chief, to the Leonard Islands.
Soon after this event, finding the disputes between
the Republicans and Royalists in the colony of Mar-
tinico to run very high, and being earnestly pressed
by the latter to effect a descent on the island, Major-
General Prince landed with 3000 men, but that officer judged it expedient to reembark almost immediately, being satisfied that the Republican party
was too strong to afford just hopes of success in the
Royalist cause.   Admiral Gardner now returned to
England, and in the following year bore a part in the
action of June 1st, under the gallant Earl Howe.
On this occasion his conduct was conspicuous in the

extreme, his ship having suffered more than any other in the fleet, with the exception of the " Brunswick." In consequence he was not only particularly thanked by the Commander-in-Chief, but was appointed Major-General of Marine, and created a Baronet of Great Britain. On the 22nd of June, 1795, Sir Allen Gardner was present at the action off the Port L'Orient, when the French fleet only saved itself from total destruction by timely flight. Two years after this event, when a dangerous mutiny had broken out at Portsmouth, he manifested a degree of firmness and resolution during that trying period worthy of his high character as a British naval officer. From this time he continued to serve in the Channel Fleet, till the close of the year 1799, when he was sent with sixteen sail of the line to reinforce the fleet off Cadiz, and in the Mediterranean. Perceiving, however, that little danger was to be apprehended in these quarters, he returned with nine sail of the line, accompanied by the envoy from Lisbon.

In 1800 he served in the Channel Fleet, but soon afterwards was, being previously raised to the dignity of an Irish peer, appointed to succeed Admiral Kingsmill, the naval commander in Ireland. This command he continued to hold till the year 1807, when he hoisted his flag as Admiral of the Channel Fleet, which ill health, however, soon obliged him to relinquish. He died in 1810, and was buried in the Abbey Church of Bath, with the grandeur and solemnity due to his rank and merit.

Lord Gardner's political career was not distinguished by any circumstance of great moment. He sat in three successive parliaments. His first election took place in 1790, when he was returned for Plymouth. In 1796 he was colleague to Mr. Fox in the representation of Westminster. On this occasion he was opposed by Mr. John Horne Tooke, whose wit, satire, and eloquence, were more alarming to the Admiral than ¡a shower of cannon balls from the enemy's fleet. Notwithstanding, he once more offered himself for the same city, and was successful. At this time Mr. Fox, in addressing the electors, said, " A noble Admiral has been proposed to you. I certainly cannot boast of agreeing with him in political opinions; but whom could the electors pitch upon more worthy of their choice than the noble Lord—in his private character universally respected, and a man who has served his country with a zeal, a gallantry, a spirit, and a splendour, that will reflect upon him immortal honour."

MARY HOWITT.

In a copy of " My own story," which belonged to the late Thomas Hart, Esq., banker, of Uttoxeter, is this pleasing note in that gentleman's handwriting, occasioned by early remembrances called up by a perusal of that interesting little book—" I remember this Mary Howitt well, and think I see her now bringing home large bunches of flowers, which she was fond of gathering in the fields." Uttoxeter may be truly proud that it has been the birth-place of this lady, who ranks amongst the most distinguished and pleasing writers of the day. She was born early in the present century. Both her parents were descended from ancestors of honourable reputation. Her father was Samuel Botham, Esq., surveyor, and her mother was of the family of Wood, the Irish patentee, about whose halfpence, minted under a contract of the Government of George II., Dean Swift raised such a disturbance with his "Draper's Letters," preventing the issue of the coinage, and saddling Mr. Wood with a loss of £600,000. Sir Robert Walpole resisted all recompense for his loss, although Sir Isaac Newton, who was appointed to assay the coinage, pronounced it better than the contract required, and Mr. Wood, of course, justly entitled to remuneration. His son, Mr. Charles Wood, the grandfather of Mrs. Howitt, and who became assay master at Jamaica, was the first to introduce platina into Europe. Many of her ancestors, who were attached to the Society of Friends, have suffered for the assertion of their rights in religious matters.

Mrs. Howitt, who was brought up in the religious tenets of the Quakers, pursued her early studies under her father's roof, in association with her elder sister (now Mrs. Harrison), where they made proficiency in Latin, French, and chemistry. At this period she also made stealthy draughts at those sources of literature which were looked upon as vain, and strictly forbidden by the rules of the religious society to which she belonged; and to satisfy the taste thus acquired,

such books as were in the neighbourhood were laid
under contribution. She was at this early period,
too, an observer of nature, and an admirer of its
varied beauties. Nor less so was her sister. How
beautifully her love for flowers is spoken of by Mr.
Hart. She had also a love for poetry, which led
her to make available for metrical illustration such
subjects as she deemed suitable; and these, which
were handed about in manuscript, fell into the hands
of Mr. Howitt, a young poet of kindred mind, and
of the same persuasion in religion. This circumstance led to their early marriage, and in 1823 their
first and joint production appeared, under the title of
" The Forest Minstrel," and was warmly welcomed
by the public. She continued to devote herself to
literature, and in 1827 " The Desolation of Eyam,"
a touching subject, pathetically treated, was published, with a selection of lyrics, also the joint production of Mr. and Mrs. Howitt. Mrs. Howitt next
published " The Seven Temptations," in which she
eschewed outward objects, and painted the struggles
of the inner being. The three-volume novel was at
this time in the ascendant, and she resolved in her
succeeding literary effort to meet the taste of the day,
and gave to the reading public, " Wood Leighton,"
in three volumes, which met with considerable success, and has several times being re-issued in a cheap
form. This book has been much read in Uttoxeter,
and there is a general impression 'that it is intended
throughout as a description of persons, events, and
scenes, belonging to the neighbourhood of her birth,

and altogether as real and distinct as any to be found in history. With respect to " Wood Leighton," and other ficticious works this lady has written, she kindly writes, in a letter respecting them, as follows :—" Although Uttoxeter has been the groundwork of a good deal I have written, yet I have allowed myself the privilege of a writer of fiction, and not felt the necessity of adhering more closely to the details of facts than first suited my purpose. I have filled up any gap or *hiatus* according to my own fancy, and as best perfected my picture ; so when strict accuracy is requisite I am not in such works wholly to be depended upon." This passage will enable many of the readers of " Wood Leighton" to surmount some of their misapprehensions of many of the characters and localities described in the work.

In the year 1837 Mr. and Mrs. Howitt made a tour in the Scottish Highlands', where they gleaned information for subsequent literary use. During their journey they travelled over the space of more than five hundred miles. They afterwards made Esher, in Surrey, their place of abode, it being surrounded by scenery of a varied and most beautiful description. About this period Mrs. Howitt wrote the series of books for the people and their children, of which " My Own Story" is one. They consist of thirteen distinct books, and it is not saying too much, that they possess a charm which can be found in no other works of a similar kind. After their completion Mr. and Mrs. Howitt went to Germany for the education of their children, and resided at Heidel-

P

burg for three years.   Form thence they visited every
principal part of the German States, and made themselves acquainted with the literature and social life of
the people.

The works of Miss Bremer having fallen into the
hands of Mrs. Howitt about this time, she applied
herself successfully to the acquisition of the Swedish
language, to enable her to present them to English readers.   The work of translation was admirably
executed, and by this means the works of Miss Bremer have justly obtained a popularity co-extensive
with the English language.   She was equally fortunate with the Danish language, from which she has
translated the beautiful story of the " Improvisatore"
of Hans Christian Anderson, and other fictions of
less importance.

In 1847 Mrs. Howitt published a handsome edition of her ballads, and other poems, to which was
prefixed an excellent likeness of the author.   At a
later period Mrs. Howitt assisted her husband in the
compilation of a " History of the Literature of the
North of Europe," in two volumes, including specimens in prose and verse, the latter metrically arranged.   She also edited, for three years, the " Draw-
ing-room Scrap-book," and illustrated by biographical
vignettes, a series of portraits of the Queens of England.   Besides having been an extensive contributor
to periodical literature for upwards of twenty years,
she has written " The Heir of West Wayland,"
" The Children's Year," " History of America,"
" Calendar of the Seasons," and other books, besides

BIRTH-PLACE OF MARY HOWITT, UTTOXETER.

having recently translated Miss Bremer's " Letters on the Holy Land," and assisted her husband in a beautiful work on the " Abbeys and Castles of England," in which the language possesses all the freshness of these gifted writers.[1]

A daughter of Mr. and Mrs. Howitt, Miss Anna Mary Howitt, (now Mrs. Alaric Watts,) has won success both as an author and artist. The " Art Student at Munich" is from the pen of this lady. She has embodied her conceptions in painting in a production entitled, " Margaret returning from the Fountain," derived from this portion of Goethe's " Faust,"—" Margaret having heard the harsh judgment of her companions at the city fountain, returns home tortured by self-accusation." A son of Mr. and Mrs. Howitt is Mr. Alfred William Howitt, a ten years' resident in Australia, who was the head of the relief party who discovered Burke and Wills, the Australian explorers, and, I believe, is the author of " A Boy's Adventures in Australia." Another enterprising son has lately met with his death on Lake Brunner, in the western district of Canterbury, New Zealand, by the upsetting of a canoe.

The house in which Mrs. Howitt was born, of which an engraving is here given, is pleasantly situated in Balance Street, with a south-westerly aspect in front. A flower garden slopes from the house almost to a brook, which runs beneath in the valley. The wooded hills and green fields beyond

(1) Men of the Time, " London Quarterly Review," 1860.

form a pleasant scene, which is commanded from the house. A row of fir trees, which were planted by Mr. Botham towards the bottom of the garden, were much thought of, but most of them have been cut down, as well as some interesting clumps of trees in the distance, in view of the house, and spoken of in "My Own Story." Many, if not all, of the filbert trees remain. The house towards the street is mantled with ivy, and has a yard, which is separated therefrom by iron palisades.

EDWARD RUDYERD.

This individual was minister of Uttoxeter. In 1615 he published " The thunderbolt of God's wrath against the hard-hearted and stiff-necked sinners.' He was descended from an ancient Saxon family who settled at Rudyerd, temp., Canute the Dane, 1030. Of the same family was Sir Benjamin Rudyerd, a noted wit, poet and statesman of Charles I. reign; the friend of Lord Pembroke, Pym, and Hampden, and upon whom Ben Jonson wrote several epigrams. John Rudyerd, the architect of the second Eddystone lighthouse in 1706, was also of that family. [1]

CAPTAIN DANIEL ASTLE.

This person claims a brief notice as the author of a little local book entitled " A Prospect from Barrow Hill," dated Uttoxeter, June 25th, 1777, and printed by Pearson and Robinson, Birmingham. He was

[1] Reliquary, 1861.

educated at Barton-under-Needwood, and was the son of Mr. Daniel Astle, keeper of Byrkley Lodge, and brother to the learned antiquary, Thomas Astle, Esq., F.R.S., F.S.A., &c., &c. He served in the army under General Howe, and was at the attack of the American forces at Bunker's Hill. He subsequently became clergyman at Bromshall church for a great number of years. He is said to have been a friend of Dr. Johnson, and to have made the pen and ink sketch represented in the engraving on page 119. The figure of Astle is recognized as a faithful outline by those who knew him. He closes his book with these words, " With the woman one loves, with the friend of one's heart, and a good study of books, one might pass whole ages here and think it a day." He died in 1826, aged 83 years, and was buried at Uttoxeter.

THE EXTENT OF UTTOXETER;
ITS PRIMITIVE APPEARANCE; NOTED
BUILDINGS OF ANTIQUITY; COURT
HOUSE AND COURT LEET; FIRES WHICH
HAVE HAPPENED; POPULATION
OF UTTOXETER;
INSTANCES OF LONGEVITY, &c.

EXTENT OF UTTOXETER.

IT will be observed by the ancient plan of Uttoxeter that it differs very little in extent at the present time from what it was in 1658. Leaving out the Heath and Balance Hill, the map will warrant, I think, the opinion, that there were more houses in Uttoxeter at that period than there are now. On the Heath there were but ten cottages, and they were probably by the side of the turnpike road, on the left hand in going out of the town, the rest being an open common, or heath, of about sixty-four acres and thirty-five perches. The Heath is now the size of a large village. On Balance Hill there were eight cottages, but now there are twice that number.[1] Through the

---

(1) Lightfoot's Survey of Uttoxeter.

middle of the churchyard there was a row of houses, and one at the church gate was called a cell.

As before intimated, Uttoxeter is remembered to have had a very quaint and ancient appearance. Almost within memory the houses were all but entirely of the frame-timber class, with the spaces filled in with watlings of wood, covered with tempered clay, with an outer coating of plaster. The chimneys were almost entirely constructed in a similar manner. In most instances the gable ends came to the street; and it will be perceived by the plan, as is also remembered, that to many of the houses were porches. The only one remaining till recently was that at the White Bear Inn, in Carter Street, which is here engraved as a curiosity. It is also curious that at the west end of Carter Street several of these houses, as will be observed by Mr. Lightfoot's plan, projected to about the middle of the street. It is not less curious, that when the roof of one of these old houses almost opposite the White Hart, in Carter Street, was taken away, it was found to have been originally thatched with ling.

Modern improvements, however, have swept away many of these primitive residences, and whatever of sentiment there may be in clinging to old associations, it must be confessed that there is more of comfort and health to be enjoyed in those by which they are superseded. A few of the old patches remain, the most complete of which is in Carter Street, consisting of several houses, which, from their appearance, must be many hundred years old. The house in which I reside, in the same street, is of the same

class, but not quite so old,   It bears an inlaid date
on a door, which is thus " P. 1664, W.E."   Portions
of the Old Talbot are very ancient, as well as the
Black Swan, Buffalo's Head, and Mr. Bamford's
house at the corner of the sheep-market.

THE WHITE BEAR INN.

Happily the sites of several interesting places or
antiquity in Uttoxeter can yet be pointed out, and
one or two still remain almost intact.   The entire
ancient chief or manor house has continued intact,
except that its frame-work is covered with a coating
of what is called " *slap-dash*."   For many years it has
has been known as the schoolhouse of Miss Sutton, in

Carter Street, near the Independent chapel, and is at present occupied by Mr. Mills. It has two gables to the street, and one towards the west. The building of the ancient court house is also in existence, in the Market Place; but it has been converted into dwelling-houses and shops, which are occupied by Mr. Parker and Mr. Norris. It is traditionally said to have been the building where the soldiers, who had the defence of Uttoxeter during the civil wars, had their rendeszvous and depôt of ammunition and arms. The Court Leet of Uttoxeter was held here; and it appears that the common oven—the one in which the inhabitants of the town by feudal prescription in the ancient charters of the lords of the manor baked their bread—was in connection with the manor court, and in, or perhaps rather previous to, 1658, was held by one Laurence Bradshaw, according to the terms expressed in the following particulars :—" The furnace, or common bakehouse, with the highest room over it (the middle room being reserved to the use of the town for a Common Hall), and the bakehouse connected to a dwelling-house, with shop and cellar, at the rent of xl. ij. yearly."[1] This cellar is probably the underground kitchen of Mr. Mace.

The Court Leet is of very great antiquity, and has the same meaning as " View of Frankpledge," which was granted by Earl Ferrers to Uttoxeter in the thirteenth century, although it is probable this was only a confirmation of a right then already existing.

(1) Lightfoot's Survey of Uttoxeter.

The word " leet" is derived from the Anglo-Saxon *lathian*, or *gelathian*, to assemble, both lath and leet indicating, under different modifications, a district in which the free male resiants (residents), or indwellers, assembled at stated times, as well for preparation for military defence, as for purposes of police and criminal jurisdiction.[1] The borrow-holders, or borhes-alder, or seniors of the pledges, who were responsible for the good conduct of each of their co-pledges, who appear to have had authority analagous to that still exercised by the constable, an officer elected by the resiants, for the preservation of the peace, are thus mentioned in Lightfoot's Survey, " The Third-borrow Fine or Frith-silver paid at the leet by two borough-holders chosen by the jury, being yearly xvijs."

Behind the Common Hall and Town Oven there was a building in which the maltmill for the town then was ; and there are some outer places there at this time, which, from their appearance, may have been portions of malthouses. There are also two small mill gritstones in existence in the yard of Mr. French, on the High Wood, which are said to have belonged to a mill of some kind situated at the same place.

Another interesting place was " Mr. Wood's Hall," which was " swept for King Charles when at Uttoxeter in 1642," not any portion of which, however, is in existence. Its site is at the highest part of the

---

[1] Penny Cyclopædia.

field at Bull's Bank, opposite the New Grammar
School. The interest attaching to it is increased by
the fact of its having been the ancient residence in
Uttoxeter of the Mynors family, and it is, no doubt,
the same as that referred to by Erdeswick in his Survey of Staffordshire, in these words, " In Utcester is a
house of the Mynor's; very ancient gentlemen are
they," and not Hollingbury Hall, as has been supposed. It was sold early in the seventeenth century,
as will be more particularly noticed hereafter, to Mr.
James Wood, son of a citizen and salter of London,
one of the last of whom in Uttoxeter was a solicitor.
It was a half-timbered building of very great antiquity, and of considerable dimensions, and contained
altogether about forty rooms, some very lofty and
spacious, one of which was used as a gallery. There
were two gables towards the street; but these had a
retiring centre betwixt them, with, it is said, an embattled parapet; and there was a coach-yard in front.
It was several stories high, and the roofs had numerous dormer windows along their sides, the roof of
the central part being flat. There were secret places
at a chimney back, and elsewhere; and it is traditionally stated that King Charles was on one occasion
secreted in one of these places, though this belief is
perhaps more likely to refer to the time when it was
swept for him. The building has very many strange
ghost stories associated with it; but of curious things
of this kind it will be sufficient to preserve some
amatory lines remembered to have been inscribed
upon one of the old green glass windows—

> " I bleeding at your feet do lie,
> Unless you yield ; or else I die,
>   Harmless Anne Wood.
> Soul and body murdered here,
> I shall never rest till I see my dear."

A notion of the most improbable circumstance is also in existence, and widely credited, that a secret subterranean passage connected this ancient residence with Tutbury Castle.

There has been an hermitage at a former period near Dove Bridge, rather a conspicuous vicinity for those who passed their days " remote from man," and so found their business in prayer and their pleasure in praise ; and there has also been a moated residence on Uttoxeter Heath, a little distance below the Three Tuns Inn, where the new road to Beamhurst has gone across a portion of the site ; but the house has been destroyed a very long time : nothing but the moat was observable even two hundred years back. The land on which it stood formerly belonged to the Mynors, and was called the Little Park, or " Mott Close," so that it is not improbable that the ancient house at some time belonged to a branch of that family. [1]

Considering the character of the buildings in Uttoxeter at a past period, it is not surprising that at different times fires of an alarming description have happened to them ; but it is far more surprising for the same reason, that more have not taken place.

---

(1) Lightfoot's MSS. Survey of Uttoxeter.

One of the most destructive fires took place in the sixteenth century, and Erdeswick mentions it in his " Survey," saying, " That it (Uttoxeter) was reasonably well built, but pity it hath suffered of late great losses by fire." In the Church Register is also preserved an interesting note relating, no doubt, to the same fire—" The towne was burnte the xxist of Auguste ano domni, 1596. The vicarage house was burnte then, and almost all his goods, to his greate hurte —— years paste." The name of the minister was, apparently, William Barns, for that name as minister of the parish, with the names of his children, appear on the same cover of the register as the entry about the fire. The register is of vellum or parchment, and is very much burnt, an injury it no doubt sustained at the time. Another serious fire broke out in 1672, in the rear of a Mr. Cludd's house,[1] and burnt most of the lower part of the town. According to Lightfoot's MS. Survey, which was taken previously, Mr. Cludd resided in a house next to the Black Swan Inn, which bears, by the internal wood-work, I am told, evidence of fire, so that it spread from this publichouse to the lower corner of the Sheep Market, and along Balance Street, which agrees with the account of its consuming the " lower part of the town." Whether from wilfulness or carelessness as to the origin of the fire, or from some dispute amongst the owners of the lost property, does not transpire, but Sir Edward Bagot

(1) Parochial Accounts.

and the constables, and Mr. Kynnersley came to Uttoxeter about it, and a Mr. Edge and a Mr. Chamberlyn were sent to Stafford to the judge with a petition respecting the unfortunate occurrence. Since then several fires have happened. One about forty years ago broke out in Tinker's Lane, and destroyed two houses. In the old houses which stood opposite the White Hart, when pulled down in 1860, it was found that some of the beams were burnt half through; and such was also found to be the case at the White Bear, in Carter Street, when repairs were being effected in the year following.

The number of publichouses in Uttoxeter at the period—two hundred years ago—to which reference has been more particularly made, was few, comparitively to those in existence at this day. There was the " Crown" at the north side of the Market Place, belonging to the heirs of Townsend, and in the tenure of Henry Morton; the " Old Crown" at the corner of the Sheep Market, which consisted of two burgages and a half at ijs. vid., and being now Mr. Bamford's house, which belonged to Mrs. Sneyd, and previously to an Archbold, gent. (the same whose memorial is in the church), and in the occupation of John Startin; the " Old Swan," where Mr. Shipley's premises are, in the Market Place; the " Cock," which was in exstence till it was absorbed into the brewery premises, after a duration of more than two hundred years, as appears from documentary evidence, and it belonged to, and was held by, Thomas Gilbert; the " Greyhound," at " Bell's Corner," which has also been remembered to have been in existence, belonged to Thomas Kynnersly, Esq., and was in the tenure of widow Goodwin; and the " White Hart," which was at the corner of Carter Street and the Market Place. The " Old Swan" here mentioned, existed in the time of Queen Elizabeth, and an interesting character, named Edward Toyke, who figures as a correspondent of Mary, Queen of Scotland, stayed at it one night. He applied to the Queen by letter for one hundred double ducats, on the ground that his father had some acquaintance with her — it is supposed through a negociation for a marriage with her of Robert, Earl of Leicester. The latter fell into the hands of Sir Ralph Sadler, who suspected some secret matter lurked underneath it, and examined him to see if it was so. In his examination he mentions having slept at the " Old Swan." It proceeds thus—" Firste, this examinate saithe that he came from the Forest of Fechan, and lay with one Shrewe there half a year, a tenant of his father's, and from thence he came to Wedsberie, Tewesday, where he lay all nighte at an alehouse, not knowing his host's name. Wednesday he came to Utceter, and then he lay all nighte at the sign of the Swanne. Thursday he came to Ashbourne," &c. &c. Signed, E. Tokey.[1]

Seeing that the extent of Uttoxeter has not much altered in the space of two centuries, it would be interesting to ascertain, if possible, the relative amount of population therein at that and the present time;

[1] Notes and Queries, September, 1862.

and this, I think, it is possible pretty accurately to do.
Exactly two hundred years ago, 622, if not five more,
firehearths were made,[1] or a tax under that name
was levied, upon that number of houses or families
in Uttoxeter.   Now the population of Ireland[2] has
been attempted to be ascertained by multiplying the
number of houses by 5½.   The same rule may just
as appropriately be applied for arriving at the extent
of population in Uttoxeter at the period mentioned,
especially as it is adopted by government for such
purposes, and found to give as correct results as can
by any other means, short of actually taking the
census of each house, be obtained.   Multiplying, then,
627, the number of fire-hearths in Uttoxeter levied
in 1662, by 5½, we find as the total of inhabitants in
Uttoxeter at that time, about 3,348 persons of all
classes, and this gives an excess over the population
in 1801, when it was 2,779 only, of 669 persons.
That this is as correct a mode of obtaining the sum of
the population, indiscriminately, as can be adopted,
viz., by multiplying a given number of houses or
families by 5½, is provable by applying it to the census returns for Uttoxeter in 1811, the number of
houses being 605, and the population 3,155.   It will
be seen to give an excess over the exact population of
272, whilst multiplying by five would give a de-
ficiency of 130.   But if, in reality—which is probably not the case, as an allowance must be made for

(1) Parochial Accounts.

(2) " Illustrated London News," September, 1861.

circumstances varying with places—the population of any one locality bears with another, as a general rule, a relative proportion to the number of houses. According to this principle, then, it is demonstrable to the value of a fraction, that the proper multiplier is $5\frac{1}{4}$, and, applied to the return of houses in Uttoxeter in 1811, gives the total of the population in the town within seven persons.

The population in 1831 was 4,864. In 1851 it was 4,990, and when the census was taken in 1861, the number of inhabitants, as given by the local registrar at the time, was 4,810, of whom 2,324, were males, and 2,486 females. The result shows a decrease since 1850 to the extent of 180 persons; but on the whole two hundred years, an increase of 1,372. But by what law a decrease of the population in the space of one hundred and fifty years, or thereabouts, has taken place, to the extent of 357 persons, which was the case in 1801, and then have gone on in an opposite direction till a surplus is attained of 1,372 persons in so unmigratory a place as Uttoxeter, it is perhaps impossible to say. The decrease during the last eleven years may, however, be attempted to be accounted for, although, from there having been an accession of new houses, the fact may appear somewhat puzzling. In 1850 a many navvies who were employed on the Churnet Valley Line, or in making the branch to the wharf, were in lodgings in Uttoxeter, which was not the case in 1861, and about four or five years ago a many children were carried off by diptheria; and then during the

Q

ten years many persons have left their native place
to enlist their energies in the more promising hives
of industry, places which have been found to have
swelled by such accretions during the same space of
time to an enormous extent.   It may even be added
that the great improvements in the town, extending
to localities which at one time were deemed almost
repulsive, have excluded a great number to whom
any thing like respectability, decency, and daylight
do not promise much for their avocations.

Although diptheria is mentioned as having visited
Uttoxeter in common with other places, yet the town
appears to have had an immunity from most other
epidemics, which, when they happen any where,
often decimate the population.   Indeed, Uttoxeter
is noted for its great salubrity.   When in 1646 the
plague was blighting to an alarming extent several
of the towns about—as Lichfield, Stafford, and
Ashbourne, as well as the adjoining place, Clifton—
Uttoxeter appears to have escaped ; and, although
so much oppressed by the exactions occasioned by
the Civil Wars, was in a position to afford relief in
sums of money to each place,   To Ashbourne it sent
a contribution of £3, to Clifton, 5s., and to Lichfield
the sum of £2, 9s., with a further sum of £2 to
Stafford, all collected in the town, with the exception of 6s. 8d. given from the parish rates.

It is asserted, however, in the Staffordshire Direc-
tory, that the plague did visit the town ; but there is
nothing in the constable's accounts to bear it out.
A stray soldier or two pestered with it got into the

town, and it must have been respecting them that warrants were taken out. That it was confined to these men is the more probable from the determination to isolate them from the inhabitants, by placing them in cabins which were erected for the purpose at, doubtless, the outside of the town. All this precaution proves how great an alarm was produced from its dreadful nature; but as there is no further mention of it, it is almost certain that the inhabitants happily escaped.

It is, also, owing to its healthy situation that Uttoxeter has obtained a distinction for the great age which many of its inhabitants have attained. Dr. Symon Degge, son of Sir Symon, was the first person to notice this circumstance specially in a letter preserved in Sir Symon Degge's copy of Dr. Plott's "Natural History, of Staffordshire," at Cambridge. The letter is dated August 27th, 1726, and he says, "In the three weeks I have been at Uttoxeter there have been buried four men and two women, one woman aged ninety-four, the other eighty-three; one man eighty-one, another eighty-seven, another eighty-two, and one young man sixty-eight. Yesterday I talked with a man of ninety who has all his senses, and walks without a staff. About a month since he had a fever; he was speechless two days. His daughter is sixty, and about six month's since he buried his wife, who had lived sixty-three years with him, and was aged eighty-five years. In this town are now three men, and their wives, who have had fifty-three children, and each hath the children now alive. They

are all young men, the oldest being above sixty. . . .
I will only tell you, that in 1702 there died three
women, their years as follows:—one, one hundred
and three; second, one hundred and twenty-six; and
the third eighty-seven." Jno. Archbold, Gent., died
at the age of one hundred and three, in 1619, as
already seen by his epitaph.

Sir Symon Degge, himself was a remarkable instance of longevity, he having lived to the age of
ninety-two years. With respect to his family on the
subject of long life, he states in a note to his copy of
Dr. Plott, page 313, sec. 8—" I had seven brothers
and sisters, besides myself, all living together not
long since, and the youngest sixty years of age.[1]

Similar observations might have applied to inhabitants of Uttoxeter many times since, and the following instances, of a recent date, have an interest not
much less. Mary Blood, a native of Spath, and said
to have been the last person baptized at Crakemarsh Church, died a few years since at Uttoxeter,
at the age of one hundred and six. In 1814 Samuel
Bell died at the age of eighty-six. John Hill at the
age of ninety, and Catherine, his wife, in the same
month in her eighty-sixth year, and as previously
noticed, there is a tombstone in the churchyard to a
Mary Powell, who died at the age of one hundred
and thirty two, on the 1st January, 1812. William
Adin's mother died a few years since, at the age of
ninety-seven; and Mary Hodgkinson, in Tinker's

---

(1) I am much indebted for these extracts to the Rev. F. Martin,
Burser of Trinity College, Cambridge.

Lane, quite recently, at the age of ninety-five. Mr. John Ault died in 1861, June 4th, aged ninety-six, and to the last was quite active. On the 11th of the same month of June four persons died, whose united ages were three hundred and twenty-six years. Their names and distinct ages were Mary Machin, eighty-three; Joseph Twigg, eighty-seven; Mary Kynnersley, eighty-one; Ann Banks, 75. A tombstone in the churchyard informs us that Mr. John Crossley died at the age of one hundred years and eight months, on September 20th, 1836, and his wife at the age of eighty-five, in 1812. There are many persons living, quite active and hale at seventy-seven and eighty years of age, and some few who are upwards of ninety.

ANCIENT FAMILIES OF UTTOXETER,

AND

FAMILIES OF DISTINCTION.

THE family of Mynors is one of great distinction and antiquity in Uttoxeter. Their pedigree goes back to the time of King John, early in the twelfth century, the first of whom there is any account being Roger de Mynors, who had a son, Stephen, to whom and his heirs Robert de Ferrars granted lands at Barton-under-Needwood, and, by another charter, land lying near White Heath, for their homage and service with house-boot and hay-boot through the whole ward of Barton, and twenty hogs, quit of pannage. The land granted by the second charter was what was afterwards called Blackenhall, of which Sir John Mynors, Knight (son of John Mynors, Steward of Tutbury, tenth, Edward II., by Sybel his wife, daughter of Sir William Bagot), was Lord, sixth, Edward II., and by Cicely, his wife, daughter of Thomas Noel, of Newbold, county Leicester, left Thomas Mynors, lord of this manor, fourteenth, Richard II., and Robert Mynors, his second son, from whom those of Uttoxeter, the Woodlands, and other places, were descended. A grant was made to the Uttoxeter branch for the fishery of the Dove, from Dove Head to Dove Foot, and five miles up Bentley Brook. Captain Richard Mynors, to whom belonged Hollingbury Hall, flourished in the seventeenth century, and served with great bravery in the Dutch wars, and also against the rebels at Colchester. Several others were eminent and prosperous navigators, particularly William Mynors, son of Richard Mynors, Gent., of Hollingbury, near Uttoxeter, who safely returned eleven times from the East Indies about 1660. It has generally been asserted that the property of the family at Hollingbury Hall, which was on the High Wood, where a farmhouse stands on its site, near Toot Hill, had been wasted in the seventeenth century; but the enterprising character of its owners strongly contradicts it; and besides, in Mr. Lightfoot's Survey, finished in the middle of that century, it does not appear that any of it had been sold, and indeed it is now in the possession of their descendants; and although Erdeswick says there was in Uttoxeter a house of the Mynors, it has been supposed to refer to that on the High Wood. The property which was dispersed was that at Uttoxeter; and it is singular that this was not known by Mr. Samuel Bentley, who in the last century seems to have had no knowledge of there having been one of the family in the town, and mentions the wasted property as belonging to Hollingbury, in the " Gentleman's Magazine," in 1788. The extent of each estate is exhibited in the following survey, from Peter Lightfoot's MS.,

from which it will be observed that the homestead at
Uttoxeter, known, when standing, as Uttoxeter Hall,
the one in which King Charles I. was entertained,
was bought by Mr. James Wood, who resided at it
in 1642 :—

MESSUAGES AND LAND WHICH BELONGED TO WALTER
MYNORS, ESQ. :

	A.	R.	P.
One capital messuage or mansion-house at the north-east end of the town, with garden, orchard, and yard, and one close adjoining, called House Close	6	0	35
One close of meadow adjoining, called Amber Lands	6	2	15

These were bought by Mr. Wood.

	A.	R.	P.
One close of pasture, divided into two parts, called The Flatts	19	3	35

The nearer was sold to Mr. Dawson, and the further, divided into two parts, to Mr. Cotton.

	A.	R.	P.
One little piece of meadow adjoining ...	0	1	17
One close of meadow adjoining, called Mastall Meadow	5	1	25
One close of pasture adjoining, called The Mastall...	22	0	9
All those pastures adjoining to Strong-shall, and extending to the Heath, called The Great Parks	88	2	5

These were bought by Mr. Cotton.

	A.	R.	P.
One close of pasture in Bromshullfe Field	1	2	35
One close shooting north upon Stonyford	4	2	30

One tenement and four closes of pasture,   A. R. P.
adjoining to the High Wood, near
to the Jackmires, called the Oowlers,
or Owleys 31 2 0
Bought by Thomas Smith and Nicholas Mynors.
One close of pasture adjoining to the
Woodfield 14 0 0
Bought by Edward Ouldfield.
Two tenements, and certain closes near
Beresford Green, the closes in which
the houses stand 5 0 15
One close adjoining, called Little Meadow 2 0 5
One close adjoining, called Buddie Close 6 0 10
One close called Corn Close, and one
close called Newlands 23 1 10
The whole farm is conceived to be called Newlands.
One parcel of Land in Woodfield ... 1 2 20
One tenement and piece, called Mustard
Field by the Wood... ... .. 22 0 20
One close in Woodfield 1 2 0
One parcel of land lying in Netherwood 12 0 0
Bought by John Milward, Esq.
Three closes of pasture lying in Tynset
Park, called George's Park ... 39 1 0
Bought by Peter Lightfoot, sold to Manloves in 1634.
Two parks adjoining called Middle Park,
late Townsends 35 3 35
One close of pasture adjoining to the
Heath, in which there is a moat,
called The Little Park in Moat Close 7 2 30
Bought by Edward Villiers, Gent.
_____
Total of 357 3 2

TENEMENTS AND LAND WHICH BELONGED TO THOMAS
MYNORS, ESQ., OF HOLLINGBURY HALL:

Thomas Mynors, Gent., holdeth divers lands and
tenements, purchased of divers several persons, part
copy, part freehold, at the yearly rent of xxxs.
viijd., viz.,

	A.	R.	P.
One capital messuage adjoining to the High Wood Side, with the barns, stables, court, and yard, called Mynors of the Hill, or Hollingbury Hall, and the close called Kitchen Croft, one close called the Barn Yard, and one large close of pasture or meadow adjoining	13	2	20
One tenement on the east side of the wood, and three closes adjoining, in the tenure of Elliott, late of Basford	13	2	0
One close adjoining to Woodford Land called the Sevenacres	9	0	5
One close on the west side of the wood, called Dimble Close...	6	2	15
One tenement and certain lands adjoining to Blount's Green, called Green Fields	10	3	30
Three closes of pasture and meadow in Woodfield adjoining to Grisslesich	4	1	35
Nine lands lying open in the same field	1	3	1
One land in the same place	0	0	30
Four lands more in the same place ...	0	13	5
Part of one close in Woodfield... ...	0	ſ	25

One half-acre lying in Little Broad Meadow	0	2	0

In Bromshullfe Field.

One piece of land there	0	1	32
One other piece in the same furlong ...	0	2	25
One piece lying in Rycroft	0	3	35
One piece lying to Stoneyford	0	2	10

In the Botham Field.

One close adjoining to Blake Meadow ...	0	2	20
One land lying in a croft in Botham Field	1	0	0
One acre lying open there	0	3	10

His lands in Netherwood.

One half-acre adjoining to the Critcks ...	0	2	0
One acre more there	1	0	0
One rood there	0	1	0
One acre in Frambolt's Meadow ...	1	0	0
One small piece there in Netherwood ...	0	0	20
	70	0	8

The house or hall at the north-east side of Uttoxeter passed by purchase from the family of Wood to Mr. Copestake, jeweller, with the land adjoining, and subsequently to the late Thomas Hart, Esq., who destroyed the building, The present representative of the family is John Mynors, Esq., of Eaton Dovedale, a gentleman highly esteemed in the neigbhourhood, and owner of the Knypersley estate in the Woodlands. Hollingbury is still in the family of the Mynors, it being at present enjoyed by Mr. Edwin P. Mynors, mercer, of Uttoxeter.

A branch of the ancient family of the Floyers, of
Hants, Devon, formerly lived at Uttoxeter, one of
whom was Thomas Floyer, mercer, of Uttoxeter,
whose son Richard was lord of the manor of Weston-
in-the-Moorlands, and he purchased Uttoxeter Moor,
upon the sale of it, from the crown. Richard Floyer,
his grandson, married Elizabeth, daughter of Sir
Richard Weston, one of the barons of the exchequer.
Thomas Flier, who was slain in Uttoxeter, was of
the same family, as well as Richard Flier, Esq., mentioned in Lightfoot's " Survey," who possessed most
of the land called therein " Demesne Land," of
which there were 343a., 1r., 1p., besides most of
which a Richard Flyer, Esq., probably the same, had
30a., 1r., 26p. A Francis Flyer, Esq., was also owner
of about 4a., 1r., 27p. of land at the same period.
A representative of Robert Tixall, in the time of Edward III., was Richard Tixall, butcher, of Uttoxeter.
The heirs of Tixall had in the Manor of Uttoxeter,
11a., 2r., 3p. of land. Leese Hill became possessed
by the Tixalls, by the marriage of William Tixall
with a daughter of the Normans. Sir Walter
Raleigh was of an ancient Uttoxeter family, as was
Sir Symon Degge, as already stated. The family of
Hart was an old family in Uttoxeter, and John Hart,
Gentleman, temp., Charles I., had an estate of
285a., 3r., 36p. The male line is extinct in the late
Thomas Hart, Esq., whose only son died in his in-
fancy, and whose only daughter married the Hon.
Richard Cavendish, and is since deceased. The
family of Cauldering, also, were of Uttoxeter, owning

42a. of land; besides whom there were branches of the families of Norman, Manlove, Berisford, Bowyer, as well as other old and respectable families, as those of Bakewell, Warner, Ouldfield, and Woolridge, a name which goes centuries back, and gives name to Woolricheshay, and most of those benevolent persons who have left charities to Uttoxeter. Among these the heirs of Richard Middleton had about 113a., 2r., 36p. of land; John Shawcross, Esq., 53a., 22p.; Thomas Mastergent, 22a., 2r., 38p. Many or most of these names are extinct in Uttoxeter, and I presume the instances are but few in which direct descent can be traced from any one of these families, and still rarer in which the property has descended in hereditary succession.

THE MILWARD FAMILY.

In connection with the foregoing notices of old families of Uttoxeter, I have much pleasure in adding the following interesting details respecting the families of John Archbold, gent., of that town, and of Sir William Milward, epitaphs to both of whom, of the seventeenth century, as they appear in Uttoxeter Church, have been copied, and transferred to these pages. For the following particulars I am indebted to Mr. E. J. Milward Barnard, of Greenwich, who is a descendant from both of these worthies, and who has bestowed much time and trouble in collecting the arms, pedigrees, and other matters relating to his ancestors, and their various branches, from the "Heralds' Visitations," and from churches and private

sources. Sir William Milward married Catherine,
daughter of John Fleetwood, of Caldwich. He had
three sisters; the first of whom, Elizabeth, married
John Archbold, gent., of the Woodlands, Uttoxeter,
and also of London. His descendant, Colonel Henry
Archbold, was with Penn and Venables at the conquest of Jamaica, where he settled. By his wife,
who was the daughter of Colonel Byndloss, he had
many children, who are now represented by some of
the families possessed of property in the island. His
second sister married Thomas Chambers, and his
third married Walter Mynors. His father married
Margery, daughter of William Dethick, of Newhall.
His earliest recorded ancestor was Owen Mylward
(so spelt in the "Herald's Visitations"), who lived
in the year 1392. Of his subsequent ancestors,
one was married to Joane Pembridge, who was descended from an ancient Herefordshire family. Another was of the Kniveton family, of Kniveton,[1] near
Ashbourne. Another has married Felicia, who,
through her mother, represented the ancient families
of Daniel, Baguley, and Cheadle, and was daughter
and co-heiress of Sir John Savage, whose father had
married Catherine, daughter of Sir Thomas Stanley,
afterwards Lord Stanley, and who himself commanded the left wing at the battle of Bosworth, and

---

[1] ".Kniveton hath given both name and seat to the famous family
of Kniveton, of whom is St. Leo. Kniveton (an antiquary), to whose
study and diligence I am so much indebted."—CAMDEN.

The first recorded parliamentary representative for the county of
Derby was Henry de Kniveton, who served that office in the twenty
third parliament of Edward I.

was very instrumental, with Lord Stanley, his uncle, afterwards made Earl of Derby, in promoting Henry VII. to the throne.

Sir William Milward, above-mentioned, died in 1630; and his son, Sir Thomas Milward, of Eaton, the celebrated Chief-Justice of Chester, married Thomasine, co-heiress of Henry Berisford, of Alsop-in-the-Dale, county of Derby, her sister having married a member of the ancient family of Coke.

As family documents, which are much enquired after by compilers of local histories, are always of interest and importance, I am enabled to give two extracts from such which relate to freehold property in Balance Street, of which W. Condlyffe, Esq., of Leek, is the freeholder in a lineal descent, commencing with his great-grandfather, who was succeeded by his grandfather, and after passing through the two sons of the latter, John and Joseph Condlyffe, came to himself as the only surviving son of Joseph Condlyffe; and it is presumed that not any freeholder on a small scale will take a priority.

On the 20th of July, 1705, the present ancient house in Balance Street, Uttoxeter, now, and for many previous years, in the occupation of Mr. William Harvey, shopkeeper, was purchased for £35, the description of the premises in the title-deed being as follows, viz. :—

" All that messuage-house or tenement, situate, standing, and being in Uttoxeter aforesaid, in a certain street there, called Balance Street, adjoining to the land of Rowland Manlove, Gentleman,[1] on the west, to the land of James Snape, of Uttoxeter aforesaid, on the north, and the aforesaid street called Balance Street on the south.   All which said premises now or late were in the tenure, holding, possession, or occupation of Mastyn Green, and the ground whefeon the house stands was lately purchased by Richard Mottram, of Uttoxeter aforesaid, blacksmith, of and from William Green, of Uttoxeter aforesaid, brazier, but the house was built by the said Richard Mottram since his purchase of the said ground.[2]

By a subsequent purchase-deed, dated 16th June, 1731, from James Snape, yeoman, James Horobin, of Uttoxeter, shoemaker, and Thomas Bentley, blacksmith, of the first part, and the great-grand-father of Mr. Condlyffe, of the other part—

" All that piece, moiety, or parcel of ground consisting and being five yards and thirteen inches and half in length, & three yards & six inches in breadth, having the land of the said James Snape on the north, and to the said house on the south, & to ye house now in possession of James Snape, party to these presents, the east, & and to the house in the tenure, holding, or occupation of Daniel Wood on the west." The purchase-money was £3, 13s. 6d.

(1) Rowland Manlove, Gent., was living in 1658, and he had various closes of land, making 42a., which he held at the rent of xxijs.

(2) The land was probably left unoccupied till then, subsequent to the fire which destroyed all that portion of the town, for before the fire the land had houses upon it.

Among persons of distinction who had possessions in the manor of Uttoxeter but who did not live there are these two—Lord Cromwell had one croft adjoining to the parson's yard; and Sir Thomas Wolsey held freely two-third parts of the reputed manor of Little Bromshullfe, by the yearly rent of 8s.[1] Mr. Wood, purchaser of the property of Walter Mynors, Esq., was a gentleman of considerable wealth, for he also bought the whole of the glebe land, consisting of 34a. 25p., and 62a. 1r. 10p. of other land, belonging to the dean and canons of Windsor; but these he had to restore again. Rowland Cotton, Esq., of Crakemarsh Hall, also, anciently, had much property in Uttoxeter, both in messuages and land.[2]

The family of Lightfoot was one of great respectability, and had property in Uttoxeter, and more than one member of the family has risen to considerable eminence.

JOHN LIGHTFOOT, D.D., MASTER OF ST. CATHERINE'S COLLEGE, CAMBRIDGE,

Was the son of the Rev. Thomas Lightfoot, Vicar of Uttoxeter, in the county of Stafford, a man not to be named without a preface of honour and respect. He was born in a little village called Shelton, in the parish of Stoke-upon-Trent. He was a

(1) The land at the west side of Uttoxeter went by the name of Bromshullfe Field. The quantity of assert land (supposed) for which no rent was paid, was 158a. 2r. 35p.

(2) For much of this information I am indebted to "Lightfoot's Survey."

R

man of exemplary piety, and of indefatigable industry, and was one of the greatest examples of the
last age for his constant care of those souls which
were committed to his charge.   This he showed by
his constant preaching, and diligent instruction and
catechising of the youth of his parish, from which
his preaching did not excuse him.   He was a
burning and shining light, and showed his love to
his Great Lord and Master by the unwearied care
of his sheep.   He was in holy orders six-and-fifty
years, and thirty-six years vicar of Uttoxeter above-
named.   He died July 2nd, A.D. 1658, and in the
eighty-first year of his age.

The Rev. Thomas Lightfoot married Miss Elizabeth Bagnall, a gentlewoman of very good family in
Staffordshire, three of whose family were made
knights by Queen Elizabeth, for their martial prow-
ess and valour in the then wars in Ireland against
the rebels.   She was a woman of exemplary piety,
and died January 24th, A.D. 1636, at the age of
seventy-one years.

The inscription on the Rev. Thomas Lightfoot's
monument in Uttoxeter Church was written by his
son, Peter Lightfoot, the physician, as stated, and
furnished to Strype by the Rev. Michael Edge, then
Vicar of Uttoxeter, who printed it with the life of
Dr. Lightfoot, in the folio edition of his works.   The
monument still exists in Uttoxeter Church.   Strype
also adds, as a *curiosa*, an epitaph, which the same
Rev. Thomas Lighfoot had prepared for himself, and
which was found in his study after his decease.   This

I subjoin, to let the world see somewhat as well of the pious and heavenly breathing mind, as the scholarship of that man from whom our doctor was derived—

THOMAS LIGHTFOOT,

Olim superstes nunc defunctus alloquitor amicos
       suos, qui in vivis sunt.

En med tam multis puppis quassata procellis,
Nunc tendem, portum, practa quietis habet.
Nil scopulos ultra bibulas nil curat armas.
Istius aut mundi quæ mare monstro. parit,
Namque mare est mundus puppis vaga corcus
    obumbrat,
Atque animam signat navita quisque soam
Portum quem petimus calum est; sed ea aura
    salutis,
Quæ navem impellit, spiritus ille Dei est,
Solvite felices igitur portumque tenete
Post ærumnosi tuo bida demna maris.
Sed non ante datur portum contingere quam
Fracta per undosum vestra carina mare.

The Rev. Thomas Lightfoot had five sons—the eldest was Thomas, the only one of all his sons bred to a secular employment, being a tradesman at Uttoxeter, though his burial is not to be found there. The second, John, of whom we will say more below. The third, Peter, a very ingenious man, and practical physician in Uttoxeter; and besides his art he was of great usefulness in that county, and often in commissions for ending of differences. He had intended to write the life of his brother, Dr. John Lightfoot, but was prevented by death.   He was the compiler of the " Survey of Uttoxeter," which has been useful in writing this work ; and he also constructed a plan of the town.   He appears from the Survey to have been a person of property, and his place of residence was in Balance Street, about where the Black Swan Yard is, but it was burnt down by the fire of 1672.   He was also the author of a tract called " A Battle with a Wasp's Nest."   The next was Josiah, who succeeded his brother, Dr. Lightfoot, in the charge of his living of Ashby, though he was never inducted to the living, but acted as curate to his brother, who gave him the profits of the benefice ; and upon the doctor's death, in 1675, a son of this brother, also named Josiah, a graduate of the University of Cambridge, and Member of St. Catherine's College, was inducted to the living, that " the old man (as Strype adds) might enjoy it during his life, and his son after him."   But, alas ! for all human plans and forethought, both father and son died in the year 1683, and were buried at Ashby, that of the father on August 24th, and that of the son on the 17th of November following ; and descendants of the former were resident at Ashby till within this last few years.   The last of the family buried there was Mr. John Lightfoot, who died in 1847.   We are indebted for some particulars illustrating this notice to another member of the family, Mr. William Tomkinson Lightfoot.

The youngest son of the Rev. Thomas Lightfoot was Samuel, who was a Member of Christ's College,

Cambridge, and took the degree of B.A. in 1631, and M.A. in 1635, and entered into holy orders, but died young. His signature occurs in the Ashby register, as curate in the year 1632; but where else he exercised his ministry, and the place and date of his death, have not been ascertained.

The arms of the family are barry of six, *or* and *gules*, on a bend *argent* three escallops of the second.

Crest, a griffin's head erased, gorged about the neck with a collar charged with three escallops.

Evidences of these arms still exist in the seal of Dr. John Lightfoot, attached to letters of his to Dr. Edward Bernard, and preserved in the Bodleian Library, Oxford; on the portrait of the Doctor engraved by White, of which a fine impression is in the print-room of the British Museum; and on the seal of the Rev. John Duckfield, Rector of Aspeden, Herts, who married Joice, the eldest child of Dr. Lightfoot, attached to letters preserved in the manuscript department of the same museum.

Amongst the owners of the principal landed property at the present day are the Hon. Richard Cavendish, Thomas Bladon, Esq., W. J. Fox, Esq., Mr. Mynors, T. Spencer Stone, Esq., and others; and how great the number of respectable families is, the many handsome residences scattered through the town and its vicinity sufficiently prove. The ancient name of Kynnersley is omitted here because of the notice shortly to be given of Loxley.

ANCIENT CUSTOMS.

MAY-GARLANDS AND MAY-POLE; SACRED WELLS;
OMENS AND SUPERSTITIONS; SPORTS AND
PASTIMES; CIVIL USAGES.

ONE of the principal and most interesting of old customs still observed in Uttoxeter takes place on the 1st of May, and it is that of groups of children carrying garlands of flowers about the town. The garlands consist of two hoops, one passing through the other, which gives the appearance of four half-circles, and they are decorated with flowers and evergreens in much profusion, and surmounted with a bunch of flowers as a sort of crown, and in the centre of the hoops is a pendant orange and flowers. Mostly one or more of the children carry a little pole or stick, with a collection of flowers tied together at one end, and carried vertically, and the children themselves are adorned with ribbons and flowers in a profuse manner. Thus they go from house to house, which they are encouraged to do by the pence they obtain, and so, unsuspectingly, perpetuate a custom of the highest antiquity; for, like others, it is a relic of heathenism, the Druids observing the 1st of May in honour of the goddess Flora. Nearly a

hundred years back Mr. Bentley appears to have
been pleased with the observance, which, were he
living, would delight him as much as when he thus
commemorated it—

" How oft has thy rural parade,
　　So fam'd on the first of sweet May,
　With garlands bedecking each maid,
　　Delighted me through the long day.
　O May ! with thy beautiful train,
　　How joyous thy happy return ;
　But wishing thy stay is in vain,
　　And only thy swiftness we mourn."[1]

Another observance at Uttoxeter was the festivity
of the May-pole, to which a space, about where the
Wesleyan Chapel stands, was devoted some two hundred years back.　But interesting as the custom was
from its Celtic antiquity, the observance of it has
been discontinued in Uttoxeter a long time—

" No more the May-pole's verdant height around,
　　To valrous games the ambitions youths advance;
　To merry bells and taber's sprightly sound,
　　Wake the loud carol and the sportive dance."

There is much interest attached to several ancient
wells at Uttoxeter, one of which is Penny Croft
Well, in the Flatts, at the north-east of the town.
It has lately been turned into a common drinking-
place for cattle ;　but is recollected to have been kept
in neat order, when flowers, especially the Marsh-

(1) River Dove ; a Lyric Pastorale.

mallow, which appears early in the month of May, were strewn about it. This well was supposed to possess curative properties, for which purpose it used to be much resorted to, and it is probable it derived its name of Penny Croft Well from the pence the afflicted offered for the use of its healing virtues.[1]

Another of these wells was called Marian's Well[2] anciently,[3] but in more modern times Maiden's Well, or Maiden's *Wall* Well (*wall* having the same meaning as well), and is situated on the ascent to the High Wood, by the road side, nearly opposite to the public-house there, but it has since been taken into the field. The waters of this well have also been famous for their virtues in healing; and the grandfather of an aged female living in Uttoxeter wished in his dying moments to have a bottle of water from it to drink, on account of its remarkable properties; so that its fame remained great until less than a hundred years back, although, perhaps, not six persons' at this time, except by this notice, know any thing about it. But what is also remarkable about it is, that it was believed to be haunted by the ghost of a handsome young lady, on account of which people were much afraid of going past it at night—a superstition origi-

(1) See opinion in " Reliquary," 1860-1.

(2) Should Marian be a corruption of Mary this well would doubtless be a baptistry in early times, in connection with Uttoxeter Church, which is dedicated to St. Mary.

(3) Lightfoot's Survey.

nating, probably, in a former belief of the well having been inhabited by spirits, there being superstitious beliefs of this kind in Scotland at this day.

These, doubtless, were two of the Holy Wells of a remote age, and which were regarded sacred amongst the Britons; for of similar wells in Cornwall Borlaise says the Druids pretended to predict future events. On the subject of holy wells in Staffordshire, Dr. Plott has these interesting observations— "They have a custom in this country, which I observed on Holy Thursday at Breewood and Belebrook, of adorning their wells with bows and flowers. This, it seems, they do, too, at all gospel places, whether wells, trees, or hills, which being now only for decency's sake is innocent enough. Heretofore, too, it was usual to pay this respect to such wells as were eminent for curing distempers on the saint's day whose name they bore, diverting themselves with cakes and ale, and a little music and dancing. But whenever they begin to place sanctity in them—to bring alms and offerings, or make vows at them as the ancient Germans and Britons did, and the Saxons and English were too much inclined to, I do not find but they were forbid devotion in those times as well as now, this superstitious devotion being called wellworship, and was strictly prohibited by Anglican counsels as long ago as King Edgar, and in the reign of Canutas."

There is a striking identity betwixt the mode of adorning wells in this county, as described by Plott, and the manner in which the far-famed wells of Tis-

sington were decorated about eighty years ago. I
learn from a very old man that when he was a boy
green hawthorn was cut down in Dovedale, where,
from the warmth of the situation, verdure would be
the earliest, and was conveyed to the village and
stuck in the ground about the various wells, when
flowers were strewn over them and tied to them in
the form of garlands. This fact, I think, clearly
fixes the practice of the interesting custom in the
village before the introduction of any Christian cere-
monies, and probably proves that it has been continued there almost uninterruptedly from British and
heathen times. [1]

Somewhere near the Dove a well was formerly
known as St. Cuthbert's Well—the saint to whom
Doveridge Church is dedicated—and was probably
the well of an ancient baptistry, in connection with
the church. [2] I believe it existed near the ravine on
the hill side overlooking the Dove, and, therefore,
a little north both of Doveridge Church and the
Hall. The ravine marks the course of the old road.

Amongst omens in which many persons at Uttoxeter place credence, and which it is perhaps difficult

[1] I am fortunate in being enabled to present here two views showing the manner in which the wells at Tissington are decorated at the
present day, by the use of two engravings kindly lent by Mr. Jewitt,
F.S.A.

[2] " The general subject of holy wells and springs, and the legends,
superstitions, divinations, and customs connected with them, is worthy of extended investigation, and the collecting together of notes
and illustrations by this means will be doing good service to archæ-
ology." Mr. Jewitt, in the " Reliquary," 1862.

TISSINGTON WELL DRESSING.—THE HALL WELL.

TISSINGTON WELL DRESSING.—THE TOWN WELL.

for educated people to shake off, are the chirpings of
the cricket, the creaking of furniture, the howling of
dogs, and the falling of the weights of the clock,
which have been so strictly observed by some that
they declare that when they have happened a death
in the family has invariably taken place.

It is also believed that if people will bow nine
times to the new moon they will have a present; and
the moon is likewise an object of superstition in de-
terring people from killing pigs when the change
takes place. Bad luck, it is also particularly declared,
will follow those who marry or make any fresh undertaking on a Friday. Witchcraft has been no less
popular, and from a pool somewhere not far from
Dove Bridge having some two hundred years past
been called in ancient writings " Witches Pool," it
is likely this was a place where unfortunate witches
have been drowned when the practice of witchcraft
was punished with death.

The formerly dense woods in the neighbourhood of
Uttoxeter appear, generations back, to have been
peopled by frightfully imaginative beings, as fiends;
and hence there was a *Hob* or Fiend Hurst, and
a Hob Lane, hob meaning fiend. There is, also, still
in existence a Gendall's Wood, which has most likely
a similar import; for Gendell is probably a name derived from Grendall, which is a myth of Scandinavian
and German mythology or superstition, and bears
in meaning, according to Dr. Latham, in his " Eth-
nology of the British Isles," an analogy to our devil.
If this is so, such an identity of early superstition
is interesting.

Some civil and feudal customs have been already incidently described—some interesting occcurences as having taken place at the pillory—an instrument of Saxon origin—the last person placed in which was a blind man, for nearly killing his wife with a large stone ; and it is remembered that the town was in a state of excitement through it during the day. It is in tradition that a man was once hung at the pillory. It is not improbable it was the man who slew John Scott in Uttoxeter, at the time of the Civil War. As stated, the stocks and cuck-stool—for re-repairing which in 1667 Anthony Blake was paid 10s. 6d.—were connected with the pillory. The gibbet, which was claimed very early for Uttoxeter was, by tradition, situated on the High Wood, at the Four Lane Ends. Persons, who in despair have committed suicide, have had the barbarous custom perpetrated upon their bodies of being buried at the Four Lane Ends, at Kiddlestitch, and in Timber Lane, with stakes driven through them.

Bull-baiting was a particularly favourite sport in Uttoxeter, in former times, but it was suppressed through the exertions of a number of gentlemen about forty years back. The scene of the sport was in the Market-place, the ring being a few yards south-east of the conduit. The game of foot-ball used to be an exciting play here also, but, without any interference of authority, it is almost entirely disregarded. But trap and ball—a game which can be traced back to the fourteenth century[1]—is in

(1) Strutt's " Sports and Pastimes."

much repute amongst the working-classes, and appears to have been so time out of mind. Nine pins, and bowling on the green, are still more in fashion, to the comparitive neglect of the more manly game of cricket.

In theatrical amusements the town of Uttoxeter was well cared and catered for till the beginning of this century; for during the theatrical season it supported one and two theatres—one at the Black Swan Inn, and another at the Red Lion Room. Stanton's company catered for the admirers of the drama in Uttoxeter for many years, and were well patronised by all classes in the neighbourhood. Mr. Samuel Bentley wrote several prologues for them in 1767. One of these was recited by Master S. Stanton, when a benefit was being given for the children of the company. Another of these compositions was spoken by Miss Stanton in 1770, when the Right Hon. Sir Henry Cavendish, Bart., the Right Hon. Lord and Lady Vernon, and many other persons of distinction, were present. But to a late period Mr. Bentley favoured the Stanton company with effusions of this class, and to the last was one of their patrons and friends.

It was at Uttoxeter, with this company, that Miss Harriett Mellon first made her débût on the stage. At the time she stayed at a house in Church Street, occupied by the friends of the late Mrs. Baxter, who recollected carrying her luggage to the room of the Red Lion Inn, where the performances took place. She remembered this her first appearance very well,

and spoke of her as not less amiable and kind in
disposition, than handsome in her appearance.   But
the celebrity of this lady is, perhaps, more especially
due to her becoming the wife of Thomas Coutts,
Esq., the wealthy banker, and afterwards, on the
death of Mr. Coutts, being married to the Duke of
St. Albans.   Mr. Coutts had been previously married, but lost his wife, by whom he had three daughters, all of whom were married to noblemen of the
highest rank.   Mr. Coutts was a munificent patron
of the meritorious actors of his day, and it is supposed his intimacy with Miss Mellon originated from
this circumstance.   She proved to him the greatest
blessing, and made him the happiest of men.   His
immense wealth was left to her.   At her death, however, at which time she was a duchess, she, having
no children of her own, bequeathed her riches to
Miss Angela Georgiana Burdett, daughter of Sir
Francis Burdett, who had married Sophia, third
daughter of Mr. Coutts, by his first wife, accompanying the inheritance with the condition that she should
assume the name and arms of Coutts.   This lady is
Miss Burdett Coutts, whose munificence in doing
good is so well known.[1]

Edward Knight, the comedian, also took part with
a company at Uttoxeter.   He was born in Birmingham, and was brought up as an artist, but made
choice of the stage as a profession.   At Uttoxeter
he appeared in " Arno Silvester Daggerwood," and

(1) " Gentlemen's Magazine," 1822, and " Men of the Time."

" Signo." Some of his personifications have been instanced as the most chaste and truly natural on the British stage. One day, at Uttoxeter, Mr. Knight received a note requesting his attendance at the inn adjoining the theatre, and intimating that he would receive information which would be of advantage to him. On hastening to the inn he found a gentleman of the name of Phillips, who recommended him to apply in his name to Mr. Tate Wilkinson, manager of the York theatre, who was a person of very eccentric character. Mr. Knight immediately wrote a polite note, in the name of Mr. Philips, to Mr. Wilkinson, and in a very short time he received a very laconic epistle, which utterly extinguished his glittering expectations. The note runs as follows :—

" Sir,—I am not acquainted with any Mr. Phillips, except a rigid Quaker, and he is the last person in the world to recommend a person to my theatre. I don't want you.

TATE WILKINSON."

Recovering from this uncivil and mortifying repulse, he wrote, in the bitterness of his anguish, a second letter to the manager, which is as follows :—

" Sir,—I should as soon think of applying to a Methodist preacher to preach for my benefit, as to a Quaker to commend me to Mr. Wilkinson. I don't want to come.

E. KNIGHT."

This letter was too much in Mr. Wilkinson's own peculiar style to meet with an unfavourable reception, but nothing resulted from it at the time. At the end of the year, however, during which time Mr. Knight remained with the Stafford Company, he was agreeably surprised with a second letter from his former correspondent. In brevity and elegance it was no wise inferior to his former epistle, but the matter of it sounded more sweetly to his ears. The following is a transcript of it:—

" Mr. Methodist Parson,—I have that produces 25s. a week. Will you hold forth?

TATE WILKINSON."

Mr. Knight, thus engaged, continued to perform at York, Leeds, and other places, and was afterwards promoted to Drury Lane, and to the Lyceum ; so that what was played upon Mr. Knight as a jest at Uttoxeter, ended in his permanent benefit. He died in 1826.[1]

(1) The " Mirror."

MARKET, TOLLS, FAIRS, AND TRADE OF
UTTOXETER.

IT does not appear at what time markets were first granted to Uttoxeter. It is evident, however, that one was held at this town by Robert de Ferrars, and it was subsequently confirmed, first to Edmund, Earl Lancaster, 21st Edward I., 1292, and afterwards to Thomas, Earl of Lancaster, in the 2nd of Edward II. Before that time markets were held chiefly on Sundays and holidays, for the convenience of dealers and customers brought together for hearing Divine service; and perhaps this may be one reason why groups of people are seen congregating in numbers in many churchyards at the present day before service commences. Uttoxeter market has long been noted as one of the best in the kingdom, and it is mentioned as such in the Harleian manuscripts. Before cheese fairs were established, cheese, as well as butter, used to be one of the commodities with which it was supplied.

Uttoxeter market has always been, and still is, particularly depended upon for its supply of butter, which has been done up at different periods in various ways, to suit the taste and convenience of both

s

the manufacturer and the buyer. It is at present
chiefly turned out of hand either in the shape of rolls,
and, consequently, called "'rolled butter," or from
round butter prints, with pleasing figures cut upon
them, such as of a cow, a domestic fowl, a wheat
sheaf, a heart, a cluster of acorns, nuts, or flowers,
with suitable borders round the edge. Some years
ago the prints were nearly eliptical in shape, with
lozenge-shaped designs cut in. Very different was
the mode of getting up the butter for the market
two hundred years back in this neighbourhood, at
which remote period it was sold in " butter pots,"

which were coarse, cylindrical, unglazed vessels, the
making of which then formed a considerable branch

of the pottery trade in Staffordshire. An account of these curious vessels, as manufactured for Uttoxeter Market, and some legal restrictions respecting them, is given in Dr. Plott's " Natural History of Staffordshire :"—" The butter they buy by the pot of a long cylindrical form, made at Burslem, in this county, of a certain size, so as not to weigh above six pounds at most, and yet to contain at least fourteen pounds of butter, according to an Act of Parliament fourteen or sixteen years ago (about A.D. 1661, 13 and 14, Charles II., cap. 26), for regulating the abuse of this trade in the making of the pots, and false packing of the butter, which before was good for a little depth at the top, and bad at the bottom ; and sometimes set in rolls, only touching at the top, and standing hollow below at a great distance from the sides of the pot. To prevent these little moorlandish cheats (than whom no people are esteemed more subtle), the factors keep a surveyor all the summer here, who if he have any ground to suspect any of the pots tries them with an instrument of iron made like a cheese-taster."

The use of the butter pots was continued to about seventy or eighty years ago. The observations of Dr. Plott are accompanied by the remark, that the London cheesemongers, who had set up a factory at Uttoxeter, laid out on a market day as much as £500 in cheese and butter alone.

Butter pots, however, are mentioned in the parochial records of the town forty years before Dr. Plott wrote ; for five pots of butter were sent from Uttoxe-

ter to the garrison of Tutbury Castle, on the 7th
of May, 1644, and had been bought at the sum
of 12s. As this was seventeen years before the
Act of Parliament for the regulation of the sale
of butter in pots, it is difficult from this to judge
of the exact price of butter per pound at Uttoxeter at that remote period. And yet it may be
reasonably inferred that the pots of 1644 were of the
size of those manufactured after 1661 ; for it appears
the act was passed more for the prevention of any
irregularity in the size of the pots, and the mode of
packing butter in them, than for any actual altera-
tion of the size the pots were understood to be. If
so, butter then at Uttoxeter was worth but about
twopence a pound, supposing the five pots of butter
sent to Tutbury, costing 12s., contained fourteen
pounds of butter each. About fifty years before butter was retailed throughout the kingdom at seven-
pence per pound ;[1] but this was regarded an enormous price, which, Stowe says, " was a judgment for
their sins." It is highly probable, therefore, that
the pots contained fourteen pounds of butter, which
consequently was twopence per pound at Uttoxeter,
when the five pots were bought, especially as it cor-
responds with the price of cheese at that time in the
town, as to which the old parochial accounts have
preserved very distinct information, the sum of
£7 15s. 10d. having been paid for 8cwt. 2qrs. 7lbs.,
which was also for the beseiged at Tutbury. Six

(1) Chronicum Preciosum, by Bishop Fleetwood.

chickens about the same time cost two shillings, or fourpence each, for Lord Goring when at Uttoxeter.

At this distant period the tolls, fairs, and markets, with the borough court, were held by the heirs of John Gorenge, at the yearly rent of £4 13s. 4d. [1]

Corn, instead of being offered in samples, as now is the case, was, like cheese, brought in quantities in bags and offered to buyers, and for the quantity bought a certain measure was taken in toll. Corn thus taken, when the tolls were taken by the lord of the manor, was stored in a room called the granary, over, or in connection with, the courthouse, and it was reached by a flight of steps at the outside of the building; and, whether correct or not, it is stated that it was ultimately ground to flour—such as was wheat—and sold to the poor at a very low price. Against this house a market bell used to be rung at ten o'clock by the collector of the tolls, to prevent chapmen forestalling or buying marketable articles before the town was supplied.

Cheese was discontinued being brought to the market for sale in the year 1818, when in the month of March a meeting was convened, consisting of some of the principal gentlemen and agriculturists in the neighbourhood, with the late Lord Waterpark in the chair, to petition Lord Talbot, who held the manorial rights, to allow three cheese fairs to take place at Uttoxeter during the year, and to be toll pickage free. [2] The request as to the fairs was granted,

(1) Lightfoot's Survey.

(2) See the " Staffordshire Advertiser" for the time.

although it does not appear that a legal charter was obtained for them from the crown (in which case, I presume, like markets established without charter, they cannot be legal, the parties setting them up being liable to be called upon to show by what warrant such a right is exercised), for in the same month of March the first cheese fair ever held in Uttoxeter took place, and proved successful.[1] There being no documents accessible to the public containing any further information relating to the origin of the cheese-fairs, except the one from which these particulars have been derived, nothing further can be said about them, except what has transpired in the course of the litigation about the tolls. Till then, however, the proprietors or lessees of the tolls did not enforce the payment of toll upon cheese, pitched in the fair, upon parishioners, but only upon parties living without the boundaries of the parish. Of the origin and result of the lawsuit it will not be unimportant to give such a *resumé* as reports occurring at the time will enable me to furnish.

The dispute about the tolls originated in 1857, in the case of Moss *v.* Buckley, which was heard before the late R. G. Temple, Esq., Judge of the County Court, on Saturday, January 24th of that year. The defendant, as lessee of the tolls, had seized a basket of apples, which the plaintiff alleged he was carrying through the Market Place on a market day, owing to a refusal to pay the demand of a penny for

---

(1) " Staffordshire Advertiser," 1818.

alleged toll. The money, however, was ultimately paid, and the apples restored to the owner, and the action was brought to recover the penny, with damages, or more correctly speaking, to test the legality of the claim. Judgment with costs was given for the plaintiff, on the evidence that the goods were not exposed in the Market Place for sale, but were merely being taken through to a person who had bought them, and that therefore the distress was illegal.

The case caused considerable excitement, and led to the insertion of a letter in one of the local papers[1] of March 11th, not likely to allay it. It called in question the validity, either by charter or act of parliament, of the right of any toll on cheese set down in the Market Place for sale on the cheese fair days, and urging resistance to the demand for toll until it was proved that the claim was lawful.

The proprietors, however, remained firm in their demand, and issued placards announcing that the demand for toll for cheese would be strictly enforced at the fair on September 2nd, 1857, and although there was much opposition, the requisition was generally complied with. But at the fair on November 12th of the same year many farmers refused to pay, and the names of several were taken, with the view of suing them, and amongst them that of Mr. Deoville, of Thorney Lanes, who took the position of defendant, though with the prospect of being sup-

(1) " The Era."

ported by his brother farmers in the case an action against them for refusal was brought. Subsequently several letters appeared in the same paper, professedly to produce an amicable arrangement betwixt the opposite parties, followed by one on the 9th of December, 1857, from a person who contended that the document upon which the proprietors of the Town Hall and tolls rested their claim for toll was a feudal law of the time of John of Gaunt. The result was a public meeting at the Red Lion Room, on January 13th, 1858, to discuss measures by which the vexed question of cheese-toll might be settled. Although this meeting did not terminate in any decisive issue, the parties concerned shortly afterwards arranged to have the question brought to arbitration. For this purpose an eminent legal gentleman, C. H. Scotland, Esq., was mutually fixed upon by the parties, and he attended at the Town Hall, Uttoxeter, on the 20th of May, 1858, and the day after, when the plaintiffs were represented by Mr. Crompton Hatton, and the defendants by Mr. Grey, of the Northern Circuit. The plaintiffs rested their claim on the ground that the soil and freehold of the Market Place where the cart of the defendant stood belonged to them, and Mr. Fradgely, architect, and Mr. E. S. Bagshaw were examined, as witnesses to repairs, cleaning, and the erection of the weighing machine in the Market Place by the plaintiffs. The plea put in for the defence rested upon two points— first, that although the Market Place belonged to the plaintiffs, the defendant exercised only right of road

as one of the Queen's subjects ; and second, that the
Market Place belonged to the lords of the manor,
for that by the court rolls, the lords of the manor
amerced a person for breaking up the soil of Bear
Hill, part of which is in the Market Place, and a
number of witnesses were called to depose to having never paid any toll.

No award was immediately given on this evidence,
for several meetings were subsequently held in London, at which translations of documents of great
antiquity were produced on the part of the defendant
affecting the question, the principal point in dispute
at which being, " whether or not the freehold and
soil of the Market Place belonged to the plaintiffs,"
as already stated, and which they contended did, and
were, consequently, entitled to the cheese-toll in
question. The defendant strenuously disputed the
ownership of the soil, and contended that the soil
of the Market Place and the tolls were distinct,
although it was admitted that the plaintiffs were the
owners of the tolls, which they were empowered by
their charter to levy on certain days, but not on articles not included in their charter, and on days never
mentioned in it, and at fairs established subsequently
to their charter, the tolls at which had always been
disputed. The award was at length made, and it
decided that no toll was payable by the defendant
in respect of cheese exposed for sale at a fair held
in the Market Place, not on a Wednesday, and
that the Market Place was not the property of the
plaintiff.

Notwithstanding this decision, a demand for toll was made at the cheese fair on November 11th, 1858, and complied with, except in a very few cases.

The Market Place, from that year till 1861, remained unrepaired and uncleaned, when a complaint was made against the proprietors of the market tolls for non-repair. Mr. Dunnett, on their behalf, at the Petty Sessions of June 12, stated that when the case first came before the magistrates, the defendants considered, from the nature of their tenure of the Market Place, that they were not liable to repair it, but that the subject had been carefully looked into, and they then admitted their liability. At the same time he repudiated the alleged wilful neglect, and complained that the greatest fault rested with the proprietors of the different houses in the Market Place, for breaking up the surface for the repairing of drains and not properly replacing the materials.

Besides the fortnightly cattle market on every alternate Wednesday, Uttoxeter has cattle fairs on May 6th, September 19th, November 11th and 27th; colt fairs, September 1st and 19th; cheese fairs, March 12th, September 3rd, and November 12th.

For many years Uttoxeter had an annual show of fat cattle. The last was held in a field in Short Lane, December 12th, 1855, and was one of the most successful of any that had taken place. At the annual dinner the chair was taken by H. Meynell Ingram, Esq.

The North Staffordshire Agricultural Meeting was held, for the first time, at Uttoxeter, in September 1857. The trial of implements was made on land on the High Wood, in the occupation of Mr. James Bakewell, of the Moorhouse Farm. In every respect, although the day turned out exceedingly wet, the meeting, both as to the things living and manufactured, and the attendance was the best of any up to that time. It is intended again to be held at Uttoxeter in the present year, 1864.

The trade of Uttoxeter is principally of a local description, like that of most other market towns situated in the centres of agricultural communities. In this respect it has, however, somewhat improved of late, but not in a way to add materially to the prosperity of the town. The Uttoxeter Brewery Company has extended its operations, as well as the Messrs. Cope, leather and glue manufacturers; and an iron foundry has been commenced on a moderate scale, by Mr. Bewley, at Brook House. Cork manufacturing is also extensively carried on in the town.

Uttoxeter, however, has had its manufactures, and one branch has gained for it a remarkable notoriety, not only as to its ancient existence in the town, but as being in extensive practice at the present day. How frequently it is seriously asserted in books of reference, that Uttoxeter is " surrounded by iron forges !" which is enough to give a stranger an idea that it is one of the busiest places in the kingdom. Still if the stereotyped remark does not hold true as to the present, it does, to some extent, as to the past; for in the fourteenth century it had two iron forges, and besides the manufacture of iron from its raw state, it is probable it was also a great centre for the conversion of it into articles and implements of use for the honour of Tutbury generally, trade being very wisely equalised in those feudal times amongst the several towns of the honour, for their reciprocal benefit. In fact, it was the only staple trade of the town, and most likely the people for the greater part got their livelihood either at the forges for making iron, in the making of implements, or by the merchandise of the same, many persons probably being severally engaged in each.

Fortunately the place where these forges stood when in operation five hundred years ago is ascertainable, and it will not be uninteresting to my readers if I now point out the site. It is certain they must be sought for by the side of a stream of water, and if refuse of such places can be discovered in the vicinity of some stream near the town, it may justly be concluded that it was there the forges existed. Various mechanical contrivances are now employed, independent of a running stream, to produce the blast necessary to smelt the iron, but in those days the only motive power for the purpose was that of a fall or current of water. The Hockley Brook is the only stream close to Uttoxeter, and it is by this, at the bottom of Pinfold Lane, at the north-west side of the bridge over this brook that the refuse of a forge, or of forges, has been found. In the course of making foundations for buildings, tan-pits, and holes for gate-posts, on their premises here, Messrs. Cope have found quantities of this refuse (a large piece of which, bróught to me by Mr. William Cope, I preserve), which leaves no doubt that the forges existed at that spot.[1] The meadow betwixt Messrs. Copes' and the Hockley Road was, doubtless, wholly occupied by these iron works, for many years ago it was covered by hillocks, ; and when the ground was levelled and drained, about fifty years since, much refuse of iron works was observed : and, what may be geologically interesting, a number of owler trees were found at a considerable depth, as submerged when the land might be a bog.

Betwixt two and three hundred years ago there was a trade at Uttoxeter in fulling cloth, but whether this was of as high antiquity in the town as the bleaching established at Newborough, and woolcombing at Tutbury at the time the iron-works were established at Uttoxeter, there are no means of showing, unless the non-mention of it in the documents in the office of the Duchy of Lancaster may be considered decisive against it. However, a fulling-mill existed in connection with this town more than two hundred years back, and it was at the

---

(1) It was by the side of the Hockley Brook that the ancient corn-mill for Uttoxeter stood, but much (higher up the brook, and above the Hockley fishpond, for the remains of one were found when the railway was made past there. There is a piece of land there called " Pool Meadow Shutt," and this probably was the fishery of the Pool of Uttoxhather, and the mill wheel was probably turned by the water falling from it.

Tean Brook, a little higher up than the " Old Mill House," which now stands close to the foot-road going to Crakemarsh. It was in the occupation of Sir Thomas Milward, but was subsequently converted into a corn-mill, when it was held, with some land there, by the heirs of Sir Thomas Milward, and Walter Mynors, Esq., at the yearly rent of £14 6s. 7d.[1] A very ancient mill, independent of another to be mentioned, stood at the brook, a little below the bridge, on the turnpike road for Spath, within the memory of some old people ; and almost any one recollects some cottages standing there till within the last eighteen years, so that probably it was the ancient mill used for fulling previous to being employed as a corn-mill.

At a more recent period, indeed at the last and at the commencement of the present century, the jewellery trade was carried on to a great extent in Uttoxeter ; and it occasionally happens that the wonderful business, the extensive range of shops, and other matters which appertained to them, are the subject of conversation among those whose reminescences reach so far back. The buildings comprising the jewellers' shops, which were of the half-timber class, and several stories high, occupied an extensive site opposite to Silver Street, with a large yard in front coming up to the road. Two brothers, of the name of Copestake, are recollected to have had this business. They did a considerable foreign trade, besides being

(1) Lightfoot's Survey.

under the patronage of the British Government, for whom they executed many important contracts, stars of honour of great value being amongst them. Altogether they employed about one hundred and forty men and eighty apprentices. The lapidaries, who were also numerous, did the polishing of stones at their own houses in various parts of the town ; and there still lives an old man in Uttoxeter who served his apprenticeship with them to the lapidary business. It appears the trade left Uttoxeter about fifty years ago, in obedience to those changes, it is presumed, which are produced by competition, cheaper manufactures, and the application of mechanical contrivances, by which extensive manufactures are generally drawn to common centres.

Calico and linen weaving, as well as the jewellery trade, have been extensively carried on in Uttoxeter to within the last forty or fifty years at several "jenny shops," at which about eighty or one hundred hands found employment. One of these places occupied the whole of the north side of the triangular enclosure facing the New Grammar School, and another took up the whole space of the side of the yard and part of the garden of Mr. R. D. Barns, in Carter Street.

Then, about a half a century back too, there was a cotton mill over Tean Brook, where the " Old Mill House" stands ; and in those days Stramshall corn mill was also used as a cotton mill.

But of not much inferior importance was the lace trade, which was introduced by Miss Grace Cope-

stake, famous in " My Own Story," who lived at Uttoxeter Old Hall.   Here she employed many young
women of the town in embroidering lace, at which
they cleared a guinea a week.   She also let out
quantities to the towns and places about.   With
these branches of trade and manufactures giving
employment to so many persons, it is surprising that
Uttoxeter, which at the apparently less prosperous
time of the civil war furnished such large sums of
money for political purposes, was found to be so far
oppressed by poor's-rates in 1788 as to have the common enclosed, specially for the relief of the inhabitants burthened by them.

The business of bookselling has been mentioned as
introduced into Uttoxeter by Michael Johnson ; but
it was not until many years later that printing was
brought into it, the first printer being Mr. Richards,
who established a printing-office about eighty years
ago, he having previously been in the same trade at
Duffield.[1]   It is not to be expected that the Uttoxeter printers have turned out of the press many works
beyond such as have been of local import; and yet
it may not be without interest to collectors of local
literature, which is often illustrative of local history,
to enumerate some of. the pamphlets and books
which have come into existence through the medium
of the Uttoxeter printers.   Perhaps the earliest
specimens of printing done in Uttoxeter are the
copies of two pieces of poetry reprinted in connec-

(1) Father of Mr. Richards at the Post Office.

tion with this book—one on " Peace," and the other
on his " Birthday," by Mr. Bentley, the printer of
both probably being the late Mr. Richards. I have
also seen a poem on " Patriotism,"—the patriotism of
Sunday Schools,—a rather superior performance, also
from the press of Mr. Richards, and, if I recollect
rightly, from the pen of one of the Saddlers. Mr.
Richards also printed for a London house an edition
of " La Perous's Voyages," with plates, and an Arith-
metic, as well as a tale for a Mrs. Holebrook, of
Sandon, the name of which I cannot discover.
Amongst the books printed by Mr. Norris have
been three editions of Uttoxeter Church Hymn
Book, and an edition for Marchington Church. For
the Rev. Dr. Bevan, formerly of Leigh, he has
printed a Catechism, and a Scripture History; and a
collection of Letters and other pieces by persons in
humble life, edited by Mr. Blagg. These are the
productions of persons in the neighbourhood at the
time, and must be considered remarkable for those
they were written by. The " Christian Wreath of
Flowers," by the Rev. Mr. Armstrong, was also from
this press. It is a small collection of original poems,
of which two copies only were on large paper. Mr.
Norris has also printed a lecture on " Botany," and
another on the " Philosophy of History," by the late
Rev. T. P. Jones, of Alton. For Miss Robotham he
printed a poem on Alton Gardens, with some pleasing verses added. Recently he has published a sermon, on the death of the late respected Mr. Vernon,
founder of free Sunday Schools in Uttoxeter, by the

T

Rev. John Cooke; and still more lately, " Pictures of the Lowly," by Mr. G. Wakefield ; also lithographic views of Uttoxeter Church and Alton Towers. The late Mr. Kelly printed two " Statements," large pamphlets by Mr. Rushton, solicitor, which had respect to Alleyne's Grammar School. Mr. Kelly also printed an able sixpenny tractate, by Mr. Gould, at the time there was so much discussion betwixt the church parties, it having reference to the subject in dispute. Mr. Kelly started the first Uttoxeter newspaper in 1855, under the title of the " Uttoxeter New Era." It· is continued by his successor, Mr. Smart, its day of publication being Wednesday. Mr. F. Davis printed a funeral sermon on the death of Prince Albert, which was preached in Uttoxeter Church by the Rev. H. Abud, vicar.

The following Traders' Tokens of the seventeenth century were struck in Uttoxeter :—

Obverse—WILLIAM CARTWRIGHT, 1668=within the inner octagon, in a shield, the Mercers' Arms.

Reverse— IN VTTOXETER HIS HALF PENNY. A pair of scales between two flowers.

This is an octagonal token.

The Mercers' Arms are *gules* a Demi-virgin couped below the shoulders, *proper*, vested *or*, crowned with an Eastern crown, her hair dishevelled and wreathed about the temples with roses of the second, issuing from clouds, and all within an orle of the same, *proper*. The orle of clouds is frequently, as in this instance, omitted.

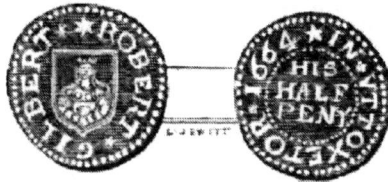

Obverse—ROBERT GILBERT=In the field, without an inner circle, the Mercers' Arms, in a shield.

Reverse—IN VTTOXETOR . 1664=In the field, HIS within the HALF inner circle, PENY.

Obverse—IOHN HALSEY . 1668=In the field without an inner octagon, the Mercers' Arms, in a shield.

Reverse—   * IN *
VTTOX   The lines divided by rows
* ETER *   of dots.
HIS HALF
PENY,

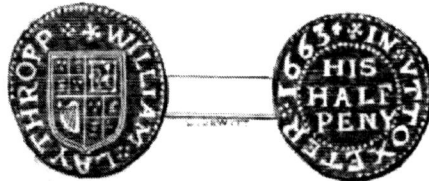

Obverse—WILLIAM LAYTHROPP=In the shield, the
Royal Arms. No
inner circle.
Reverse—IN VTTOXETER 1663=In the field, HIS
within the HALF
inner circle, PENY.

The issuer of this token was probably an inn-keeper, the royal arms being the sign of his hostlery, the " King's Arms."

Obverse—WILLIAM . LEESE . 1668=The Grocers' Arms.

Reverse—IN VTTOXETER HIS HALF PENY=In four
lines across the field.

This is an octagonal token.

The grocers' arms are *argent*, a cheveron *gules* between nine cloves, six in chief and three in base, *sable*.

Obverse—JAMES LOYED=

Reverse—VTTOXETER . HIS HALF PENY, 1660=

Obverse—IEFFERY POWER . OF=St. George and the Dragon.

Reverse—VTTOXETER . 1666=In the field, HIS within the HALF inner circle, PENY.

This was probably an innkeeper's token, the sign being the " George and Dragon."

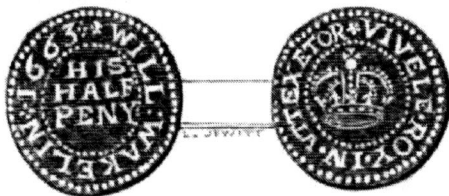

Obverse—WILL . WAKELIN . 1663=In the field, HIS within the HALF inner circle, PENY.

Reverse—VIVE . LE . ROY . IN . VTTEXETOR=In the field, within the inner circle, a crown.

Probably an innkeeper's token, the issuer keeping the " Crown."

LIBRARIES

AND

LITERARY INSTITUTIONS.

THE mention of books and printers almost naturally recalls to mind the name and times of Michael Johnson. Much as he plodded to Uttoxeter with books, there could have been only comparatively few readers in the town in his day, and no very extensive variety of books for the choice of those who did read. Fifty years ago books were very rare in Uttoxeter, but there was a circulating library established before 1824, and in 1830 Mr. John Bowers Smith opened a small one at the bottom of High Street. This worthy example was followed by Mr. Norris, in the establishment of a more extensive one, to which readers had recourse for many years. Perhaps, however, few readers are prepared to say what one of its most frequent visitors has asserted, that " he has read all the books in it, and some of them several times over." The Permanent Library at the room of Mr. Norris is supported by the respectable classes in Uttoxeter and neighbourhood, and consists of a valuable and extensive collection of modern books; and in connection with it is a supply of the high class monthly and quarterly journals and reviews. Recently a supply of books from Mudie's library has formed a valuable appendage to it. The terms are a guinea entrance fee, and an annual subscription of the same amount.

From the consideration of Circulating Libraries to that of Mechanics Institutes " is but a step." The first in Uttoxeter was formed about the year 1839, under the title of " The Uttoxeter Society for the Diffusion of Useful Knowledge and Mechanics Institute," and its meetings were held in the room over the stationary shop of Mr. Norris. The opening lecture, which was an able disquisition on " The Philosophy of History," was delivered by the late Rev. T. P. Jones, of Alton, and was printed in 1841, with a dedication to the late Robert Blurton, Esq., of Smallwood, both of whom were members of the local committee of the London Society for the Diffusion of Useful Knowledge. It had a small beginning, for its first catalogue of books, printed in 1844, did not number more than seventy-one distinct works; but great discretion was exercised in their selection, for at that time a better collection, for the extent to which it went, could not have been found for the purpose. Yet this society did not realize general public support, and in 1845 a rival one was commenced—the same which has borne the title of the Uttoxeter Literary and Scientific Institution, which has lately undergone a change, and now has the name of Mechanics' Literary Institution. The Society for the Diffusion of Useful Knowledge, if it was not over prosperous before, now became inactive, and its library was sold to the committee of the new undertaking for about £20.

The rooms of the new society were, in the first instance, in the Market Place, but as the number of members increased, a more commodious and convenient place became necessary, and the building in High Street, formerly a bank, but now the offices of Mr. Welley, solicitor, were rented, and used for several years for the library and reading-rooms. The institution has now rooms at the Town Hall, which it has occupied since its completion in 1853. At this time, or thereabouts, the society was in its height of success, and its treasurer had as much as £60 in hand, a great part of which was expended in buying furniture for the new rooms. It was declared by Dr. Hudson, in a work on Mechanics' Institutes, to be the most prosperous of any in the kingdom. Although it was declared so flourishing by this gentleman at the time he wrote, it could not have been so to the extent represented, from the amount of population; and even comparatively speaking—that is, by contrasting it with similar institutions in larger towns—it could not have carried the palm, judging of it on those principles of self-support which are the only criteria for measuring the innate vitality and relative superiority, in a financial sense only, of such societies. In thus looking at the institution at that period, it ought to be remembered that it received many handsome donations from some of its patrons, as from the late Joseph Mallaby, Esq., and support to an extent, and in a way, of which the public will not probably be made acquainted, from its then worthy president, Thomas Bladon, Esq. But of course, such external support could not always be expected. Once fairly started, its advantages and benefits, being so evident to the whole town, it ought, with proper management, to have held on its way, free from the burden of debt, to the benefit of the locality. This, however, was not the case, and when the novelty of the institution had somewhat subsided, in 1859 it was found to be seriously involved in debt, and the only question was whether it should be allowed to die a natural death, or whether some extraordinary effort should be made to retrieve something of its former prestige. Perhaps one of the causes of decline were the worse than profitless soirees and lectures, which invariably involved a serious outlay and loss. It was determined to try in that year an experiment, and a fete was fixed upon, and by permission of T. C. S. Kynnersley, Esq., was held in Loxley Park. The proceeds of this, with a public subscription, and the benefit of a soiree, given by ladies and gentlemen of the town, raised sufficient to meet the claims against the institute, and leave a surplus in hand, which, had a due regard been paid to the expenses of the fete, might have been very much larger. A fete was also held in 1860 at Doveredge, and, although the day was wet, preventing so large an attendance as at the one in the previous year, it produced a balance, after defraying expenses, of £14. Since that time another soiree and several expensive lectures have again tended to involve the institute in debt, which at Christmas, 1861, amounted to nearly £40, and presented an almost sure prospect of its final close. Phœnix-like, it has, however, after some modifications and a little kindly help, again risen into life; and surely the attraction of the newspapers supplied, and the library, which certainly will bear recruiting with fresh books (which it cannot be without the support of the town, at the very moderate rate of 5s. per annum, the amount paid for individual membership), ought to be sufficiently great, without any special pleading, and without naming any other motive, to induce a sufficient support to so useful an undertaking. But similar vicissitudes have been common to many other like institutions with the one at Uttoxeter.

Since its formation the Literary Institute has had for patrons—T. P. Heywood, Esq., the late J. Mallaby, Esq., and Lord Waterpark. Of presidents there have been these gentlemen—A. A. Flint, Esq., Thomas Bladon, Esq., W. J. Fox, Esq., G. Cooper, Esq., and the Rev. John Cooke has acted almost the whole of the time as vice-president. At the present time it has neither patron nor president.

The library of the Institute comprises about one thousand two hundred volumes. Many gifts of books have been made to it, especially by the late Joseph Bladon, Esq., of which, special mention may be made of a copy of the " Encyclopædia Britannica," " Pictorial History of England," and other very valuable works.[1]

The Town Hall, besides comprising rooms which were purposely included for the Literary Institute, also contains offices for the police department and savings' bank. It owes its existence to the enterprize of the proprietors of the tolls, which passed into their hands by purchase a little while before it was erected in 1853. The building stands in High Street, where it has a frontage of ninety feet four inches. It contains on the ground floor an entrance hall, twenty feet six inches, by sixteen feet two inches, approached under a stone portico; a lobby (separated from the entrance hall by a glass screen), twenty feet six inches by eighteen feet four inches, which leads into the large room, or hall, which is sixty-eight feet four inches long, thirty feet wide, and thirty-four feet high, for the use of the magistrates, public meetings, and lectures. A gallery runs round the two sides and south end; at the opposite end is an orchestra. On the same ground floor is also the great staircase to the upper rooms; also on it is the the savings' bank, the magistrates' consulting-room, reading-room for the subscribers to the Literary In-

---

(1) Since this was written the library belonging to Mr. Norris has been purchased by the proceeds of a fete at Sudbury, on the grounds of Lord Vernon, so that now the attractions to membership to the Institute are trebly increased. There is, also, now a reading-room at the Town Hall, separate from the Mechanics' reading-room, for One Guinea subscribers only. The Earl of Shrewsbury also permitted a fete to be held at Alton Gardens in the summer of 1863.

stitute, and the police offices. These are approached
by two doors, one on each side of the principal
entrance. The last-mentioned department is kept
totally distinct from the other portions of the building, and is entered by a passage at the side of the
hall. On the first floor, immediately on the landing,
is a large ante-room, from which the galleries round
the great hall are approached; the ladies' retiring-
room, thirty-five feet six inches, by sixteen feet; the
library belonging to the institution, twenty-three feet
by fourteen feet; the honorary members' reading-
room, twenty-nine feet six inches by seventeen feet;
the female singer's retiring-room; and the sitting-
room and three bed-rooms of the police department.
Under the ground-floor is cellaring, which is let to
the Brewery Company. There are also prisoners'
cells under the police department. The architect
was Mr. Fradgely, and the builder Mr. W. Evans,
of Ellastone. The cost of the building was between
£3000 and £4000.

The corner-stone of the Town Hall was laid by
Lord Waterpark on the 26th of August, 1853, the
trowel being presented to Lord Waterpark by Dr.
Taylor. After this the architect deposited a bottle,
containing the various current coins of Her Majesty's
reign, in an orifice cut for the purpose in the founda-
tion-stone, and the place was covered with a brass
plate, bearing the following inscription, with the
names of the proprietors:—" The corner-stone of
this Town Hall, erected by the following proprietors, was laid on the 25th day of August, 1853, in

the sixteenth year of the reign of Queen Victoria, by Henry Manners, Lord Waterpark."

The names of the proprietors are—Mary Sneyd Kynnersley, Anne Fox, Herbert Taylor, Joseph Mallaby, Thomas Rushton, John Vernon, and Thomas Bladon.

The Smithfield Market at the back of the Town Hall belongs to these proprietors, and was arranged at the time the Town Hall was built. It occupies 1a. 1r. 5p. of ground. The stalls and pens will contain eight hundred head of cattle, eight hundred and forty sheep, and two hundred and twenty-five pigs. The entrance for cattle is in Smithy Lane; for sheep and pigs in High Street. The disposition of the stalls and pens was made by the advice of Mr. John Etches, of Harley Thorn Farm, near Stone. The Smithfield cost about £1500.

The Town Hall was opened November 29th, 1854, under circumstances of a deeply interesting character. Then was progressing the ever-memorable Crimean war, which left so many widows and orphans of soldiers to the mercy of their country, and the opening was made the public occasion of an appeal on behalf of the patriotic fund. The hall was densely crowded. The chair was taken by Clement Thomas Sneyd Kynnersley, Esq. The object of the meeting was introduced by Herbert Taylor, Esq., M.D., which was the opening of the hall in connection with so patriotic a cause. Various resolutions were proposed by the late John Vernon, Esq., the Rev. Henry Abud, the late Joseph Bladon, Esq., the

late Joseph Mallaby, Esq., the Rev. Peter Holland,
Catholic priest; the Rev. John Cooke, Independent
minister; the Rev. William Parkinson, Wesleyan
minister; Thomas Bladon, Esq., Thomas Rushton,
Esq., A. A. Flint, Esq., and others. The amount collected in the town, with the proceeds of the opening
of the hall for the patriotic fund, was the sum of
£250. This was a large sum to raise in Uttoxeter
for such a purpose, considering that £100 had been
collected in the previous January, for the poor of the
town during the extremely severe weather.

PUBLIC SCHOOLS.

ALLEYNE'S GRAMMAR SCHOOL.

THIS school was founded May 24th, 1558, by Thomas Alleyne, Allyn, or Allen, priest and clerk, who founded and endowed it, and constituted the Masters, Fellows, and Scholars of Trinity College, Cambridge, trustees of his charity. The extent to which it was endowed was £13 6s. 8d. per annum; but in 1847 Trinity College, Cambridge, consented to raise it to £144 annually, with the advantage to the town of one free pupil. In 1855 documents were discovered which revealed the extent of the property of Mr. Allen, and it was conceived Uttoxeter had a right to a greater beneficial interest in it. An information was consequently laid against the college, and the cause, Attorney General *v.* Trinity College, Cambridge, was heard before the Master of the Rolls on January 29th and 30th, 1856. The prayer was, that the court would declare the Uttoxeter and other schools entitled to the increased income of the testator's estates, or to some share thereof, and that a proper scheme might be framed for the management of the property of the said charity, for the regulation of the Uttoxeter and other schools, and for the

management of the said charity generally. The
Master of the Rolls decided, February 7th, 1856,
that the college was entitled to the beneficial interest
in the surplus which had accrued in the case, and
added that a great deal might be said whether the
college was trustee of the schools, with trusts to be
properly performed, and if so, that the trust was to
form a free grammar school, not to be solely for
Church of England purposes, and that would be a
trust to maintain the school sufficiently, having regard to the neighbourhood and its wants. He also
thought that rules and regulations might be made
for the government of Uttoxeter school, and admission of scholars into it, which might extend the
benefit, and make it unnecessary to interfere.

The informants, however, were heard before the
Master of the Rolls, Sir William Romilly, on the
2nd of August, 1856, who dismissed the information.
The suit was not fruitless, though partially unsuccessful, for it was the means of securing a more
liberal mode of admission to the advantages of the
school; of increasing the number of free scholars;
and of greatly extending the limits as to the reception of pupils on the foundation, as well as a handsome new building for the school.

The legal proceedings incurred an expence of
about £700, towards which Mr. Rushton gave £150,
Mr. Joseph Bladon, £50; the executors of the late
Mr. John Vernon, £150; Mr. Thomas Bladon, £50;
Mr. G. G. Bladon, £50. But some of these gentle-
men afterwards—but particularly the executors of

Mr. Vernon—gave additional sums for the same purpose.

The tercentenary of Alleyne's school took place in 1858, and was duly recognized. The New Grammar School, which was erected in 1859, is pleasantly situated on Bull's Bank, adjoining the residence of the Head Master, then the Rev. W. Harvey, M.A.[1] The present Head Master is Mr. Rhodes; the Second Master, Mr. Jarman. The original school was in Bridge Street. The first building was, probably superseded by the one of brick recently destroyed, which stood about one hundred yards from the bridge on the side next the fish-pond. The same street is, also, or rather used to be, called Schoolhouse Lane, and the Dean's Row, from the school having been there, and from the tithe-barn formerly standing in the same field as the school.

The estate of the donor, according to one of the "statements" by Mr. Rushton, was of great extent and value. In land there are about one thousand three hundred, or one thousand four hundred, acres, several manors, numerous dwelling-houses and buildings, and several tenements in London. These estates are let principally on leases. The rents *reserved* therein amount annually to above £413 in

---

(1) The death of Mr. Harvey took place very suddenly on the 4th of February, 1864. He was held in the highest esteem as a model teacher. A costly and handsome mural tablet has been erected to his memory in the school by his old scholars. An obelisk is also about to be erected to him in the cemetery, and it is also decided to found Harvey Prizes in books, for the boys of Alleyne's school.

money, eighty-five quarters of malt, and about three hundred of wheat. As fines were taken in the granting of nearly all the leases (thus anticipating the future proceeds) the amount of the reserved money and corn-rents bear not the slightest proportion to the actual rental of the estates; and it is admitted that the fines taken on granted existing leases amounted to £9488, 6s. 8d. The oldest of these was granted in 1837, and the remainder in 1842.

The particulars in the will of Mr. Alleyne fully justified the Master of the Rolls in the view he took of the "information" already referred to; and although it is of considerable length it will be sure to be perused with interest—

WILL OF THOMAS ALLYN, MAY 20TH, 1558.

Will of Thomas Allyn, clerk, parson of the Parish Church of Stevenage, in the County of Hertford, respecting his personal estates only, appoints John Langley, citizen and goldsmith, of London (who married testator's cousin Joanes), and Thomas Allen, of Shirland, in the county of Derby, his executors.

He appoints his god-son, Edmunde Kympton, of Weston, in the County of Hertford, gent., and his cousin, Christopher Edwards, citizen and haberdasher, of London, supervisers and overseers of his testament.

The executors to do nothing without the counsel, advice, and consent of of the said Edward Kympton.

May 24th, 1558, the said testator made a will concerning his real estate, of which the following is a copy :—

In the name of God, Amen, the 24th day of May, in the year of our Lord, 1558, and in the fourth and fifth years of the reign of our most gracious Sovereign Lord and Lady, Phillip and Mary, by the grace of God King and Queen of England, Spain, France, both the Sicilies, Jerusalem, and Ireland, Defenders of the Faith, Archduke of Aústricke, Duke of Burgundy, Myllayne, and Brabant, counties of Hasburge, Flanders, and Tyrole, I, Thomas Allyn, clerk, parson of the Parish Church of Stevenage, in Stevenage, in the county of Hertford, having an earnest zeal, desire, and mind to set up and maintain for our soul's good and laudable works, as may and shall be to the honour and glory of Almighty God my Maker, Saviour, and Redeemer, do make, declare, and ordain this my last will, touching and concerning the law, order, and disposition of all and singular my manors, messuages, lands, tenements, and heriditaments, with all and singular their appurtenances whatsoever they be in the realm of England, in manner and form following :—that is to say, I give, devise, and bequeath unto the Masters, Fellows, and Scholars of Trinity College, in Cambridge, of King Henry the Eighth's foundation, all that my manor of Wheston, with the appurtenances thereunto belonging in the county of Leicester : and all that my manor of Wry, Hellsham, with the appurtenances, in the county of Kent : and all and singular other my manors, lands, tenements, heriditaments in the county of Leicester, and in the county of Kent, and in the county of Hertford aforesaid, and in the county of Stafford, and in the city of London, amounting to the clear yearly value of four score pounds, or thereabouts : and all and singular deeds, evidences, charters, court-rolls, muniments, and writings, concerning the said manors and other premises, or any part or parcel thereof, to have and to hold the aforesaid manors, lands, tenements, hereditaments, deeds, charters, witnesses, muniments, and all other the premises and their appurtenances, unto the Masters, Fellows, and Scholars and their successors, to their only proper use and behoof for evermore, to the intent hereafter followeth :—that is to say, that they, the said Masters, Fellows, and Scholars, with part of the rents, revenues, issues, and profits, coming and growing of all the same manors, lands, tenements, and other the premises with the appurtenances, shall from the day of my death for evermore, keep, find, and maintain three separate Grammar Schools, one of them at Uttoxeter, in the county of Stafford, the second at Stone, in the county of Stafford, and the third at Stevenage aforesaid, in the said county of Hertford : and shall contract and pay every year to every schoolmaster of the said three mentioned schools, £13, 6s. 8d. of lawful money of England, and in their several wages and stipends : and also make and ordain, note, and covenant statutes, orders, rules, and constitutions, for and touching the direct order and good government of the schoolmasters and scholars, and for learning of good authorers, and praying for me their founder morning and evening, with the psalm of de profundes, and other suffrages thereunto occasioned with the collect Inclinademine, Amen, &c. : and I will that Marcus Petrus Danus shall be the schoolmaster of the school to be kept at Stevenage aforesaid, and have the teaching of the scholars there during his whole life, with the consent of the Masters of the said college for the time being, he doing his duty therein as to that office appertaineth.

And I will and devise that the Masters, Fellows, and Scholars, and their successors, with part of the said rents, issues and profits coming and growing of the manors and other premises, with the appurtenances, shall, from and after my decease, keep, find, and maintain for ever one honest chaplain, being of good name and fame, and being unpromoted of any and unto any spiritual benefice or service, and having no pay, or stipend, or wages, to say and sing mass two days in every week at the least perpetually : that is to say, upon the Wednesday and Friday, and oftener when he is so disposed, within the Parish Church of Sudbury, in the county of Derby, and in that mass to pray for my soul, my father and mother's souls, for my brother and sister's soul, and all christian souls, with the psalm of " de profundus," and the collect of suffrages thereunto accustomed, and shall contract and pay to the said chaplain yearly for his salary or wages £13, 6s. 8d. of good and lawful money of England, or more or less as the said Master, Fellows, and Scholars, and the chaplain for the time being can agree : and I will that Sir Robert Glasyer, now my chaplain, have that service during his life, if he will so long serve there.

And I will and devise that the said Master, Fellows, and Scholars, and their successors shall with part of the rents and revenues aforesaid, keep and sustain once in the year for me perpetually four several obiits or anniversaries solemnly by note, with all divine service accustomed for all dead folks to be done for my soul and all Christian souls, whereof the one to be kept and done in Stevenage aforesaid, the others in Thornell aforesaid, and the third in Shirland, in the county of Derby aforesaid, and the fourth at Sudbury, in the county of Derby, at about such time of the year as I shall fortune to die, on which Placibo and dirge solemnly by note on evening, and mass and requiem solemnly by note on the morrow following, spending and bestowing yearly at every of the said obiits forty shillings of good and lawful money of England : that is to say, every priest that shall help to sing dirge on night, and sing or say mass on the morrow twelve pence, and to every clerk helping to sing dirge on the evening and mass on the morrow sixpence, at every of the said obiits, *and the overplus and residue of the said several sums of money to be dealt and distributed to the needy and poor householders of every of the said parishes, the same time by the discretion of the parson, churchwardens of every of the said parishes for the time being.*[1]

And I will and devise, give and bequeath yearly, for evermore, to four old poor men, being householders and dwellers in Stevenage aforesaid, to pray unto Almighty God for the wealth of my soul, and all Christian souls, the sum of £5, 6s. 8d. equally amongst them to be parted and divided : that is to say, to every of them £1, 6s. 8d. of good and lawful money of England, to be paid and delivered to every of them at four times of the year : that is to say, at the feast of the nativity of St. John the Baptist, St. Michael, the Archangel, the birth of Our Lord God, and the annunciation of our blessed lady St. Mary, the Virgin, or within twelve days next ensuing every of the said feasts, by even portions, the first pay thereof to begin at the first of the said several feasts which shall first and next happen after my decease : and I give and bequeath for and towards the finding or exhibition of one poor scholar within the same college yearly for evermore, forty shillings of lawful money of England : and I give, grant, and will unto James Allen, of Sherland aforesaid, one annual

---

[1] The obiits, of course, are done away with, but it appears to be a question if this clause of the will does not imply as much as a perpetual charity to the poor of these places, whether they have it or not.

rent of £10 of lawful money of England, yearly going out
of my said manor of Wheston, with the appurtenances,
and out of all other my lands, tenements, and hereditaments in Wheston aforesaid, and Blaby, and Counties
Thorpe in the aforesaid county of Leicester, to have, levy,
and receive the said yearly rent of £10 to the said *James
Allen, and his heirs and assigns for ever*, and to be paid at
the feasts of the year : that is to say, at the feast of St.
Michael the Archangel, and the annunciation of our
blessed Lady, St. Mary, by even portions, to be paid, the
first payment thereof to begin at the last of the said two
feasts which shall first and next happen after my decease.
And I will that if it shall happen the said yearly rent
of £10 to be behind in part or in all after any the said
feasts at the which that ought to be paid by the space of
one month, and that being lawfully asked, then I will
that it shall be lawful for the same James Allen, and his
heirs snd assigns in the said manor of Wheston, and other
the premises in Wheston, Blaby, and Counties Thorpe,
with the appurtenances, to enter and distrain, and the
distress so taken to bear, lead, drive, and carrying, and the
same to retain and keep until the said James, his heirs and
assigns, of the said yearly rent and every parcel thereof,
with the arrears of the same (if any such shall fortune to
be) shall be unto the said James Allen, his heirs and assigns, fully contented and paid.

And I heartily pray the said Masters, Fellows, and
Scholars of the said college, to demise, grant, and let to
farm the said manor and all other premises in Wheston,
Blaby, and Counties Thorpe, unto the said James, his executors, administrators, and assigns, for the term of fifty
years next ensuing after the day of my death, yielding
and paying unto the said Masters, Fellows, and Scholars,

and their successors yearly during the said term of fifty years the yearly rent of £20, with the reasonable covenants to be contained in the said lease. And I will that the said James shall yearly default, abate, and deduct £10 of this said yearly rent of £20 for his and their said yearly amount of £10 during the said term of fifty years.

And I will that the Masters, Fellows, and Scholars, and their successors, shall well and efficiently uphold, repair, and maintain all the manors, edifices, and buildings in and upon all and singular the premises from time to time when and as often as need shall require for evermore.

And I will and devise that the said Masters, Fellows, and Scholars, and their successors, with part of the said rents, revenues, issues, and profits of the said manor, lands, tenement, and other the premises, shall as well content and pay unto the said James Allen, his heirs and assigns, the said amount rent of £10, before by this my last will and testament given and willed unto the said James, his heirs and assigns, as also the said sum of £5, 6s. 8d. before given and bequeathed to the said four old poor men of the said parish of Stevenage for evermore. And I will that my said executors shall have and receive all the rents and services of all the said manors, lands, and tenements, and other the premises, that shall be due for the same, at the feast of St. Michael, the Archangel next after my decease.

Also I will that Nicholas Jacendeze shall have and enjoy during his life, all that tenement wherein he now dwelleth, situated and being in Stevenage aforesaid, and all such lands, meadows, and pastures now let him, and occupied with the same, the same Nicholas yielding and paying for the same during his life to the said Masters, Fellows, and Scholars, and to their successors, such yearly rent as heretofore he hath used to pay, anything before expressed to the contrary notwithstanding, in witness whereof I, the said Thomas Allen, clerk, have ratified and allowed this my present last will and testament in the presence of Edward Kimpton, gent. ; Sir Robert Glasyer, chaplain ; John Huckyll, John Clerke, Thomas Clerke, Edward Clerke, Robert Norris, Thomas Robynson, and divers others.

Proved by John Langley and James Allen, the executors, in the Prerogative Court of the Archbishop of Canterbury, on the 7th February, 1558.

LIST OF ANNUAL SUMS DIRECTED BY THE WILL OF THOMAS ALLEN TO BE PAID OUT OF HIS REAL ESTATES :

	£	s.	d.
Uttoxeter: Schoolmaster	13	6	8
Stone : do.	13	6	8
Stevenage : do.	13	6	8
Sudbury: Chaplain to say mass ...	13	6	8
(or so much as the Chaplain, Masters, Fellows, and Schoolmasters agree to.)			
Stevenage: Obiit	2	0	0
Thornhill (Yorkshire): Obiit	2	0	0
Shirland: Obiit	2	0	0
Sudbury: do.	2	0	0
Stevenage: Four poor men	5	6	8
Trinity College, Cambridge: Exhibition of one poor scholar...	2	0	0
James Allen: Perpetual annuity ...	10	0	0
	£78	13	4
For repairs yearly	1	6	8
Estimated clear rent	£80	0	0

Mr. Allen, in the will of his personal estates, directs the residue thereof to be sold, and the money thereof coming to be given, disposed, and distributed in alms and deeds of charity, to and amongst the needy and poor people, for the wealth of his soul and all Christian souls.[1]

NATIONAL SCHOOL.

The present school-rooms, which stand in Bradley Street, were erected in 1855. There are a class-room, and two school-rooms, one for boys and another for girls. They measure each fifty-three feet in length by eighteen feet in width. The former school-room was only twenty-four feet by twelve feet. Mr. Ryder is the teacher of the boys' department, and Miss Bennett of the girls.

NORMAL SCHOOL.

This is called the New Day School, and the teacher is Mr. Harris. The school-room is the largest in the town, except the Town Hall; and there is a class-room adjoining. The building is in High Street, and was erected for the Wesleyan Sabbath School.

MR. BLADON'S SCHOOL.

This school is in Pinfold Lane, and was erected by the late Joseph Bladon, Esq., and conducted at his expense. It is well furnished with every school requisite, and has a play-ground attached, where every necessary apparatus exists for the exercise and amusement of the children.

(1) Lightfoot's Survey of Uttoxeter.

UTTOXETER CHARITIES.

INQUISITIONS respecting Uttoxeter Charities have been held at the following places:—1690, October 24th, at Lichfield Close; 1727, May 10th, at Uttoxeter; and in the same year on June 20th, at Wolsley Bridge. The following account of Uttoxeter Charities is carefully abridged from the Charity Commissioners' Report. Time and circumstances have, doubtless, made alterations necessary in the mode of applying some of the gifts:—

JOHN DYNE'S CHARITY.

This is a gift by will, bearing date, January 12th, 1644. It consists of the Talbot public-house and premises, and a croft, called "Botham Croft," containing 1a., 2r., 29p., which produce a rent of about £68 per annum. The money is applied in apprenticeing poor boys of Uttoxeter to trades, a premium of £8 being given with each boy, payable by yearly instalments of £2. One-half of the charge of the indenture is also paid from the fund of the charity.

GIFTS OF BAGNALL AND OTHERS.

This is a gift by indenture of feoffment, bearing date, June 1st, 1686. It consists of a close of land

called " The Parks," comprising 6a., 2r., 7p.   The
rent is £18 a year.

GIFTS OF OAKOVER AND OTHERS.

Dorothy Oakover and others, by will, dated May
6th, 1627, gave to the poor of Uttoxeter £40, as a
constant standing stock.   Stephen Spencer, by will,
dated August 27th, 1625, for the same object gave
£10, to be disposed of in land.   On June 20th, 1727,
Richard Heaton also gave to the poor of Uttoxeter
£40.   These three sums were employed in purchas-
ing for the poor of Uttoxeter three closes of land,
called " Thorney Fields," and " Russell's Spring,"
containing in the whole 15a., 1r., 29p., which are let
at about £25 per annum.

GIFTS OF SAMPSON ALKINS AND SIMON WAKELIN.

The former by indenture dated December 2nd,
1670, and the latter by will, dated September 3rd,
1697.   The property is the " Red Hills," abbutting
on Pool Meadow, and is a field containing 2a., 1r., 2p.,
and is let at £10 a year.

DYNE'S LANE.

Dyne's Lane belongs to Uttoxeter Charities, it
having been purchased since 1727, by several sums
of money then in the hands of the trustees undis-
posed of, and arising out of charity lands.   The land
consists of about twenty acres, producing a rent of
about £30 a year, which forms part of the annual
distribution to the poor.

ELLEN MIDDLETON'S GIFT.

This was by will, dated August 29th, 1657, and consists of " Wilgs Croft,"[1] of 1a., 0r., 2p., producing a rent of £5 a year, which is applied to the benefit of poor widows.

ROBERT COX'S GIFT.

This was by will, dated October 22nd, 1621, and is 40s. a year, payable out of " Monk's Field." The land belongs to the vicar, it having been purchased by Queen Anne's Bounty. It is employed in the purchase of shoes.

GILBERT'S GIFT.

Robert Gilbert's will, dated February 12th, 1648, left 20s. for shoes for two poor men, yearly. The money is payable yearly, out of the Nag's Head public-house.

CHAMBERLAIN'S GIFT.

Francis Chamberlain devised on the 22nd October, 1651, the annual sum of 13s. 4d. out of land in Bothams Field, for honest widows and widowers.

MIDDLETON'S GIFT.

Richard Middleton, by will, dated April 6th, 1668, gave to James Wood a yearly rent-charge of 40s. out of Dove Close, or Bushby's Great Close, to be expended in shoes for the indigent.

(1) The name of this piece of land may be derived from Willow, which in the Northumbrian dialect is called " Willey."

BLOUNT'S GIFT.

Mrs. Mary Blount, by will dated April 23rd, 1594, bequeathed £100 to the town of Uttoxeter, to the help and relief of such persons as should fall into decay by fire, or death of cattle, sickness or otherwise, providing such persons found securities for the repayment of such sums as might be lent. By lying in hand the sum increased to £140, which Walter Mynors, Esq., *for his love to the town*, was pleased to take for a yearly rent-charge of £14, from the close called the Swetholme.

POKER'S GIFT.

William Poker, by will, dated January 8th, 1636, left a parcel of ground 1a. 0r. 23p. in extent, called the Quitch, for the poor of Uttoxeter and Marchington. The rent is £4 per annum, which is laid out in loaves on Good Friday.

MYNORS' GIFT.

William Mynors, Esq., of Hollingbury Hall, by will, dated October 27th, 1666, gave £100 to be put forth in the purchase of land, the moiety of the profits thereof to be for the apprenticeship of poor children in the Woodlands, and the other moiety for the relief of the poor living near Hollingbury Hall. Nicholas Mynors, for the use of the £100 granted a yearly rent-charge of £5, issuing out of messuages and lands at Gorsty Hill, in the parish of Cheadle, for the uses aforesaid.

SHALLCROSS'S CHARITY.

William Shallcross, by will, dated May 25th, 1719, gave 20s. yearly, to be paid to the vicar on St. Thomas's day, for a sermon on that day ; and a rent-charge of £5 yearly, to be distributed on the same day to poor housekeepers in Uttoxeter having no pay from the parish, deducting a land tax of 10s. 6d. The amounts arise from premises in the parishes of Stoke and Uttoxeter.

AFTERMATH AND MEADOWS.

These are the Broad Meadow and Netherwood Meadow, comprising together about one hundred and twenty acres, besides seven acres of land *anciently enclosed* from Broad Meadow. *Time out of mind* the profits of the aftermath and meadow were applied to the repair of Dove Bridge,[1] and other bridges and causeways, and public uses in Uttoxeter, but did not then amount to more than £7 per annum, as the inhabitants allowed them to lie common part of the year, and took the benefit to themselves when they should have kept them enclosed, only taking sixpence a cow, and a shilling for a horse, contrary to a decree made October 24th, 1690, after which time Dove Bridge was made a county bridge. By a decree of the Charity Commissioners, founded upon the inquisition taken May 10th, 1727, it was determined

---

(1) Dove Bridge was built in the 13th century. During the Spring of this year (1864) it has undergone repair, including the removal of the decayed stone at the bed of the river, and the substitution of fresh stonework in its place.

that, for the future, the aftermath should be made
the best use of for the repair of the bridges in the
town, and in defraying the expenses of bringing
water to the town, the surplus to go to the general
charities. On the 8th of August in each year · the
right of the trustees to the aftermath commences,
and the gates are locked and the cattle excluded till
the last week of the same month, when horses are
taken at 7s. each, and cows at 4s. each, and young
stirks in proportion. From three hundred to four
hundred head of cattle are then turned on the aftermath for a fortnight annually.[1] The average produce of the ley is about £50 a year. The sum of
£10, or thereabouts, is for the repair of bridges (four
foot-bridges in the Woodlands, over Netherland Lane
Brook ; a cart-bridge at Quee Lane ; and two foot-
bridges near Wills' Lock). The expenses of the
waterworks from Bromshall are about £30 annually,
any residue being applied to the charities. ·

CATHERINE MASTERGENT'S GIFT.

Catherine Mastergent, by will, dated March 20th,
1646, gave a yearly rent-charge of £3 6s. 8d., to be
paid out of Pool Meadow to three poor widows of
Uttoxeter, of honest and religious conversation,
in the purchase of gowns, and after to others, the
best of the inhabitants of Uttoxeter: and also her
barn in Carter Street, with all belonging to it, to be

---

(1) The aftermath is now let by auction, and makes more than by
the usual way.

employed for the habitation for three poor widows, directing them to be made into habitations after her decease. The houses have since been rebuilt by subscription.

WRIGHT'S GIFT.

John Wright, by will, dated March 23rd, 1729, gave £10 yearly, for ever, out of Snape's Field, Hatchet Wood, and Tinker's Lane Croft, subject to a deduction of £1 for one poor widow occupying the Almshouse he left by the same will in Carter Street.

LATHROP'S ALMSHOUSES.

William Lathrop, by will, devised, in the year 1700, four dwelling-houses in Carter Street, and two parcels of land in Broad Meadow and the Netherwood, in Uttoxeter, in trust, as to the houses, for the use of poor widows; and as to the rent of the land, to be applied in the repair of the said houses, and the overplus, if any, in the purchase of fuel. The land is one acre in each of the said meadows, an acre of enclosed land on Balance Hill, and a rent of £1 0s. 6d. out of a close in Rye Croft Lane. The income is about £14 0s. 6d. yearly. Lathrop's Almshouses were rebuilt in 1848, at a cost of £300.

PYOTT'S GIFT.

Mrs. Margery Pyott, by indenture, dated March 1st, 1622, left a field called Mansholme, comprising 6a. 2r. 14p. The rent thereof amounts to about £23 a year, to be applied in providing twelve twopenny loaves, to be distributed at the church, to twelve poor men or women of Uttoxeter who should have been that morning at church, the overplus, except 5s. for the trustees for their trouble, to be for the relief of such poor persons of Uttoxeter as should be unable to attend. The trustees do not receive the 5s. Mr. Jeremiah Ives was one of the trustees.

RUSSELL'S CHARITY.

Edward Russell, of Chester, by will, dated June 7th, 1666, devised 50s. out of land in Great Broughton, county of Chester, and other land lying in Great Broughton, for providing bread for the poor of Uttoxeter, his native place, some part of it to be distributed every Sunday, as the churchwardens should think proper. Fourteen penny rolls are considered satisfactory for this gift. He left a similar sum yearly to the poor of Chester.

CLOWNHOLME'S GIFT.

Thomas Clownholme, by will, dated June 8th, 1702, gave to the poor of Uttoxeter a rent-charge of 20s., to be given in bread on St. Thomas' Day. The land from which it arises is Goose Croft.

HARRISON'S GIFT.

Edward Harrison gave yearly, for ever, out of a tenement at Spath, £1, to be given to the poor of Uttoxeter on Candlemas day.

BARN'S GIFT.

Edward Barns, in 1697, devised £2 a year, for ever, to the poor of Uttoxeter Woodlands, on St. Thomas day, out of land on the High Wood. It was not invested in the trustees of Uttoxeter Charities till 1860, when application for that purpose was made to Sir W. B. Riddell, Bart., at the County Court, and granted. Previously those who held the land disposed of the charity themselves.

BEQUEST TO THE POOR OF UTTOXETER, BY MISS ELIZABETH JOHNSON, OF BURTON-ON-TRENT.

Miss Elizabeth Johnson, of Burton-on-Trent, by will, dated 24th December, 1861, for the love her mother had for Uttoxeter, devises as follows:—" I direct my executors, hereinafter named, to purchase the sum of £200, at £3 per cent., consolidated bank annuities, in the names of the official trustees of charitable funds, upon trust, to divide the annual income arising from the same amongst six poor men and six poor women, inhabitants of the parish of Uttoxeter, every Christmas, to be selected by and at the discretion of the churchwardens for the time being of the said parish of Uttoxeter."[1]

BEQUEST OF JOSEPH BLADON, ESQ.

Joseph Bladon, Esq., of Old Field House, whose demise took place January 12th, 1863, left, by will, to the poor of Uttoxeter, £50 a year for five years, to be appropriated as his trustees, Thomas Bladon, Esq., and George Goodwin Bladon, Esq., his ne-

[1] The will of the deceased is at the office of A. Welby, Esq., High Street, and for this extract therefrom I am indebted to Mr Cowlishaw.

phews, might deem the best. The first £50 was
expended by these gentlemen at Christmas, 1863, in
coal, which was distributed amongst the class for
whose benefit the money was bequeathed. The same
benevolent gentleman likewise built a number of cottages for aged persons, who were allowed to live in
them for a mere acknowledgment, which was always
returned, and they are still so occupied. The cottages are at the back of a school-room, which he also
built, and chiefly supported for many years, in Pinfold Lane, Mr. Bladon, had great confidence, and
justly so, in the efficacy of education in diminishing
human misery, and in promoting social order and
happiness, and, therefore, he was one of the first to
aid by his liberality so powerful an instrument for
the public weal.

GIFT OF WILLIAM PHILLIPS, ESQ.

William Phillips, Esq., of Springfield House, in
the Parish of Uttoxeter, by will, dated September
12th, 1863, and whose demise took place on the 21st
October of the same year, gave and bequeathed the
sum of £800 to the Vicar and Churchwardens of
Uttoxeter, and their successors, in trust, and the annual income thereof to be applied in the purchase of
suitable clothing, bed linen, and blankets, to be distributed by the discretion of the major part of them
from year to year, for ever, amongst the poor of the
same parish of Uttoxeter, and in such shares, at such
times, and in such manner, as the said Vicar and
Churchwardens should think fit.

The same testator, by the same will, devised £100 to the Masters and Fellows of Trinity College, Cambridge, for the use and benefit of Alleyne's Grammar School, in Uttoxeter aforesaid, in such manner as the said Masters and Fellows should decide.

And also by the same will, the sum of £400 to the Vicar and Churchwardens of Burton-on-Trent, the income thereof to be applied in the purchase of fuel, clothes, meat, or bread, for the poor of that parish, from year to year, for ever.[1]

UTTOXETER UNION.

This Union comprises the parishes of Uttoxeter, Rocester, Coxden, Leigh, Bramshall, Marchington, Marchington Woodlands, Draycott, Newborough, Abbots Bromley, Blythfield, Kingstone, Gratwich, and Field, county of Stafford; and Doveridge, Somersall, Sudbury, and Boylestone, county of Derby, all forming an area of sixty-three miles.

PETTY SESSIONS.

These are held on a Wednesday, at the Town Hall, at Twelve o'clock. The late Lord Waterpark presided at these sessions during a period of about thirty years. His lordship, in various other ways, gave his influence and time for the promotion of the

[1] The particulars of this gift I have been permitted to extract from a copy of the will in the possession of the testator's solicitors, Messrs. Blair, Jervis, and Gould, of Uttoxeter, to whom I beg to tender my best thanks for the truly kind and gentlemanly way in which they have permitted me the unlimited use of their copy of the "Manuscript Survey of Uttoxeter," by Peter Lightfoot.

interests of the town, which, he frequently stated, gave him great pleasure to do, when called upon. The other magistrates are Sir William Fitzherbert, T. P. Heywood, Esq., T. C. S. Kynnersley, Esq., J. Broadhurst, Esq., H. M. Ingram, Esq., T. Webb, Esq., W. J. Fox., Esq.

THE BANKS.

The banks at Uttoxeter are a branch of the Burton, Uttoxeter, and Ashborne, Union Bank; and one recently formed of the Midland Bank.

NOTICES OF PLACES

IN THE

NEIGHBOURHOOD OF UTTOXETER.

LOCHELER OR LOCKESLEIA.

A junior Ferrers of Tutbury held Loxley, which is about two miles west of Uttoxeter, in Henry II.'s reign, and in the time of Henry III. it belonged to Robert de Ferrers. In 1327 John de Kynardesleye married Johanna, daughter to a second Thomas de Ferrers. John Kynnersley was owner of Loxley eighteen Edward III. Thomas Kynnersley, twenty-second Charles I.; Craven Kynnersley, seven George II.; and Clement Kynnersley, ten George III., were sheriffs. An ancestor of the Kynnersley's was seated at Kynnersley Castle, Herefordshire, at the Conquest. There is a horn preserved at Loxley, with the proud name of "Robin Hood's Horn," which was formerly in the family of Ferrers, at Chartly. There is no particular reason given for its being Robin Hood's Horn, although it bears his initials; but from bearing three horse-shoes (two and one) it probably belonged to the Ferrars, and came into the family of Kynnersley by the marriage of Johanna, daughter of

Thomas de Ferrers, to John de Kynnardesleye, through which marriage it is supposed Loxley also came into the possession of the Kynnersleys. Loxley Hall is a modern residence, the previous ancient house having been destroyed about sixty years ago, and the ornamental stone work of it, with the ancient sculptured arms of the family, have been formed into a beautiful grotto. The entrance-hall of the present house contains the emblazoned arms of all the chief families of distinction in the kingdom, and

paintings of the family for generations back. The present proprieter is C. T. S. Kynnersley, Esq., who resides at the High Fields, near Uttoxeter.[1]

Loxley has attained a degree of celebrity as being, if not the birth-place of Robin Hood, at least the scene of many of his bold exploits. An old chronicle of the date of 1621 relates, that after his return to

(1) The monuments of the Kynnersleys in Uttoxeter Church are represented in an engraving in this volume.

Loxley from his visit to his uncle Gamewell, in Warwickshire, after certain inquiries concerning his men,

" Clorinda came by,
The queen of the shepherds was she,"

with whom he fell in love,

" Sir Roger, the parson of Dubridge, was sent for in
haste :
He brought his mass book, and bid them take hands,
And joined them in marriage full fast."

According to the traditions of the neighbourhood the
honeymoon was spent in the beautiful demesne of
Loxley; and many engaging stories have been related by the gardener of Loxley ninety years ago—
the maternal grandfather of a friend of mine—respecting both the rendezvous and doings of this celebrated outlaw. These lines are supposed to have
reference to the gallant freebooter, on his return to
Loxley, after the marriage with his wife—

" Bold Robin Hood and his sweet bride,
Went hand in hand into the green bower ;
The birds sung with pleasure in those merry green
groves ;
O this was a most joyful hour."

A vessel of Etruscan form is said to have been
found near Loxley, in the last century, and to have
been reproduced in fac-simile by Josiah Wedgwood
in his beautiful red ware.

BLOUNT'S HALL.

About a mile to the west of Uttoxeter is Blount's Hall, where the Blounts had a seat. The branch here were descended from John Blount, third son of Sir William Blount, Knight, who had lands in Burton and Rolleston. Edward Blount, tenth Richard II., died without issue, and his property passed to Elizabeth daughter of Walter Blount, younger brother of Thomas. Sir Thomas Pope Blount was the founder of Trinity College, Oxford. In Clerkenwell Church was inscribed on a stone, " Ann Blunt, daughter of Walter Blunt, of Blunt Hall, and sister to the lady Paulet, and to the lady Sidenham, died 24th April, 1503." John Blount, of Blount's Hall, 1527, was High Sheriff for this county. The Hall was taken down in 1770, but the moat may still be seen. When the estate was held—about 1658—by Sir Henry Blount, it amounted to upwards of five hundred acres of land, the greater part of which belongs now to the Loxley estate.

STRAMSHALL.

Straguicesholle, Stranshall, Stronshall (Stramshall), is about a mile slightly to the north-west of Uttoxeter. In the twentieth year of the Conquest it was held by Abricus, and afterwards Roisia de Verdun was lady of Stramshall. A church was built there in 1852, by Mr. Evans, from a design by Mr. Fradgeley, architect, of Uttoxeter.

KINGSTONE.

Kingstone, which is about four miles west of Uttoxeter, belonged to the Gresley's, and was sold in the

KINGSTONE CHURCH, NOW TAKEN DOWN.

J. Redfern del.

sixteenth century, by Sir Thomas Gresley, to Sir Edward Aston. It now belongs to the Earl of Shrewsbury and Talbot. The many old yew trees near to the site of the old churchyard, indicate the site of the ancient residence and grounds, the mote of which remains. Kingstone Church, which was probably of the fourteenth century, was destroyed in 1860 or 1861. Part of the rood screen remained.

Kingstone Church was the burying place of Symon Degge, who was buried in a chapel which he erected at the north side. On one church bell was inscribed " Ora pronobis Sancte Jacobe" (pray for us St. James); and on a second bell, " Ora pronobis Sancte Edwarde" (pray for us St. Edward); and on the third, " God Save the Queen, 1595." The new church was erected at Kingstone, at the east of the other, by the Earl of Shrewsbury in 1861. The architect was Mr. Brandon, of London; the builder, Mr. Evans, of Ellastone. It was opened and consecrated by the Bishop of Oxford, October 21st, 1861. Leese Hill is a member of Kingstone, and was the inheritence of the Tixall's and Norman's; but afterwards by marriage came to Henry Goring, of Kingstone. Wanfields belonged to the Manloves, and was bought by Rowland Manlove, by the wealth he obtained in the naval service under Sir Walter Leveson, it having previouly belonged to Sir Walter Chetwynd. It was enjoyed by his son Alexander in 1660. Dr. Wilkes, who made extensive collections towards a history of Staffordhire, in 1725, married Rebecca Manlove, of Leese Hill. Wanfield has come to the family of Lawrence.

BROMSHULFE AND GROTEWICHE.

Bramshall.   Robert de Stafford held Bramshall of the king, in the twentieth year of the Conquest.   The Erdeswicks, Willoughby de Brooke, and Sir Faulke Greville, have been lords of it.   A great portion of it belonged to Loxley estate.   Dr. Lassitter occupies the old manor-house, which has been traced to have been, with the farm, in the family of the late Roger Warner, successively, about four hundred years.   The old church at Bramshall, built in the time of Edward III., was destroyed in 1835, and the present one was built from a design by Mr. Fradgley, architect, of Uttoxeter.   The tower appears to have been of wood, and it must have stood more to the south than the present church   It did not contain any monuments.   Gratwich, near to, was a manor of the Chetwynds and Gorings, and has a church.

LEGHE AND FEELDE.

Leigh, which is about six miles north-west of Uttoxeter, was held in the Conquerer's time, 1114, by Ormus, from Galfrid, Abbot of Burton, at 100s. rent for sixteen years.   The church is cruciform.   It contains an altar-tomb, with recumbent figures of Sir John Aston, and the Lady Johanna, his wife, granddaughter of Judge Littleton.   The church was restored in 1845, when " some mouldings of the Anglo-Norman style were dug up."[1]   An incised slab bearing a foliated cross, lies in the churchyard,.   Withington and Nobut are in this parish.   Field, in the

(1) Natural History of County of Stafford, by R. Garner, Esq., F.S.A.

same parish, was held in fee from Burton Abbey by Sir John Bagot. In the time of Henry I. it was given by Geoffrey, abbot of Burton, to one Andrew, in fee farm, for 20s. per annum. Sir Harvey Bagot built a house there for his seat. In 1680 a Switch Elm was felled at Field of gigantic size. It took two able men five days to stock it. It was one hundred and twenty feet long. Its girth in the middle was twenty-five feet six inches. There were sixty-one loads of firewood in it. To saw it asunder two saws were fastened together, with three men at each end, and eighty pairs of nathes were got out of it, and eight hundred feet of sawn timber, in boards and planks; and the sawing, as the price of labour then was, cost £12. It contained ninety-six tons of solid timber. Its size was attested by Lord Bagot and all the workmen, by their signatures.[2]

CHARTLEY—CHARTLEY CASTLE.

Chartley Castle, six miles west of Uttoxeter, was built in 1220, by Richard Blundeville, Earl of Chester, on his return from the Holy Land, and an import was levied upon all his vassals to defray the expense of building. After the death of the founder, the castle and estates fell to William Ferrars, Earl of Derby, whose son Robert forfeited them by his rebellion. Afterwards he was allowed to retain them. They were subsequently carried by marriage to the family of Devereux, and then to those of Shirley and

---

(2) Plott's " Staffordshire."

Townsend, and lady Northampton gave up all she could of Chartley, namely, the estate, to one of her uncles, the then Earl Ferrars, to whose descendants it now belongs. Of the castle which has been in ruins from before the time of Leland, there remain fragments of two round towers, with loopholes so constructed as to allow of the arrows being shot horizontally into the ditch. The keep was circular, and about fifty feet in diameter. The ancient manorhouse was curiously made of wood, the sides carved, and the top embattled, and the arms of the Devereux, with the devices of the Ferrers and Garnishes, were in the windows, and in many parts within and without the house. For some time it was the prison of the unfortunate Mary, Queen of the Scots, who wrought a bed that was in it. On her way to Stafford in 1575, Queen Elizabeth visited it. It was burnt down in 1781. The park is a thousand acres, and the breed of the wild beasts of Needwood Forest are preserved in it to this day. It is traditionally said that Robin Hood found asylum at Chartley Castle; and its founder, Randall, of Chester, is thus named in connection with the famed Robin, by the author of " Piers Plowman"—

" I cannot persitly my paternoster, as the priest it
  singeth ;
I can rhyme of Robin Hood, and Randall of Chester.'

This item appears in Mr. Peter Lightfoot's Survey —Robert, Earl of Essex, held freely the Castle of Chartley, by the rent of ijs.

BROMELEI.

Bromley, which took its name of Abbot's Bromley from there having been an abbey in the neighbourhood, is about six miles a little south-west of Uttoxeter. It had formerly a number of valuable priviliges, now neglected, and a market on a Tuesday. The hobby-horse was celebrated there thrice a year two hundred years ago, and an attempt has been made in late years to revive it. The horse and reindeers' heads are preserved in the church. In connection with these was a pot, preserved by one of four or five persons called the "Reeves," in which cakes and ale were put, and the money collected went towards repairing the church and relieving the poor. The church was restored in 1855, at a cost of £4000, when the floor was lowered two feet to show the base of the columns. One of the windows contains painted glass of a man in coat armour.

At the conquest one Bagod held Bromley of one Robert de Stafford; and in the time of Henry II., one Symon Bagod was owner thereof.

BLIDEVELT.

The owner of Blythfield, which is about a mile north-west of Abbot's Bromley, at the Conquest was one Hermanus. It came into the possession of the Bagots by marriage, and here they have for generations had their seat. The building is ancient, and it contains many ancient paintings. The church contains a number of altar-tombs, with effiges, and in the churchyard is a perfect cross.

WOODFORD.

This is about a mile and a half south of Uttoxeter. In the 31st of Henry VI., Woodford belonged to Ralph Woodford, grandson of Sir Robert. In the sixteenth or seventeenth centuries it is stated— "Walter Jeffreys holdeth freely one messuage, and divers lands called Woodford farm by the yearly rent of iijs., in lieu of a sparrow-hawk, at Michas, late Heath's Land."

THE WOODLANDS.

The present Small Wood and Manor House is residence of the J. Webb, Esq. The moat of the former residence is perfect, and is to be seen near to. Betwixt the two lanes near Gorsty Hill is another fine moat, which, I presume gives the name to Moat Spring. Somewhere here, probably where the moats are, was a residence which belonged to the Rugeleys. In the sixteenth century one Thomas Rugeley, according to " Lightfoot's Survey," had 16a. 2r. 20p. of land in the parish of Uttoxeter. But long before it was held by this family, it was owned by the Thirkell's, the first of whom in this county was Rowland Thirkell (son of Robert Thirkell, of Grenworth, and brother to Robert Thirkell, knight), who married Rose, daughter of John Mynors, about the reign of Edward IV. The family is extinct. A handsome new church was erected in the Woodlands in 1859, near the Manor House. Kynnersley belongs to John Mynors, Esq.

MERGHANSTONE.

Marchington is about four miles south of Uttoxeter. It was granted by the founder of the abbey at Burton, Wulfric Spott, to one Wulfag, but at the Conquest it was held of the king by Henry de Ferrers. In 30th Henry VIII., Thomas Kynnersley, of Loxley, possessed it by inheritance from the Ferrers, and it has since passed through a variety of owners. In Marchington Church there is an altar-tomb, date, 1592, to Walter Vernon, of Hound Hill. Henry Chawner, Esq., of Hound Hill, has lately founded almshouses at Marchington.

HOUND HILL.

The earliest deed with respect to Hogenhull, Hoenil, or Howenhull, is of the time of Henry III., when Sir Henry Handbury married the daughter and heiress of Hound Hill. In the time of Henry VIII. it was sold to Humphrey Vernon, third son of Henry Vernon, knight, of Haddon, in the county of Derby. Hound Hill joins Marchington, and is in that parish. In 1012 the Saxons, oppressed by the Danes, embraced King Ethelred's plan for their extermination, and Hound Hill is named by Hollinshead as the opening scene of the tragedy. The following are the words of this ancient historian respecting it:—
" Egelred being greatly advanced, as he thought, by reason of the marriage devised upon presumption thereof, to cause all the Danes within the land to be murthured in one day. Hereupon he sent privie commissioners into all cities, boroughs, and towns

x

within his dominions, commanding the rulers and officers in the same to dispatche and flea all such Danes as remained within their liberties at a certain day prefixed, being Saint Ryce's day, in the year 1012, and in the thirty-fourth year of king Egelred's raigne (the 13th of November). Hereupon (as sundry writers agree), in one day and hour this murther beganne, and, according to the commission and instructions, executed; but where it first beganne the same is uncertain: some say at Wellowyn, in Hereforth, some *at a place in Staffordshire called Hown Hill*, and others in other places, as in such doubtful cases it commonly happens." There is a tradition of a battle having been fought at Hound Hill, which may be thought confirmatory of the account of this old writer, and to this these words have reference—

" Don't let us lie here, like hounds upon a hill,
    But march into the town;"

though there is evidently, also, a play upon the names of Hound Hill and Marchington in them. At Hound Hill alabaster has been quarried. An ancient bronze key has been dug up at Hound Hill.

DRAICOTE.

Draycot, six miles south of Uttoxeter, was held by Henry de Ferrers, in the twentieth year of the Conquest, and in the second of Edward II. Thomas, lord of Boylestone, held it from the Ferrars, by the service of hunting; and in the sixteenth Edward III., it belonged to one Richard Draycot, and by his

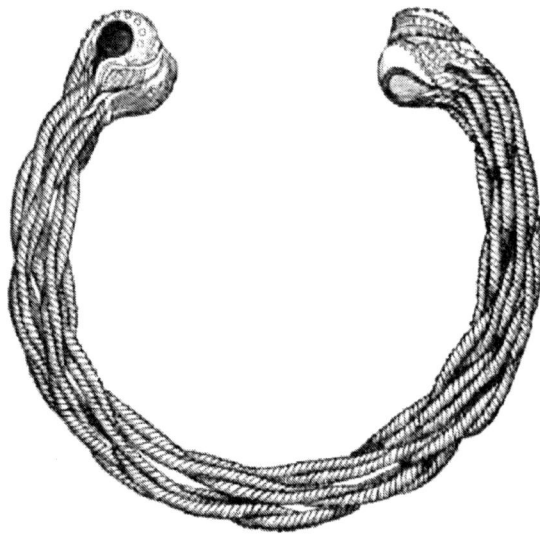

TORQUE, FOUND IN NEEDWOOD FOREST.

second wife it passed to his posterity, and in right of one of them, Johanna, to her husband, William de Pipe. It belongs now to Lord Vernon. Near Draycot, in the Greaves, Mr. Thomas Hollis, Queen's Ranger, found, in 1848, a British torque of pure gold, formed of eight twisted wires or rods, each itself formed of three other wires, and having two chaste perforated ends, and weighing fifteen and a half ounces. It is shown on the accompanying plate.

NEWBOROUGH.

Newborough, a new borough established by Robert de Ferrers soon after the Conquest. At Edgareslege (Egardsley), an hermitage was granted to the priory of Tutbury, by William de Ferrers, Earl of Derby. At the former place a Roman coin, of base silver, has been found—obverse, two heads, with wreaths; reverse, figures, with four horses in a chariot, and the word ROMA underneath. It is in the possession of Mr. R. Garner, of Stoke.

HANDBURY.

Handbury, from "hean," high, is an ancient place, the inhabitants being by Brompton called *civis bean*, or *ben*, signifying old. During the Saxon Heptarchy it was granted by Ethelbert A.D., 674, to his neice, the pious Wurburga, daughter of Wulphere, where she erected a nunnery, of which she was abbess. Her body was buried here, but on the place being afterwards overrun by the Danes, it was conveyed to Chester, where there is a splendid shrine to her, and

Hanbury Church is dedicated to her. The church was erected from remains of the nunnery and priory. About 1842, when it was undergoing repairs, some Saxon carvings were discovered, principally tombstones, with modifications of the cross and circle. It also contains a number of monuments—a recumbent figure to Charles Egerton; figures to the Agards; one of an ecclesiastic, in engraved brass, to Ralph Adderley, and others.

FELEDE.

Faulde is a little to the south-east of Hanbury, and is eight miles from Uttoxeter, south. It belonged to John de Curzon, by gift of William de Ferrers, Earl of Derby, and he dying without issue, it was carried in marriage by his sister to Nicholas, son of Adam de Burton, of Tutbury, who was living in the time of Edward I., and was witness to Burton Abbey roll, in 1321. A William Burton, says one authority (Mr. Shaw), was Abbot of Rocester; another says of Croxden. Another William was standard bearer to Henry V. William Burton, author of the " History of Leicestershire," was a descendant, and died at Fauld, and was buried at Hanbury, April 6th, 1645. Robert Burton, author of the " Anatomy of Melancholy," was another descendant. Fauld has had a church.

TOTEBERIE.

Tutbury is supposed to have taken its name from being dedicated to the Saxon deity Tuisto; but it is equally as likely to have received its name from an altar there to Tutas, the god of the Gauls. It is supposed there was a castle at Tutbury, as one of a line of forts belonging to the Celts. Offa, or Kenulph, kings of Mercia, it is conjectured, had a palace here; but it is certain Ethelred, another of these kings, made the castle there the place of his residence. Previous to the Conquest it also belonged to Ulfric Spott, founder of Burton Abbey, and was perhaps his place of residence. At the Conquest it was given to Henry de Ferrers. It was repaired by Thomas, Earl of Lancaster, and was rebuilt by John of Gaunt, when it became a place of great splendour. Bull running and the minstrel's court were instituted by him. Amongst other places this fortress became a prison of Mary, Queen of Scots. In 1831 the rich contents of the chest, which was lost in the Dove on the flight of Thomas, second Earl of Lancaster, on his rebelling against Edward II., was found, on clearing the bed of the river, and consisted of a complete series of some of the early English coins. The total quantity found was one hundred thousand. A priory was built at Tutbury by Henry de Ferrers, it being commenced about 1080. The present church is the nave of the priory, the west doorway and window being unrivalled specimens of Norman architecture. The arch of the doorway recedes from the face of the church three feet ten inches, and consists of seven principal mouldings, all richly adorned with zigzag, beak-head, flowered, and other devices. There are many other specimens of Norman device about

the building. The road entering Tutbury from Rol-
lestone or Burton is called Port Way. It is continued through Faulde and Coton, and by Draycott
toll-gate to Morton, where it terminates. It has evidently, however, gone through two or three fields to
Marchington ; and Moisty Lane, from this place to
Uttoxeter High Wood, must be the original continuation of it. If so, the Port Way at the south of
Tutbury must be a portion of the Port Way I have
described as passing Uttoxeter to the east for Stramshall and the Potteries, to Chesterton.

SUDBERIE.

The parish of Sudburie, which includes Hill Somersall and Aston, was part of the grant of Henry
de Ferrers. At an early period it came to the Montgomery family. In the reign of Henry VIII. these
manors were brought by a coheiress of Sir John
Montgomery, to Sir John, son of Sir Henry Vernon,
of Haddon Hall. This branch of the family, however, became extinct, when they went to Walter
Vernon, of Hound Hill, descended from one of the
elder brothers of Sir John Vernon, who married the
coheiress of Montgomery. Sudbury Hall, the architect of which was Inigo Jones, is the seat of
the present Lord Vernon, who is descended from
this branch. The name is derived from a town and
district in Normandy. There was a church and
priest at Sudbury at the Conquest. The present
church contains two ancient effigies of females of the
Montgomery family, and several beautiful monuments

to members of the Vernon family.   Lord Vernon is
a patron of learning.   He has organized a rifle corps
at great expense, and in the park, which is six hundred acres, has erected a range and butts.

DUBRIDGE, BROUGHTON, MARSTON, SOMERSALL, EATON.

The manor of Doveridge, about a mile and a half
east of Uttoxeter, belonged to Edwin, Earl of Mercia.
After the Conquest it was given by Bertha, wife of
Henry de Ferrers, to the priory of Tutbury.   It was,
in 1552, granted to Sir William Cavendish.   Sarah,
a wife of his descendent, was in 1792 created Baro-
ness Waterpark.   The late Lord Waterpark was a
Member of Parliament in the Liberal interest.
The family is descended from the same branch as
the dukes of Devonshire.   Doveridge Hall[1] was
built in the last century (about 1770), and has a
fine prospect.   Doveridge had a church and priest
at the time of the Norman Survey.   The present
church is of the thirteenth century.   It has some
monuments, and an arched recess, called " the holy
sepulchre," and a piscina.   The churchyard has had
a cross.   It has also one of the finest yew trees
in the kingdom.   The trunk, which is become hollow, is about twenty-two feet in circumference, while

(1) I have reason for suspecting that St. Cuthbert's Well, previously
mentioned, was rather to the south of Doveridge Hall, on the acclivity,
where there is a cluster of trees within a circular trench.   Within the
circle a little plateau has been made, on the hill-side, and such steps as
might have been used for a well have been dug up.

the branches extend about sixty-two feet. Doveridge had a market granted by the Priory of Tutbury in 1275, and a hiring market is held there now. Close to Doveridge is Lea Hill, the property and pretty residence of Miss Robotham. At West Broughton, William Parr, Earl of Essex, had an estate in 1544. In the reign of Queen Elizabeth the manor belonged to the family of Palmer. It has had a church. The manor-house at West Broughton is occupied by Dr. Williams. Marston belonged formerly to the Montgomeries. It has an ancient church, fearfully mutilated, the north aisle having been destroyed, and the old pillars and arches now appear in the outside wall. The porch has just been destroyed. The font is old, but plain, and there is remaining the place for holy water. It is curious that a rough rail forms the fastening of the door to the chancel, each end falling into niches in the walls. This, as the other places named here, are to the east of Uttoxeter. The Fitzherberts have an estate at Somersall. The hall, it is said, has been built with materials from the ruins of an ancient mansion belonging to the Montgomery family at Cubley, and is a nice old frame-timbered residence. Somersall has a church. There is a fine oak here forty-one feet round at the base, and at three feet high twenty-seven feet round. The house of Sir Thomas Milward, Chief Justice of Chester, who entertained King Charles I., was at Eaton. Over the door was placed the following inscription:—" V. T. placet Deo, Sic omnia siunt anno Domini 1576. Junii 12." The cellars only remain, and a bare tunnel communicates with them from a distance. There is a monument to Sir Thomas Milward, who died in 1658, in Doveridge Church.[1]

NORBURY.

Norbury, which is about eight miles north-east [of Uttoxeter, in the time of the Saxon dynasty belonged to Siward, the great Saxon thane. It was confiscated from him by King William, and given to Henry Ferrers. Sir William Fitzherbert, knight, was lord of Norbury in 1252, to whose ancesters it was granted in 1125. The Fitzherberts of Tissington are descended from the family at Norbury. Norbury Hall was built 13th Edward I., and was occupied by the family till 1648. Norbury had a church at the Conquest. The present church is ancient, and is remarkable for its numerous richly coloured glass windows, with memorial devices, and for its architecture. It also contains a number of altar-tombs.

ALVETON.

At Alton there was a castle before the Conquest, held by one Lunan, or, as Erdwick says, by one Juvar. The castle, of which there are ruins, was built by Bertram de Verdun. A battle was fought at Bonebury, in the year 716, betwixt Ceolred, king

---

(1) "Marriage Holme belonged to this charity (Doveridge), and was a grant from the crown, 27th April, 18th Elizabeth, to Roger Manners, Esq."—LIGHTFOOT'S SURVEY.

of Mercia, 'and Ina, king of the West Saxons, who
had invaded Mercia. Brompton the Abott of Jour-
vall, says, " Ina, king of the West Saxons, raised a
great army, fought Ceolred at Bonebury; when yet
Ceolrod (by the advantage of his strong fortifications)
so warmly received him, that he was glad to withdraw
upon equal terms, neither having much to brag of
victory." The fortress was of an irregular figure,
encompassed with a single, and in some places with
a double ditch, the whole encompassing about one
hundred acres of land. Alton Towers are built on a
portion of the site of Bonebury, where the old lodge
—well remembered—stood, and now forming a part
of the present Towers. At this entrenchment a
Saxon sword and a celt have been dug up. The
sword was given to Sir Joseph Banks. It is, perhaps, deserving mention, that at the foundation of
these early earthworks an abundance of wood charcoal was observed, when they were destroyed during
the erection of the Towers. The improvements at
Alton were begun by Charles, Earl of Shrewsbury.
A considerable part of Alton Towers, and works in
the magnificent gardens, were built after designs
by T. Fradgley, Esq., architect, of Uttoxeten[1]
This gentleman saw one of the remaining towers

(1) Besides these Mr. Fradgeley has designed other works in this
neighbourhood, some of which are already mentioned—Marchington Alms Houses, Rocester Bridge, over the Dove, a fine bridge
of one arch; Handbury Schools, Uttoxeter Town Hall (plain, according to instruction), Draycott-in-the-Clay Schools, Alleyne's
Schools, Uttoxeter; Stramshall Church, Uttoxeter National Schools,
Caldon Low Schools, &c.

of the fine old ruins of the castle fall. In Alton
Church some fine remains of Norman architecture,
consisting of a magnificent row of arches, and a
splendid pointed arch, have lately been brought to
light during a process of restoring.

TEAN.

In the twentieth year of the Conquest Tain belonged to Robert de Stafford, and has since passed
through a great many families. At Over Tean
Major Ashby, in 1728, found at some depth in his
garden a Roman vessel. In the same garden is a
spring, called " Willey Wall Well." Mr. Phillips,
late a Sheriff of the county, has a pretty seat at
Heybridge, near Tean, and is owner of the extensive
tape works there.

CROXDEN, OR CROKEDEN.

Croxden, six miles north of Uttoxeter, is remarkable for the fine ruins of an abbey, consisting of the
west front, south transept, and part of the cloisters,
founded there for the Cisterian order of monks in
1176, by Bertram de Verdun. Thomas, the first
abbot, wrote a commentary on the Bible. The curious diary of Richard de Schepeshead, thirteenth
abbot, is in the British Museum. The heart of
King John was buried here; and it was the burying-
place of the Verduns. A crucifix, with an image of
the Saviour, was found, broken, amongst the ruins,
by Mr. Carrington, who has repaired it; and it, with
a knight in coat armour, are preserved. A curious

carved oak panel of Jesus and the Twelve Apostles
has lately come to light, and been a subject of discussion at a meeting of a brotherhood of antiquaries
at Manchester.

CHECKLEY.

In the twentieth year of the Conquest, Checkley or
Cedla, was held of the king by Otha; and in King
John's time it came to the Ferrars. The church is
of the fourteenth century. The west wall within has
had some ancient and curious paintings, which have
been foolishly destroyed by *beautifying!* Some of the
windows have stained glass; and there is also in it
an alabaster altar-tomb of the date 1524, to Godfrey
Foljambe, with an effigy of himself and wife. The
font, which is Norman, is shown on the accompanying plate.

In the churchyard are three tapering stones, two
of which bear defaced figures. They are supposed
to be monumental, and Danish, and originally set up
to preserve the memory of a great battle fought between the Danes and the English, in which the latter
were victorious; and that one of the armies was totally unarmed; and that the stones represent three
bishops who fell in the engagement. Tradition also
says that a field called " Naked Field," and a place
known as " Dead Man's Green" (written in the old
register at Checkley, " Tetterton Green"), represent
the scene of the battle, where the slain strewed the
ground, and where a human skeleton has been dug up.
It is not improbable that a battle has taken place

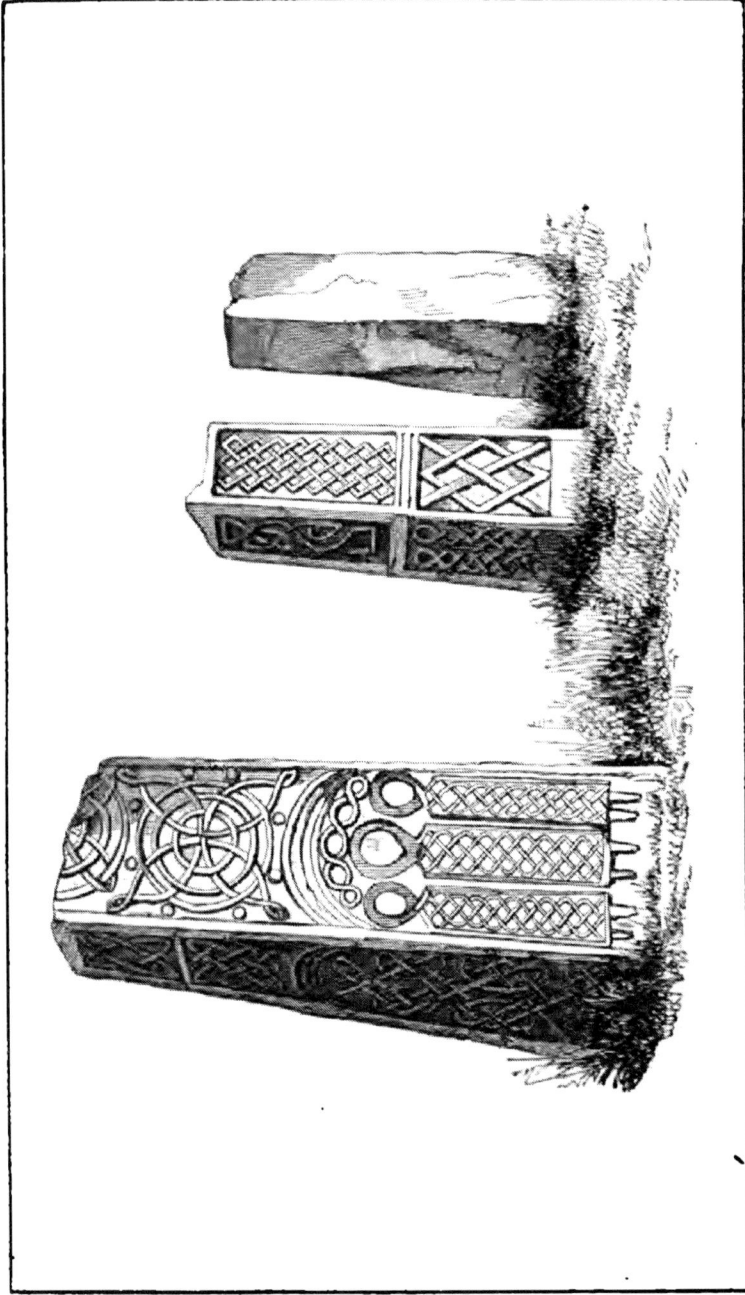

SCULPTURED STONES, CHECKLEY CHURCHYARD.

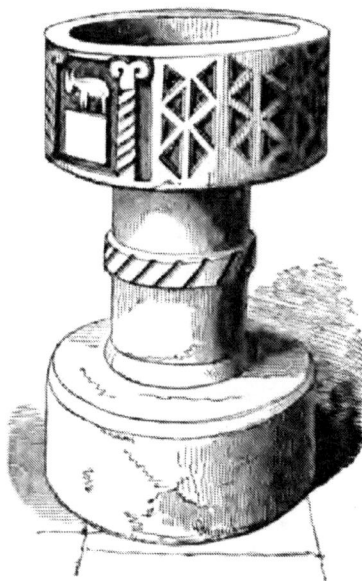

FONT, CHECKLEY CHURCH.

at Checkley; but it is doubtful whether the stones have any connection, in any way, with it, notwithstanding that such is the popular belief. I am also of opinion that the three stones were originally one monument (most likely the churchyard cross); and this, I think, would be proved (although some portions where the fractures occurred may be lost), if the parts in the earth were laid bare. However, as it is, there is sufficient evidence, I conceive, to support this view of them. If made at one time for the purpose stated (and they are all of one age, one kind of ornamention, and all of red sandstone), it might be supposed they would all be of one size. But they are not. Instead, they are of three gradations, and, if put together, would make one uniform tapering stone of about fifteen feet high, more or less, according to the length in the ground, and varying from one foot nine inches wide at the base, to about a foot wide at the upper termination, the stone without figures, which does not seem to have sustained any fracture at the top, doubtless forming the terminal part.

The ornamentation is evidently of Saxon type, but it would be difficult to decipher all the figures. One side of the widest part, or of the widest monument (speaking of them as distinct stones), has evidently contained twelve interlaced figures, of which nine remain in a very defaced form. Of the other figures, which are almost entirely defaced, scarcely any conjecture can be formed, but on both stones the cross, interlaced, is perceptible in several places.

The work has been of a superior and elaborate, interlaced description, so far as the defaced remains afford means to judge. By the side of the church is the effigy of a crusader.

Dr. Whitaker, in an interesting note in his " History of Whalley," where he is speaking of the division of the Northumbrian and Mercian kingdoms, contends that the Calclinth, which was under the control of Offa, King of Mercia, was held at Checkley, and not at an obscure place near Manchester, called Culcheth, as hitherto believed, and thereby does much towards explaining the old and singular traditions of the village, though it is not as a consequence necessary to follow Dr. Plott in his opinion about the intent of the stones. Dr. Whitaker writes : It is strange indeed. that the attention of no antiquary has been directed to Checkley in Staffordshire as the real scene of this quarrelsome and opprobrious assembly. But upon every hypothesis Checkley was far within the limits of Mercia ; and it is highly improbable that a council in the degrees of which so powerful and spirited a monarch as Offa had so near an interest, would be permitted to assemble anywhere but in his own territories. Let us see, however, on what grounds the evidence in favour of Checkley rests. First, the initial " C," in Saxon, was pronounced as ch in church. Thus Cheadde was altered in the orthography only to Chad. Calclinth then would be pronounced as Chalclinth, and the last consonants very indistinctly. Invert the two letters (c and l) in the middle of the word, and we have Chacii, or Checkley. Dr. Whitaker, in supporting this hypothesis, on the constant tradition of the village about a battle, and the slaughter of three bishops! and the memorials in the churchyard SAID to be to their memory, proceeds—" Compare these circumstances with the character of that council, which is called in the Saxon chronicle " Gefhtfullic" (a word yet retained in the Lancashire dialect, which would be, literally translated, " flitting) and the violence with which it is known to have been conducted, and there can be no doubt that the tradition is an exaggerated account of that event, whence it must follow that Calclinth is Checkley.[1]

The Saxon word appears to be in these letters— " Gefhtfullic," and translated as above would imply that the council (in this instance of so very violent a character) was not always held at one particular place, but occurred periodically at different places.

The Rev. Dr. Langley, of Checkley, translater of a portion of " Homer," wrote an account of the village, which became possessed by Mr. Shaw, who, however did not live to make any use of it in his unfinished history of the county. There have been some Lows in the vicinity of Checkley, called Werlows.

Fole, or Fauld, and Madeley, are close to Checkley, and in the ninth year of Edward II. belonged to Henricus St. Maure. At Beamhurst is the seat of H. Mountford Esq.

---

(1) " History of Whalley," p. 35.

TOOT HILL, NEAR BEAMHURST.

Since I opened Toot Hill, on Uttoxeter High
Wood, I have explored another barrow, with the
same name, on the property of W. Beech, Esq., at
the Old Wood, near Beamhurst, a little north of
Uttoxeter. The opening of this took place on the
4th of July, 1863. The mound is situated on an
elevated part of a field close to the Old Wood
Farm-house. A hedge and ditch have been carried
across its eastern margin. They were probably made
when the land was enclosed from an extensive park,
which was known as Madeley Park, and which had
belonged to the Foljambes, and where there is an
extensive site of a feudal residence. The barrow
commences on the brow of the hill, on the north
side, at about five feet deep, and it continues that
depth part way along its western side, and then
gradually diminishes in depth towards the south,
until its outline is almost lost. I thought the best
way of exploring the mound, would be by taking a
cutting, about six feet wide, across its middle. This
I did, beginning on the northern and deepest part
with the cutting. I felt doubtful whether I was
dealing with a barrow, until I came to a slight
sprinkling of charcoal, which, at the north side, lay
about five feet deep. I kept my first depth through
the whole opening, but the layer of wood ashes
gradually sloped upwards, thereby showing the natural surface of the hill, to within a foot of the present
surface of the barrow, and disappeared entirely, a
little way beyond its centre. My labours failed

failed to bring me upon any interment. Within a few inches from the surface, about the middle, I, however, met with a fragment of a smooth tapering flint, with beveled edges, not serrated, which was burnt nearly to whiteness. I, also, on replacing the clods, found a part of a flint knife, which had been dug out near to where the other flint lay. By the layer of charcoal sloping to the surface, I think it is clear that a great part of the barrow had been destroyed.

Whilst proceeding with the work I obtained a clue to associations investing the mound with an interest beyond those it claims by being a barrow. Some of the children of Mr. Marston occupier of the land, came to see what extraordinary work was going on, and a girl playfully asked me if I could run down " Tootle Field." I exclaimed, " What field is that ?" " Why," she replied, " this field." I was convinced that the field took its name from the mound, and that it was named " Toot Hill," though I had not heard it called so ; and I found, on inquiry, that it was supposed to be such.

This Toot Hill is in a very elevated place, and its name-sake on Uttoxeter High Wood is observable directly south from it, and the scenery around, for a great distance, is of the most charming description.

I have already given the derivation of " Toot," but I will here add, that the great prototype of this fabulous deity is supposed to have existed far back in the darkness of time, and in antediluvian days, and that he was the erector of engraved pillars, one

of which was standing in the time of Josephus, after
having survived the deluge ; and that they preserved
a knowledge of human and divine things, particularly of astronomy, and the great moral mystery of
the world and its Maker.   They are supposed to have
been erected in Egypt by the descendants of Seth ;
and Syriad, the place where the historian saw one of
the stones, being rendered Osiris, or Sirius, favours
the supposition.   They are spoken of in the Book of
Judges as quarries, meaning graven stones.   It is
supposed that Pythagoras derived his knowledge of
astronomy, and of the doctrine of immortality, from
the inscriptions on these stones, veiled though they
were in hieroglyphics ; and that it is the sublime
morality which they taught which lives in the writings of Plato to this day.[1]

I must, also, here add brief particulars of some
other interesting vestiges of Celtic and Saxon ages,
which I have discovered since I treated of such matters in an earlier chapter.   In a field adjoining, at
the south-east—that in which is the large tumulus,
which is infested with rabbits, standing close to the
Moorhouse, Uttoxeter, and which is one hundred
and twenty yards round, and about ten feet in height
—there are two remains, which, if they are not
Druid barrows, are most probably hut-circles, within
which, if so, there were houses of British erection,
consisting of wattled work, covered with clay, or mud

(1) " Hermes Britannicus," by the Rev. W. L. Bowles.

plaster. They are but a few yards from each other, are each twelve yards across, and are separately surrounded by a ditch about a yard and a half wide, and nearly two feet deep. The edges of the places are about two feet higher than the level of the land, but there is a dipping towards their centre, by which their regular height is much diminished. Both places have trees growing on them, and they are as much like each other as possible.

The other remain to which I have made allusion is a Saxon grave, of quite, I believe, an unique character. It is in a field to the east of, and almost opposite to, that in which are what I have named hut-circles, and is indicated by a clump of trees, which may be seen to the left of the foot-road going to Woodford. This interesting site of Saxon Christian burial is marked by a mound in the form of a cross. The four radii of the cross, which agree with the four cardinal points, are each about ten yards long, and are raised about two feet high, being about two yards and-a-half wide. The place, as mentioned, has trees growing about it, and an oak is standing at the intersection. I have given some attention to the subject of ancient modes of burial, but I have not read of, or seen elsewhere, any place of ancient interment indicated by, or existing in imitation of, a cross made of earth. Owing to this interesting remain being now exposed to the trampling of cattle, it is liable to become, in a short time, trod out of existence.

ROWCESTRE.

At Rocester there was a Roman station. In 1795 some Roman works were discovered at the mill, during some improvements. They were much like tan-pits, probably baths, in which were found several Roman copper coins, and a spear head, of brass. More

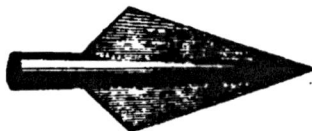

recently other Roman remains have been met with near the factory, in the shape of fragments of pottery and antler's of deer. Of these, I possess a large handle of a vessel of Samian ware, and the neck of an amphora, with mouldings round it. Several skeletons of human beings have also been found, in connection with Roman remains, in a crouching position, as if their owners had been protecting themselves from some impending calamity; and one skeleton was met with, drawn together, as in a hiding-place, in some brickwork, described to be in the form of a large drain. The father of a trustworthy old workman at Messrs. Holdsworth's fell through some brickwork, when making an excavation for some purpose, into what he imagined was an old cellar. When excavations were made for the new school, a large quantity of broken tessaræ and pottery were carted away with the soil, to form an embankment to the mill fleam, unfortunately, without any portions being preserved. A perfect jug, of Roman make, was here dug up by a labouring man, from whom it got into the Potteries, where it is preserved. There is evidently a Roman (or earlier) remain in the " *Frame Yard*" field, adjoining the church, of a square shape,

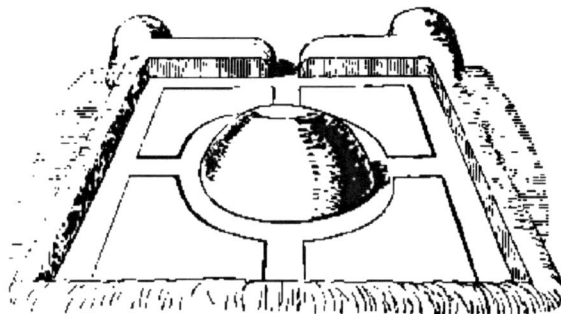

sunk much below the surface, its four sides being about forty-five yards each. In the centre is a circular mound, about forty-five feet across, resembling a tumulous, with a road round it, and with a road to it from each side of the remains. Along the southern, eastern, and western edges of the place, an earthwork, in form of a vallum, exists. This elevation along the three sides swells out at the south-east and south-west corners to two large circular mounds. There is an opening through the southern edge to the enclosure. It is possible the place was a Roman amphitheatre of small dimensions. One of the Roman roads went by Rocester, from Chesterton to Little Chester, and is now known by the name of Long Lane. At the Conquest Rocester was held by Robert de Stafford. In 1140 Richard Bacon foun-

ded a monastery of Black Canons there.   Rocester
churchyard contains a perfect raised cross slab, and

two others much defaced; and also the shaft of an
ancient cross, with interlaced work betwixt moulded
corners.   The principal genteel residence at Rocester
is pleasantly situated at Barrow Hill, and belongs to
Mrs. Dawson.   Near Rocester is, also, Woodseat, recently purchased by, and now the residence of, Colin
Minton Campbell, Esq.   Denston, close to Rocester,
has recently had a church erected, at the expense of
T. P. Heywood, Esq., of Dove Leys.   Before the Conquest, Denstone was held, with Alton, by Juvar.   It
was afterwards held by the king at the Conquest, and
subsequently passed to the Verduns and Furnivals.

In the sixteenth, seventeenth, and eighteenth centuries it belonged to the family of Madeley, whose descendants removed to Uttoxeter. A place there is called Cromwell's Green. A church has also recently been erected at Hollington.

CRACKMERES.

Before the Conquest, Crakemarsh was a demesne of Algar, earl of Mercia, and was part of the grant by the king to Henry de Ferrers. Robert de Ferrers gave Crakemarsh to his daughter Maud, on her marriage with Bertram de Verdun. It has been in the possession of the Delves (Edward I.'s time), one of whom, John, son of John de Delves, whose seat it was, was one of four squires with James, Lord Audley, at the battle of Poictiers. There is a field near Bridge Street, Uttoxeter, called Delve's Hall Meadow. Bertram de Verdun called Crakemarsh, or a place at it, his " *grove.*" Crakemarsh had formerly a church. Lady Cotton Sheppard occupies the family seat at Crakemarsh.

NEEDWOOD FOREST.

Needwood Forest, in 1656, covered nine thousand two hundred and twenty acres of land, and contained forty-seven thousand one hundred and fifty trees, including huge oaks, limes, maple, wych-elms, &c., and ten thousand cord of hollies and underwood. Before it was de-forested it contained twenty thousand head of deer. The Swilcar oak, at six feet high, is twenty-one feet four inches in girth. It is sixty-five feet high, and contains one thousand feet of timber.

ADDENDA.

In 1648 the Duke of Hamilton, after suffering a severe defeat at Preston, by a small force under Cromwell, was pursued to Uttoxeter, where he surrendered himself prisoner.

A Captain Sares was slain at Uttoxeter during the Civil War, as appears from a list of slain printed in 1660.

In 1659 Uttoxeter was in an excited condition, as appears from a letter quoted in No. xvii. of "Reliquary." Derby was in a state of revolt, and a number of militia having been sent from Staffordshire to quell it, were halting at Uttoxeter for refreshment. It would appear that Uttoxeter was inclined to be like Derby, for the shops were closed, and the inhabitants seized the militia horse, and a Captain Doughty, of the militia, espoused their side. However, the matter, both at Derby and Uttoxeter, blew over, and nothing further occurred.

Uttoxeter Church formed part of the endowment of Derby Abbey, by gift of Earl Robert Ferrers.

INDEX.

A.

Abud, 144, 149, 168, 290, 301
Adams, 160
Adderley, 340
Adin, 89, 244
Aftermath, 319
Agard, 340
Algar, Earl, 40, 41
Alkins, 316
———' Gift, 316
Allen, 88, 204, et seq
Alleyne, 169, 303, et seq.
———'s Grammar School, 303
Allen, Thomas, Life of, 204
Allyn, Will of Thomas, 306
Alport, 160, 161, 203
Altartomb, 165
Alton, 345
Alwyne Hall, 36
Archbold, 181, 182, 191, 238, 244, 253, 254
Armstrong, 289
Ash, 188
Ashcroft, 21
Ashby, 347
Ashenhurst, 81
Astle, 119, 228, 229
Astle, Dan., Life of, 228
Aston, 188, 192, 331, 332
Ault, 245
Avering, 45
Avery, 69
Ayloffe. 69

B.

Bacon, 357
Baddeley, 138
Bagnall, 258, 315
———'s Gift, 315
Baguley, 254
Bagott, 335
Bagot, 63, 95, 96, 98, 246, 333, 335
Bagshaw, 126, 145, 280
Bakewell, 253, 283
Ball, 79, 80, 184
Bamford, 232, 238
Bane, 153
Banks, 245, 326, 346
Barlow, 92
Barnes, 191, 287, 322
Barns' Gift, 322
Barnard, 253
Barker, 192
Bateman, 14, 23, 176
Bates, 205
Baxter, 213, 269
Beech, 352
Belec, 59
Belton, 65
Beltane Fires, 19
Bell, 172, 244
Bennet, 314
Bentley, 3, 32, 34, 70, 121, 169, 185, 211, et seq., 247, 256, 263, 269, 289
Bentley, Sam., Life of, 211
Beresford, 141, 253, 255

Bernard, 261
Bethel, 136, 138
Bevan, 289
Bewley, 283
Birch, 92
Bladon, 125, 145, 168, 171, 177,
    261, 297, 298, 301, 302, 304,
    314, 323, 324
Blagg, 177, 289
Bladon's School, 314
———— Bequest, 313
Blount's Gift, 318
———— Hall, 330
Blount, 64, 192, 318, 330
Bloor, 325
Blood, 244
Blundeville, 333
Blurton, 295
Blythefield, 335
Boden, 196
Bodley, 206
Bookselling, 239
Borlace, 45
Botham, 223, 228
Bowles, 354
Bowyer, 81, 253
Bradbury, 190
Bradshaw, 233
Bramshall, 332
Brandon, 209, 331
Brereton, 74, 75, 84, 85
Bremer, 226, 227
Bridgewater, 209
Britton,, 31
Broadhurst, 336
Brocklesby, 122
Brougham, 137
Brown, 13, 93, 14, 202
Brooke, 332
Bromley, 335
Broughton, 201, 213
Buckley, 278
Bull Baiting, 268
Bunting, 201
Burdett, 270
Burke, 129
Burton, 192, 206, 340
Butler, 152

Butter Pots, 274
Buxton, 93
Byles, 135, 137, 133
Byndloss, 254
Byron, 219

C.
Camden, 206, 254
Campbell, 143, 358
Carlyle, 104
Carrington, 347
Carser, 143
Cartwright, 200, 201
Caudrey, 52
Cauldring, 252
Cavendish, 253, 261, 269,
    343
Cemetery, 193
Chamberlain's Gift, 317
Charities, 305
Chartley, 334
Chamberlain, 317
Chamberlyn, 238
Chambers, 254
Chatham, Lord, 122
Chawner, 337
Cheadle, 254
Chelmsford, 139
Chester, 48, 197
Chetwynd, 332
Checkley, 348
Churches, 151, 194
Church, Inscriptions in the,
    169, et seq.
Civil War, 72
Clarence, Duke of, 66
Clarke, 9, 88, 126, 153, 172
Clerke, 313
Clownholme, 322
Clownholmes' Gifts, 322
Cloyd, 86
Cockburn, 137
Cockerell, 141
Coke, 209, 255
Cole, 143, 197
Communion Plate, 193
Condlyffe, 256
Congregational Churches, 196·

Cooke, 126, 187, 197, 198, 290, 298, 302
Cooper, 298
Cope, 95, 97, et seq., 283, 285
Copes, 15
Copestake, 96, 97, 176, 251, 286, 287
Costerdine, 198
Cotton, 184, 206, 248, 257
Coutts, 269
Cowlishaw, 323
Cox, 317
——'s Gift, 317
Crakemarsh, 359
Cranmer, 153
Craven, 67
Crichlow, 168
Crichton, 141
Cripps, 45
Crispe, 45
Croker, 189
Cromwell, 257
Crosby, 186
Crossley, 94, 245
Croxden, 347
Cumberland, Duke of, 92, 94, 102
Curzon, 340
Customs, Local, 262

D.

Daniel, 96, 97, 254
Davenport, 199
Davis, 290
Dawson, 248, 392, 358
Dees, 205
Degge, Sir Symon, Life of, 207
Degge, 3, 67, 155, 191, 192, 193, 207, et seq., 243, 244, 252, 331
Delves, 359
Denis, 218
Deoville, 279
Dethick, 254
Devereaux, 333, 334
Domesday book, 39
Dove, the river, 10, 11

Doveridge, 343
Draycot, 338
Duckfield, 261
Dunnet, 282
Dunnicliffe, 126
Dyne, 315, 316
——'s Charity, 315
—— Lane, 316

E.

Eaton, 37, 80, 243
Edge, 192, 238, 258
Edwards, 306
Egerton. 209, 340
Eglingtoun, 142
Elcho, Lord, 103
Elliot, 250
Ellis, 139, 209
Erdeswick, 41, 64, 209, 235, 332
Erne, 141
Essebourne, 52
Estaing, 219
Etches, 301
Evans, 31, 168, 170, 300, 330, 331
Extent of Uttoxeter, 230

F.

Fauld, 340
Fairfax, 85
Farrar, 153
Ferrers, 40 to 57, 165, 233, 246, 273, 327, 328, 333, 334, 337 et seq., 359
Field, 38
Fires, 236
Fish, 78
Fitzherbert, 121, 326, 344, 345
Fleetwood, 254, 276
Flier, 153
Flint, 145, 298, 302
Floyers, 252
Folk-lore, 262
Fox, 123, et seq., 145, 222, 261, 301, 326, 398
Fradgeley, 144, 280, 330, 332, 399, 346

Frambolt, 251·
Fraser, 148
French, 234
Friend's Meetinghouse, 195
Fulford, 141
Furnivall, 130, 358

G.

Galloway. 198
Gardner, Lord, Life of, 217
Gardiner, 173
Gardner, 93, 185, 213, 217, et seq.
Garner, 70, 165, 332, 339
Garnish, 334
Gell, 74 to 77
Gerrard 83
Gibson, 67
Gilbert's Gift, 317
Gilbert, 88, 238, 317, 291
Gilliespie, 158
Gisborne, 9
Glasyer, 313
Glenorchy, 196
Godbehere, 198
Goodwin, 239
Gorenge, 277
Goring, 78, 277, 331, 332
Gould, 290, 325
Greatorex, 100
Gresley, 63, 330, 331
Greville, 332
Green, 34, 256
Grindon, 52

H.

Hackett, 154
Hall, 2, 13, 14
Halsey, 291
Hammond, 173
Hampden, 228
Hampson, 200, 201
Hand, 135, 141
Handbury, 337, 339
Hannen, 139
Harding, 193
Harland, 40
Harris, 314

Harrison, 205, 223, 322
———'s Gift, 322
Hart, 166, 169, 193, 222, 224, 225, 252
Hartshorn, 148, 188
Harvey, 255, 305
Hatton, 280
Hawthorn, 107, 176
Haywood, 141
Heaton, 316,
Henry, 40
Heming, 158, 159, 160
Herring, 171
Heywood, 141, 143, 298, 326, 358
Hobson, 94
Hogkinson, 244
Hogg, 6
Holdsworth, 356
Holebrook, 289
Holland, 202, 302
Hollinshead, 337
Hollis, 339
Hone, 20
Hooper, 153
Horobin, 256
Hound Hill, 337
Howard, 135. 145
Howe, 229
Howitt, 186, 196, 222, et seq
———, Mary, Life of, 222
Huckhill, 313
Hudson, 212, 296
Hutton, 94, 96

I.

Ingestre, 134, 142, 144, 145. 146
Ingram, 141, 143, 282, 326
Ives, 322

J.

Jacendeze, 312
Jackson, 81, 192
James, 198
Jarman, 305
Jeffreys, 336
Jerringham, 29

Jervis, 325
Jewitt, 24, 25, 101, 266
Johnson, Penance of, Dr. 104 et seq.
Johnson, 104, et seq., 126, 197 229, 287, 294, 323
Johnson, Bequest, 323
Jones, 214, 289, 295, 342
Jonson, 228

K.

Kelly, 139, 290
Keeling, 176
Kerr, 141
Kingstone, 330
Kirk, 171
Knight, 270, 271, 272
Kniveton, 254
Kympton, 306, 313
Kynnersley, 103, 161, 163, et seq., 169, 172, 175, 177, 238, 239, 245, 261, 297, 301, 326, 327, 328, 336, 337

L.

Lancaster, Earl of, 49, et seq.
Langley, 313, 351
Lasbrey, 196
Lassiter, 332
Latham, 267
Lathbury, 63
Lathrop, 292, 321
————'s Gift, 321
Latimer, 153
Lawrence, 331
Ledgould, 155
Leese, 292
Leicester, Earl of, 239
Leigh, 11, 332
Levett, 141
Leveson, 331
Levies, 77
Libraries, 294
Lichfield, 105
Lightfoot, 20, 21, 35, 47, 70, 78, 79, 88, 152, 155, et seq., 173, 174, 175, 191, 192, 193, 233, 234, 247, 249, 252, 257,

et seq., 264, 277, 334, 336, 314, 345
Lightfoot Dr. Life of 257
Lilly 205
Lime Croft 38
Littleton, 332
Longfellow 127
Longevity, 243
Lothian, 141, 142
Loyed, 292
Loxley, 3. 4, 10, 77
————, 261
———— Notice of, 327

M.

Mace, 233
Machin, 245
Macpherson, 34
Madeley, 214, 359
Malbon, 169, 211, 212
Mallaby, 170, 297, 298, 301, 302
Manlove, 100, 249, 253, 255, 331
Manners, 345
Manisty, 138, 139
Marston, 343, 353
Marchington, 337
Market, 273
Marriage of the Prince of Wales, 148
Mastergent's Gift, 320
————, 253, 230
Matthews, 133
May Garlands, 262
———— Pole, 263
Meadows, 319
Mechanics' Institution, 295
Mellon, 269, 276
Mercia, Earl of, 40
Merinton, 52
Methodism, 198
Meynell, 52, 59
Middleton's Gift, 317
————, 75, 253, 317
Milward, Family of, 253
————, 177, 178, 179, 249, 353, et seq., 286, 344, 345

Mills, 233
Minors, (see Mynors)
Montague, 131
Montfaucon, 33
Montgomery, 63, 342, 344
Mortimer, 52
Morton, 238
Mosley, 47, 52, 67, 69, 70, 82, 152
Moss, 278
Mottram, 256
Mountford, 351
Mundy, 9
Murphy, 121
Musgrove, 190
Mylwarde, 254
Mynors, Family of, 246
———, 64, 97, 161, 163, 192, 246, et seq., 261, 286, 318, 336,
Mynors' Gift, 317

N.
National School, 314
Needham, 88
Needwood Forest, 7, et seq., 49, 359
Nevil, 69
Newborough, 339
Newton, 223
Nicholson, 139
Nightingale, 11
Noel, 247
Norbury, 345
Norfolk, Duke of, 135, 137
Normal School, 314
Norman, 253
Norris, 46, 119, 233, 289, 294, 299, 313
North, 141
Northampton, 75, 334
Northumberland, Earl of, 40
Nottingham, Earl of, 48

O.
Okeover's Gift, 316
———, 316
Oakley, 85

Oale, 219
Oldfield, 172, 173, 209, 210
Oudfield, 192
Ouldfield, 249, 253

P.
Pack, 141
Palmer, 136, 344
Pamphili, 135
Parker, 69, 233
Parkinson, 302
Parry, 218
Passman, 65
Peace, Invocation to, 121
Pearson, 228
Pembridge, 254
Pembroke, Earl of, 45, 49, 228
Pently, 32
Penn, 254
Percival, 88
Perry, 143
Petty Sessions, 325
Peveril, 48
Phillips, 271, 324, 346
———'s Gift, 324
Pillory, 268
Pitt, 8, 121, 161
Plague, 242
Planche, 41
Plot, 3, 11, 208, 209, 243, 244, 265, 275, 333, 350
Plymouth, Brethren, 203
Poker, 318
———'s Gift, 318
Population, 239
Porter, 192
Povey, 143
Powell, 190, 244
Power, 293
Poyns, 81
Pratt, 193
Prince, 220
Printing, 289
Prynne, 160
Puncharden, 52
Pym, 228
Pyott, 321
———'s Gift, 321

R.

Raffles, 197
Raleigh, 54, 252
Randall, 45, 334
Redesdale, 137
Reeves, 166
Register, Extracts from the Parish, 191
Richards, 288, 289
Richmond, Earl of, 62
————, Duke of, 134
Riddel, 323
Ridley, 153
Robin Hood, 328, et seq.
Robinson, 96, 313
Robotham, 289, 334
Rocester, 356
Rolleston, 52, 64
Rolt, 138, 139
Romilly, 304
Roman Catholics, 202
———— Roads, 27, 31
———— Remains, 27, 34
Rudyerd, Edward, Life of, 228
Rudhall, 184
Rudyerd, 228
Rugeley, 336
Rushton, 290, 301, 302, 304
Russell, 322
Russell's Charity, 322
Ryder, 314
Ryecroft, 38

S.

Sacheverel, 108
Sacred Wells, 263
Saddler 201, 239, 289
Sampson, 153, 154
Sanders, 121
Saville, 206
Schools, 383
Scotland, 280
Scott, 78, 82, 137, 192, 196, 268
Seckerson, 201
Seward, 105
Shallcross, 91, 253, 319
————'s Charity, 319
Shakespeare, 190

Shaw, 7, 11, 28, 58, 59, 60, 155, 163
Shawcross, 91, 253, 319
Shee, 137, 138
Sheldon, 206
Shephard, 172
Sheppard, 169, 359
Sheret. 76
Shipley, 238
Shirley, 333
Shoeswell, 45
Shoyswell, 45
Shrewsbury Peerage Case, the 128
———— and Talbot, 128, et seq., 299
Slater, 187
Smith, 100, 161, 172, 173, 193, 249, 294
Snape, 256
Sneyd, 141, 177, 238
Somersall, 343
Spelman, 206
Spott, 337
Spragg, 192
Stanley, 254
Stanton, 269
Startin, 67, 238
Stafford, 322, 357
Steele, 100
Stephens, 212
Stone, 261
Stowe, 276
Stramshall, 336
Stretton, 52
Street Architecture, 231
Strutt, 268
Stubbs, 170, 171
Stukeley, 18
St. Helen's, Lord, 121, 122
St. Leonards, 136
St. Liz, 42
St. Maure, 351
Sudbury, 14, 15, 340
Superstitions, 267
Sutton, 232
Swan, 198
Sweeting, 143

Swift, 223
Swynnerton, 64, 80
Symonds, 79

T.

Talbot, 277
Tansley, 166
" Tansley, My Lady," 166
Taverner, 100
Taylor, 93, 144, 145, 175, 192,
  199, 217, 301
Tean, 347
Temple, 278
Thesiger, 135, 139
Thirkell, 336
Thornbury, 104, 115
Thorneycroft, 143
Thorperley, 205
Tichborne, 132
Tixall, 252, 331
Toland, 20
Tolls, 277
Tokens, Trader's, 290
Tooke, 122, 222
Toothill, 352, 355
Townsend, 334
Town Hall, 299
Toyke, 239
Trade, 283
Trollope, 208, 209
Troutbeck, 140
Turner, 59, 126
Tutbury, 63 to 66, 340
Twigg, 115, 245
Twyford, 52

U.

Union, 325
Uttoxeter, General character-
  istics of, 3 to 4
Uttoxeter, Derivation of the
  name, 4 to 7
Uttoxeter, Geology, 11 to 15
————, Neighbourhood,
  7 to 11

V.

Vaughan, 81
Venables, 254

Verdun, 345 347, 358, 359
Vernon, 15, 69, 88, 198, 269,
  289, 299, 301, 304, 305, 337,
  339, 342, 343
Villiers, 349

W.

Wakefield, 290
Wakelin, 293, 316
————'s Gift, 316
Walpole, 22, 223
Waltham, 97, 98
Wanfield, 331
Ward, 40
Warner, 106, 205, 253
Warton, 82
Waste, 153
Waterford, 142
Waterpark, 277, 298, 325
Watson, 81
Watts, 227
Webb, 324, 336
Wedgwood, 329
Wellesley, 134
Welby, 296
Wells. 263
Wensleydale, 137
Wesley, 198, 200, 201
Weston, 252
Wetton, 97, 98
Whitridge, 196
Whitmore, 67
Whitehall, 210
Whittaker, 17, 350, 351
Wilkes, 331
Wilkinson, 88, 271, 272
Willes, 138
Williams, 138
Wilson, 193
Winfield, 37
Wolsey, 257
Wood, 126, 193, 223, 234, 235,
  248, 256, 257, 317
Woolridge, 253
Woodford, 336
Woodlands, The, 336
Wright, 321
————'s Gift, 321

Printed by L. Jewitt, " Derby Telegraph" Offices, Derby.

Lightning Source UK Ltd.
Milton Keynes UK
21 December 2010

164712UK00006B/49/P